Mining and Sustainable Development

Mining is a transformative activity which has numerous economic, social and environmental impacts. These impacts can be both positive and adverse, enhancing as well as disrupting economies, ecosystems and communities. The extractive industries have been criticised heavily for their adverse impacts and involvement in significant social and environmental scandals. More recently, these industries have sought to respond to negative perceptions and have embraced the core principles of sustainability. This sector could be regarded as a leader in sustainability initiatives, evident from the various developments and frameworks in mining and sustainability that have emerged over time.

This book reviews current topical issues in mining and sustainable development. It addresses the changing role of minerals in society, the social acceptance of mining, due diligence in the mining industry, critical and contemporary debates such as mining and indigenous peoples and transit worker accommodation, corporate sustainability matters such as sustainability reporting and taxation, and sustainability solutions through an emphasis on renewable energy and shared-used infrastructure. Written by experts from Australia, Europe and North America, but including examples from both developed and developing countries, the chapters provide a contemporary understanding of sustainability opportunities and challenges in the mining industry. The book will be of interest to practitioners, government and civil society as well as scholars and students with interests in mining and sustainable development.

Sumit K. Lodhia is an Associate Professor and Director, Centre for Sustainability Governance, in the School of Commerce, University of South Australia.

Routledge Studies of the Extractive Industries and Sustainable Development

African Artisanal Mining from the Inside Out
Access, norms and power in Congo's gold sector
Sarah Geenan

Mountain Movers
Mining, sustainability and the agents of change
Daniel M. Franks

Responsible Mining
Key concepts for industry integrity
Sara Bice

Mining in Latin America
Critical Approaches to the New Extraction
Edited by Kalowatie Deonandan and Michael L. Dougherty

Industrialising Rural India
Land, policy, resistance
Edited by Kenneth Bo Nielsen and Patrik Oskarsson

Governance in the Extractive Industries
Power, cultural politics and regulation
Edited by Lori Leonard and Siba Grovogui

Social Terrains of Mine Closure in the Philippines
Minerva Chaloping-March

Mining and Sustainable Development
Current Issues
Edited by Sumit K. Lodhia

www.routledge.com/series/REISD

Mining and Sustainable Development

Current Issues

Edited by Sumit K. Lodhia

First published 2018 by Routledge

2 Park Square, Milton Park, Abingdon, Oxfordshire OX14 4RN
52 Vanderbilt Avenue, New York, NY 10017

Routledge is an imprint of the Taylor & Francis Group, an informa business

First issued in paperback 2020

British Library Cataloguing in Publication Data
A catalogue record for this book is available from the British Library

Library of Congress Cataloging in Publication Data
A catalog record for this book has been requested

ISBN: 978-1-138-56293-6 (hbk)
ISBN: 978-0-367-59337-7 (pbk)

Typeset in Sabon
by Wearset Ltd, Boldon, Tyne and Wear

Contents

Figures

Tables

Contributors

Motoko Aizawa is an expert on environmental, social and governance dimensions of sustainability, and focuses on policy and legal initiatives that help governments and companies improve their sustainability performance. She currently manages InfraActiv, a research organization that examines the sustainability dimensions of economic, social and financial infrastructure. She served as Managing Director USA of the Institute for Human Rights and Business from 2014 to 2016, following more than two decades at the World Bank Group. She is the principal author of the 2006 IFC Performance Standards, and the human rights provisions in the 2012 version of these Standards. While at IFC, she was also instrumental in the creation and implementation of the Equator Principles. She began her career as a business lawyer, specializing in due diligence in mergers and acquisitions, and project financing of infrastructure projects. She obtained her BA from Hamilton College, LLM from London University and JD from Loyola University of Chicago.

Saleem H. Ali is Blue and Gold Distinguished Professor of Energy and the Environment at the University of Delaware, and also holds Adjunct Professor status for both the Global Change Institute, and the Sustainable Minerals Institute at the University of Queensland in Australia. He previously served as Chair in Sustainable Resource Development and professor of sustainability science and policy, also at the University of Queensland. Previous to that, he was professor of environmental studies at the University of Vermont's Rubenstein School of Natural Resources, and founding director of the Institute for Environmental Diplomacy and Security. His books include *Treasures of the Earth: Need Greed and a Sustainable Future* (Yale University Press) and, with Larry Susskind, *Environmental Diplomacy* (Oxford University Press). He has been recognized by the World Economic Forum as a "Young Global Leader". Professor Ali received his doctorate in environmental planning from MIT.

Alan Bond is Senior Lecturer in Environmental Management in the School of Environmental Sciences at the University of East Anglia (UK) and Extraordinary Professor in the School of Geo and Spatial Sciences, North West University (South Africa), with over 25 years' experience in Impact Assessment (EA). He runs a full-time MSc programme on Environmental Assessment and Management at the University of East Anglia; is Editor-in-Chief of the journal *Environmental Impact Assessment Review*; and has published over 75 peer-reviewed works and edited two key texts on sustainability assessment (with A. Morrison-Saunders and R. Howitt (2013) *Sustainability Assessment: Pluralism, Practice and Progress*, Taylor and Francis; and with A. Morrison-Saunders and J. Pope (2015) *Handbook of Sustainability Assessment*, Edward Elgar, Cheltenham, UK and Northampton, USA).

Naomi Boughen is a social researcher applying her skills and expertise to examine what drives trust and acceptance of extractive operations, and more importantly, why. She examines this at different scales: internationally, nationally and at local mining operations. Naomi has applied this expertise to help co-design a global data and analytics service, providing a systematic approach to articulating attitudes and experiences with mining, and guide more reflexive and effective community engagement strategies. Naomi has a background in environmental management and social research methods.

Simone Carr-Cornish is an applied social researcher examining the social impacts of industries and innovations, with a focus on how best to manage these impacts. Simone's research of what constitutes a social licence and defining related best practice stakeholder engagement has spanned across the energy, extractive and agricultural industries. She has collaborated with industry, policy-makers and communities, to generate best practice stakeholder-led solutions. Simone has a background in business, psychology and social research methods.

Yosoon Choi is an Associate Professor in Energy Resources Engineering at Pukyong National University, Korea. He received a BS degree at the School of Civil, Urban and Geosystem Engineering, Seoul National University, Korea in 2004, and a PhD degree at the Department of Energy Systems Engineering, Seoul National University in 2009. He was a Post-Doc fellow at Department of Energy and Mineral Engineering at Pennsylvania State University, USA. He has been working in the area of Energy Resources Engineering, Mining Engineering, Geographic Information Systems (GIS), 3D Geo-modelling, Operations Research, Engineering Geology, Solar Energy Engineering and Renewable Energy Systems.

Daniela C. dos Santos has practiced law in the extractive industries (oil, gas, and mining) for 20 years. She has extensive national and international experience, including in Sub-Saharan Africa, South America and Asia. She is principal at Invenient Solutions Consulting Ltd. Recent projects include working as National Researcher for Transparency International – Canada on the global project Mining for Sustainable Development. At her last corporate position with a mining multinational, Daniela led a team of more than 45 lawyers in 11 jurisdictions. She has lectured at several law faculties, including at Western University, University of Toronto and Osgoode Hall Professional Development. Her research interests include: institutional change; the role of multinational enterprises in development; human rights; law, finance and development. She graduated from the University of Rome, Italy, in International Relations, has a J.D. from Osgoode Hall Law School and an LL.M. in Natural Resources Energy and Environmental Law from the University of Calgary. She is currently a doctoral candidate at the Faculty of Law, University of Toronto, Canada.

Syed Ali Ghoreishi-Madiseh is an Assistant Professor at Norman B. Keevil Mining Engineering Institute of the University of British Columbia, Vancouver, Canada. Prior to joining UBC, Ali did his PhD and postdoctoral studies at McGill University. His research includes the study of various mechanical and energy systems with a specific emphasis on mining and petroleum industries. His research team focuses on developing novel solutions for maximizing energy efficiency, improving system performance, preventing waste of energy and replacing fossil fuels with renewable energies.

Pietro Guj is a Research Professor at the Centre for Exploration Targeting of the University of Western Australia, after a distinguished international career in both the exploration/mining industry and Government where, after a period as a finance executive for the Water Authority, he held the role of Deputy Director General of the Department of Minerals and Energy and Executive Director of the Geological Survey of Western Australia. His main interests are in project evaluation, risk analysis and in resources governance with emphasis on the formulation and administration of internationally competitive mining regulatory and fiscal regimes – fields in which he has lectured, published and consulted widely internationally, primarily for the World Bank.

Faramarz (Ferri) P. Hassani obtained his BEng (1975) and PhD (1981) in Mining Engineering from Nottingham University, England. He has been at McGill University since 1983 and many years in a leadership role. He is presently the Webster Chair Professor of Mining Engineering. His focus has been in Rock Mechanics, Mining and Energy as well as Mine Backfill. He has been advisor to number of governments on mining issues and consultant to many major mining companies around the globe as well as recipient of many patents and awards. He maintains a strong interdisciplinary research and has supervised over 170 PhD,

MEng Students and research scientists. He has contributed to over 450 scientific articles, books and reports and has chaired many international conferences such as Mine Backfill in 1989 and 2007, the World Mining Congress 2013, as well as the International Society of Rock Mechanics Congress in 2015.

Susan Joyce is a sociologist with 25 years of experience working on the community and social dimensions of the extractive industries and other investments, primarily in developing economies. She works on improving the social performance of companies implementing these activities through assessment of the social and human rights impacts and risks, development of management responses, and training and capacity building programs. She is interested in strengthening integration of human and indigenous rights into impact assessment and contributing to applied research on issues of sustainable outcomes, FPIC and cumulative social impacts. She has an MSc in Development Sociology from Cornell University.

Justine Lacey is a Senior Research Scientist and leads the Adaptive Communities and Industries programme of social and economic research within CSIRO, which researches the design and use of scientific innovations for application in sectors including mining, agriculture, biosecurity, health and the environment for the benefit of industry, government and society. Her research examines the aspects underpinning the mineral industry's social licence to operate, and how this concept is used in other resource management contexts, such as forestry and agriculture. She has a background in ethics and natural resource management.

Sumit K. Lodhia is an Associate Professor and a Director of the Centre for Sustainability Governance (CSG), where he leads research focused on sustainability accounting, reporting and governance. He has completed a Bachelor of Arts (BA) and Master of Arts (MA) at the University of the South Pacific, and a PhD from the Australian National University (ANU). He has published over 50 articles in a range of prestigious refereed journals, and is a member of the Editorial Board of several international journals. He has presented his research at conferences nationally and internationally, is a mentor at PhD colloquia associated with various conferences and is on the technical committee for several conferences. In 2014, he co-edited an extensive special issue of the *Journal of Cleaner Production* on mining and sustainability. He has strong links to industry, enabling him to research the sustainability accounting practices of major Australian organisations, both public and private, and he applies his academic research through his teaching, lecturing on sustainability accounting and reporting at undergraduate and postgraduate levels, mentoring lecturers and supervising PhD and Masters students.

Nicolas Maennling leads the economics and policy research at the Columbia Centre on Sustainable Investment (CCSI) and is a development economist with experience in the public and private sectors. His focus is on designing strategies and tools to maximize the benefits and minimize the negative externalities of extractive industry investments. He has led trainings and advisory projects in various countries on taxation systems, financial modeling, economic and infrastructure linkages to extractive industry projects, macroeconomic and revenue management in resource rich countries, and risk analysis. Prior to joining CCSI, he advised the Ministry of Finance in Timor-Leste on issues including inflation, macroeconomic forecasting and fiscal sustainability. He also spent three years in Mozambique, first as the resident Overseas Development Institute fellow in the Ministry of Industry and Trade working on the design and implementation of Mozambique's industrial policy. He then served as a consultant for a private bulk commodity shipping company, LBH Group, and the UK Department for International Development (DfID) on resource extraction projects in northern Mozambique. He received a Bachelor of Science in Economics from the University of Birmingham (UK) and a Master of Science in Economics from the University of Warwick (UK).

Fiona Haslam McKenzie was educated in Australia and the United States and has a varied academic background, including a PhD in political geography, researching the socio-economic impacts of the restructuring of the Australian agricultural industry. Over the last two decades her focus has been the socio-economic impact of the Australian staples economies. She has extensive experience in population and socio-economic change, housing, regional economic development and analysis of remote, regional and urban socio-economic indicators. She is currently researching the socio-economic impact of different regional workforce arrangements and uneven economic development in Western Australia. She was appointed director of the Centre for Regional Development at the University of Western Australia in 2015. She has served on several government and private sector boards, undertaken work for corporate and small business sectors and has published widely.

Benjamin C. McLellan has been an Associate Professor at Kyoto University`s Graduate School of Energy Science since 2010, having previously been a research fellow at the University of Queensland`s Sustainable Minerals Institute. His research is broad, covering energy, minerals and sustainability assessment – typically involving systems modelling of new technologies and their propagation and limitations in society. The minerals–energy nexus is a particular focus of his work, as well as unconventional resources such as deep ocean minerals.

Kieren Moffat is a Senior Research Scientist and leads the Resources in Society research program within CSIRO. This programme seeks to understand the relationship between mining and society across scales, geographies and time. Kieren leads global projects assessing citizen attitudes to mining in resource rich countries in partnership with the International Institute for Environment and Development (IIED) and operational level examination of the drivers of social acceptance among mining communities with a range of resource companies. Through this work to date, the views of more than 44,000 citizens in nine countries have been collected and a quantitative model of the key drivers of social licence developed at local and national scales. Kieren has a background in social and organizational psychology.

Angus Morrison-Saunders is Professor of Environmental Management, School of Science, Edith Cowan University, Australia; Extraordinary Professor in Environmental Sciences and Management, Research Unit for Environmental Sciences and Management, North West University, South Africa; and Senior Associate of the University of Cambridge Institute for Sustainability Leadership, UK. He has over 25 years' experience teaching and researching in environmental science and management with an emphasis on environmental impact assessment. He has published over 100 peer-reviewed works and co-edited two key texts on sustainability assessment (with A. Bond, and R. Howitt (2013), *Sustainability Assessment: Pluralism, Practice and Progress*, Taylor and Francis, London; and with J. Pope and A. Bond (2015), *Handbook of Sustainability Assessment*, Edward Elgar, Cheltenham, UK). He is author of the forthcoming (2018) *Advanced Introduction to Environmental Impact Assessment* (Edward Elgar, Cheltenham, UK).

Ciaran O'Faircheallaigh is Professor of Politics and Public Policy at Griffith University, Brisbane. He is one of the world's leading authorities on the interrelationship between Indigenous peoples and resource development, and has published over 100 books and articles in this and related fields. His recent publications include *Negotiations in the Indigenous World: Aboriginal Peoples and the Extractive Industry in Australia and Canada* (Routledge, New York, 2016); and *IBA Community Toolkit: Negotiation and Implementation of Impact and Benefit Agreements* (Gordon Foundation, Toronto, 2015, with Ginger Gibson). For over 25 years Professor O'Faircheallaigh has worked with Indigenous organizations and communities in Australia, Canada and Papua New Guinea on negotiation of agreements with mining and oil and gas companies, and on conduct of community consultations related to large projects.

Michelle Rodriguez is a social researcher working on issues of social licence to operate in the energy and extractive industries. Michelle contributes to the advancement of scientific understanding of social impacts of industry, technology and innovation, with an emphasis on public perception, community engagement, behaviour change and social acceptance. Michelle has a background in organizational communication.

Rauno Sairinen is Professor of Environmental Policy at the University of Eastern Finland (UEF), and also works as a scientific leader of the Institute for Natural Resources, Environment and Society (LYY Institute) at the UEF. He has been appointed as Honorary Professor in the Centre for Social Responsibility in Mining (CSRM) at the University of Queensland in Australia, and is also a member of the Board of Directors at the Geological Survey of Finland (GTK). His major research themes have concerned mining policies and its social responsibility, environmental and natural resources governance, social impact assessment, environmental policy instruments and community planning. He acted as the co-chair of the social impact assessment section of the International Association for Impact Assessment 2011–2017. During 2010–2016, he has led seven research projects on mining and society relations.

Kendyl Salcito is the Executive Director of NomoGaia, a nonprofit research organization specializing in corporate human rights due diligence. Her expertise in business and human rights is grounded in investigative research carried out in Burma, Indonesia and Canada between 2005 and 2007. Since co-founding NomoGaia in 2008 she has gained recognition as a leading practitioner of corporate human rights impact assessment (HRIA) for multinational corporations and foreign investors whose operations intersect with local communities in complex contexts. She has advised industry groups, nonprofit groups and government entities on corporate human rights performance, including the World Bank and UNICEF. She has worked as a consultant to Newfields LLC in the Human Rights Assessment Group and as a policy analyst for CO_2 Scorecard since 2008. She holds a PhD from the Swiss Tropical and Public Health Institute in Epidemiology, an MA in Journalism from the University of British Columbia and a BA in History from Princeton University.

Sara L. Seck (LLB, Toronto; PhD, Osgoode Hall) joined the Schulich School of Law, Dalhousie University, in Nova Scotia, Canada as an Associate Professor in July 2017, having served as a member of the Faculty of Law at Western University, Ontario, since 2007. In September 2015, Sara received the Emerging Scholarship Award from the Academy of Environmental Law of the IUCN (World Conservation Union) in recognition of her research contributions on sustainable mining and international environmental law. She is a Senior Fellow with CIGI's International Law Research Program, where her research examines business responsibilities for human rights affected by climate change; a member of the Editorial Board of the new *Business and Human Rights Journal* (Cambridge University Press); and a member of the International Law Association's study group on Business and Human Rights. She also serves as the Deputy Director for North America of the Global Network for the Study of Human Rights and the Environment.

Guy Singleton has a diverse educational and professional background, which support his interests in realising meaningful opportunity for regional Aboriginal communities. Guy has a first-class Honours degree in biological science and a PhD in remote Aboriginal community development from Curtin University's Business School. He has worked with and for a range of Aboriginal corporations on development projects across Australia. Since 2012, he has worked within Western Australia's resource sector for both domestic and international mining companies. He is currently employed by ASX100 listed Northern Star Resources Limited and is a director of Central Desert Native Title Services, and also an Adjunct Research Fellow at the University of Western Australia within the Centre for Regional Development.

Perrine Toledano heads the Columbia Centre on Sustainable Investment. (CCSI) focus on extractive industries and sustainable development. She leads research, training and advisory projects on fiscal regimes, financial modeling, leveraging extractive industry investments in rail, port, telecommunications, water and energy infrastructure for broader development needs, local content, revenue management, contract transparency and optimal legal provisions for development benefits. She has led projects in DRC, Liberia, Paraguay, Mozambique, Sierra Leone, Tanzania and Timor-Leste, and assisted many more government teams remotely. She also jointly developed curricula for a masters and an executive course on extractives and sustainable development taught at Columbia University. Prior to joining CCSI, she worked as a consultant for several non-profit organizations, including the World Bank, DFID and Revenue Watch Institute, and private sector companies, including Natixis Corporate Investment Bank and Ernst and Young. Her experience includes auditing, financial analysis, IT for capital markets, public policy evaluation and cross-border project management. She has a Masters of Business Administration from ESSEC in Paris, France, and a Masters of Public Administration from Columbia University.

Frank Vanclay is Professor of Cultural Geography in the Faculty of Spatial Sciences at the University of Groningen in the Netherlands. Previously based in Australia, he has had a long-term interest in the social impacts of large projects, especially the extractive industries, and was the lead author of the guidance document on social impact assessment for the International Association for Impact Assessment. He is also interested in related topics such as: social licence to operate; business and human rights; project-induced displacement and resettlement; and free, prior and informed consent.

Mark Wielga is co-founder and Director of NomoGaia. He has over 20 years direct experience with human rights in action. He has managed and performed human rights impact assessments on large footprint corporate projects in Africa, Asia and Latin America, and has worked with transnational corporations to design and implement corporate human rights policies as well as emergency responses to urgent human rights controversies. He has taught, lectured and published on human rights and corporate social responsibility in universities and institutions around the world. He is a lawyer licensed in the United States and his extensive international and corporate legal experience informs his human rights work.

Preface

This book is the culmination of a research interest in mining and sustainability spanning almost two decades. I found the mining industry to be a useful context for my PhD and having attended an industry conference on mining and sustainable development in the early days of my PhD tenure, I realised that despite perceptions of mining as a 'dirty' industry, there were fundamental actions being undertaken by mining companies to address sustainability concerns. Having continued with my interests in mining and sustainable development, I was encouraged by Professor Don Huisingh to co-edit a special issue of the *Journal of Cleaner Production* in 2012. This special issue came out in 2014 and represents one of the most extensive reviews of sustainability in the mining industry to date. My fellow co-editor Professor Chris Moran alerted me to a special book project on mining and sustainable development by Routledge and it was he who had started off this book project. I was privileged to be asked by the publishers to revive this project and would like to wholeheartedly thank the contributors for their patience and support in ensuring that this fine book was published. Many thanks to the Routledge publishing team, especially Tim Hardwick and Amy Louise Johnston for their hard work and support towards this project. My research centre, Centre for Sustainability Governance at the University of South Australia, Adelaide, Australia deserves a special mention for encouraging research that has impact for practice. Lastly, I would like to dedicate this book to my late grandparents, Harilal Ranchod Lodhia and Ganga Ben Lodhia, whose 'thirst' for knowledge continues to inspire me to this day.

Sumit K. Lodhia

1 Mining and sustainable development

Sumit K. Lodhia

The role of mining in sustainable development

Mining is a transformative activity which has numerous economic, social and environmental impacts. These impacts can be both positive and adverse, enhancing as well as disrupting economies, ecosystems and communities (Moran *et al.*, 2014). From economic development, construction of infrastructure and development of communities, to severe environmental effects during the entire mining life cycle, displacement of local communities and concerns over wealth inequities, the mining industry (also referred to as minerals or extractive industries) plays a critical role in local and national economies and communities.

The extractive industries have been criticised heavily for their adverse impacts and involvement in significant social and environmental scandals (Franks, 2015). Incidents such as those in the OK Tedi and Baia Marie mine sites (Lodhia, 2007) at the turn of the century and, more recently, the Samarco mining dam failure (Garcia *et al.*, 2017) are some examples of the adverse consequences of mining operations. This has resulted in constant scrutiny of mining activities by stakeholders and an increasing pressure on mining companies' social licence to operate (Lodhia, 2007; Lodhia and Hess, 2014). These industries have sought to respond to negative perceptions and have embraced the core principles of sustainability (Moran *et al.*, 2014; Franks, 2015; Bice, 2016).

The minerals sector could be regarded as a leader in sustainability initiatives, evident from the various frameworks in mining and sustainability that have emerged over time. Guidance such as the Global Mining Initiative and the Extractive Industries Transparency Initiative globally (Franks, 2015), and local sustainable development codes such as Enduring Value for the Australian mining industry (Lodhia, 2007), indicate the seriousness with which sustainability issues are regarded in the mining industry. It can be concluded that over time, mining companies are required to be responsive to their social and environmental responsibilities and contribute positively towards sustainable development (Bice, 2016).

This rest of this chapter is structured as follows. A framework for exploring current sustainable development issues in mining is introduced in the next section. This framework provides the broad parameters through which the major themes of this book are organised. The chapters of this book are discussed in relation to this framework. The final section presents the implications arising from this book and discusses specific issues that could be explored further in future work.

A framework for mining and sustainable development

Having acknowledged the importance of sustainability in the mining industry, a framework is developed in order to establish current issues in mining and sustainable development. There are five key elements to this framework: recognition of the increasing importance of sustainability in mining (as discussed above); due diligence mechanisms for addressing sustainability matters in mining; contemporary challenges to sustainability in the mining industry, corporate approaches towards mining and sustainability; and sustainability solutions.

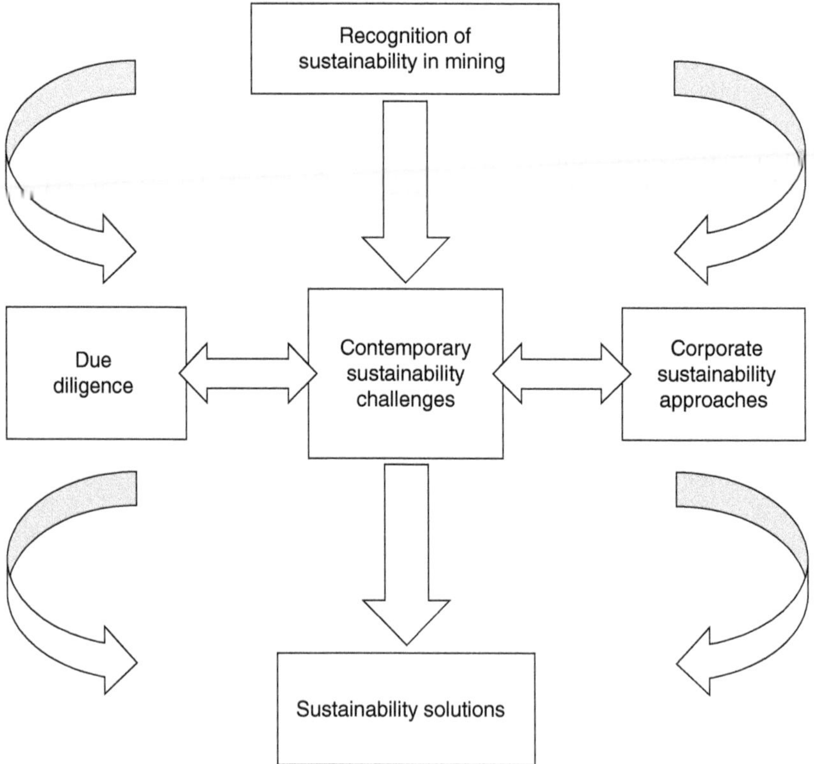

Figure 1.1 A framework for mining and sustainable development.

The framework is predicated on the premise that business as usual is no longer acceptable and that sustainability matters are critical for survival of the mining industry. In order to ensure that mining companies are contributing positively to sustainability, due diligence mechanisms in the form of social and environmental impact assessments are needed. Due diligence exercises ensure that mining companies are cognisant of the social and environmental aspects of their operations, both in relation to reducing negative impacts and enhancing the benefits provided by mining. These activities are essential for ensuring the integrity of mining operations during their entire life cycle. At the same time, contemporary challenges in sustainability and mining cannot be ignored and should be monitored on an ongoing basis. These can include both social and environmental challenges and could be specific to a particular region. Further, corporate approaches such as management and accounting (including sustainability accounting and reporting), and taxation, are also fundamental to ensuring that economic, social and environmental sustainability are addressed. These three elements are not mutually exclusive; there is often overlap between them. For instance, a contemporary sustainability challenge may be identified in due diligence and would require a corporate sustainability approach to manage this challenge. Taken together, due diligence, addressing contemporary challenges and corporate sustainability approaches have the potential to facilitate sustainability solutions, thereby highlighting that the mining industry is not the problem but, rather, part of the solution to sustainability.

Using this framework, this book examines current topical issues in mining and sustainable development. The chapters in this book provide a contemporary understanding of sustainability opportunities and impediments in the mining industry.

Current issues in mining and sustainable development

This book consists of thirteen chapters and five sections. Following this introductory section and chapter, the remaining five parts represent each element of the framework: recognition of the importance of sustainability; due diligence mechanisms for sustainability; contemporary sustainability challenges in the mining industry; corporate mining approaches that address sustainability; and sustainability solutions.

Part I provides an overview of mining and sustainable development with emphasis on the increasing importance of sustainability for mining. The chapters emphasise the changing role of minerals in society and the social acceptance of mining. Part II discusses due diligence, with discussion of social and environmental impact assessments. Part III focuses on two critical and contemporary challenges in mining: indigenous issues and transit worker accommodation in remote communities. Part IV takes a corporate focus with emphasis being on sustainability reporting, and mining taxation. Part V provides examples of sustainability solutions for mining and these include discussion of renewable energy and shared-use mining infrastructure.

An overview of the importance of sustainability in the mining industry is provided in the second and third chapters. Ali (Chapter 2) highlights the changing role of minerals in society through a focus on its supply and demand. He addresses the vexed issues of non-renewability and sustainability of minerals and applies notions of industrial ecology and the circular economy to mining. Such a systematic perspective suggests an increasingly vital role of minerals in society, leading to a need for broader and effective considerations of mineral supply and demand. Moffat *et al.* (Chapter 3) address the social acceptance and trust of mining operations by drawing upon extensive global surveys of communities. The authors posit that contact experience with corporate personnel, procedural and distributional fairness, and confidence in governance of social and environmental issues are fundamental drivers of trust and acceptance of mining. The social acceptance of mining by stakeholders has the potential to lead to a more sustainable mining industry.

Part II of this book addresses due diligence in mining operations. Due diligence in the form of environmental and social impact assessments are critical elements in ensuring that the adverse sustainability impacts of mining operation are minimised and addressed effectively. Bond and Morrison-Saunders (Chapter 4) discuss environmental impact assessment (EIA) and apply this notion to mining activities. The authors highlight that EIA has moved from a mere environmental focus to a sustainability focus with emphasis on the contribution of a proposed activity to sustainable development. The application of EIA to mining suggests a need for sustainable mining which the authors contend is feasible. Best practice EIA principles are discussed in relation to mine planning, implementation and closure. Similarly, Joyce *et al.* (Chapter 5) highlight the transition in social impact assessment (SIA) from an analysis of negative impacts of mining to management of its social impacts and enhancement of social benefits. The role of SIA in the entire mining life cycle is discussed. The authors suggest that for SIA to be successful, it needs to be incorporated into business decision making processes at an early stage. Local perspectives through engagement with communities also need to be embedded into risk and impact management.

Salcito and Wielga (Chapter 6) discuss due diligence in relation to mining operations. Fundamental tools for due diligence include impact assessments such as EIA and SIA discussed previously. The authors focus on human rights due diligence, developed as a result of the UN Guiding Principles on Business and Human Rights. This is an exploratory concept in the mining industry. Despite this, the authors contend that there is cause for optimism and that bold companies would transition to such due diligence in the foreseeable future. Aizawa *et al.* (Chapter 7) also discuss the challenges of human rights due diligence for mining companies through a focus on its financing. It is envisaged that in addition to law and policy, a number of alternative financing arrangements could ease the burden of financing human rights diligence and thereby encourage an increasing adoption of this mechanism by mining companies. These include tax incentives, financing assistance, social impact bonds and crowdfunding.

The third part of this book addresses contemporary challenges in mining and sustainable development. Two contemporary issues are addressed here. O'Faircheallaigh (Chapter 8) highlights the inherent contradiction of mining and sustainability from an indigenous perspective. However, the author suggests that mining activities could be sustainable from an indigenous perspective if their development and needs were considered. Involvement of indigenous people in environmental management of large-scale projects and the use of minerals revenue to promote economic and social development in communities that is sustained even after mining ends are perceived as critical in enabling mining to contribute to indigenous development and sustainability. The author posits that these issues are broader than mining projects and require a state-wide systematic response which empowers indigenous groups to engage with extractive industries. Mckenzie and Singleton (Chapter 9) address the push and pull factors for transit worker accommodation in remote Australian mining communities. The concern for such a mechanism is that it does not lead to development of regional communities and may impact worker's welfare. However, work flexibility and mobility, and reduction in costs for companies are perceived as beneficial. The authors suggests that mining companies, communities and governments should collaborate and ensure that regions benefit from transit worker accommodation.

Part IV of this book addresses mining and sustainable development from a corporate perspective. Lodhia (Chapter 10) discusses the evolution in studies on sustainability reporting in the mining industry. Sustainability reporting is an approach that mining companies utilise to provide accountability over the social and environmental aspects of their activities. There is much that needs to be investigated in relation to sustainability reporting in this industry and the chapter provides future research directions for research on sustainability reporting in the mining industry. Guj (Chapter 11) discusses mining taxation in minerals rich developing countries. Three fiscal approaches are discussed: those focusing on economic efficiency and equity, revenue maximisation and stability, and transparency and administrative efficiency. The author provides comprehensive guidance on improving mining fiscal regimes which he suggests will depend on the improvement of tax administration processes in host countries.

The final part of this book discusses possible sustainability solutions for mining operations. McLellan *et al.* (Chapter 12) focus on emissions from mining activities and highlight the role of renewable energy in mining. The key drivers and potential for renewable energy in the mining industry are identified. An examination of the longer-term trends in mining indicates a changing landscape for renewable energy under specific technological changes in the mining industry. Toledano and Maennling (Chapter 13) focus on another critical issue, sustainable development goals, and specify how the mining industry could contribute to them. More specifically, the authors highlight how the mining industry could provide increasing access to infrastructure. Such infrastructure has primarily been geared towards corporate activities but it could be shared and developed to meet the needs of host countries. Shared-use mining infrastructure could contribute positively to addressing the funding gaps for infrastructure development required under the sustainable development goals.

Contributions and future possibilities

The chapters in this book make an important contribution to comprehending the interplay between mining and sustainable development. They will be of relevance to mining practitioners, governments and civil society, as well as scholars and students with interests in mining and sustainability. This book has a number of broad implications which are discussed next before further areas worthy of future investigation are discussed. Overall, it highlights a shift in emphasis in the mining industry from a mere management of social and environmental issues to being proactively involved in addressing global sustainability challenges.

The earlier chapters in this book reiterate the changing role of the mining industry and a need for the industry to have social acceptance, thereby providing evidence of the increasing importance of sustainability for mining companies. Due diligence through social and environmental impact assessments are perceived as critical and a foundational step in addressing sustainability challenges in the mining industry. Contemporary challenges such as Indigenous issues are paramount for the mining industry and a need to collaborate with local communities is essential for mining companies in earning the trust of their host communities. This would ensure the social acceptance of mining. Transit worker accommodation is another complex sustainability challenge that affects mining employees and regional development, and requires cooperation among communities, companies and governments.

Corporate approaches to sustainability by mining companies are essential in addressing social and environmental issues in the mining industry. Sustainability reporting has been highlighted as a mechanism that mining companies can use to provide social and environmental accountability to their various stakeholders. The discussion of mining taxation in this book provides insights into fiscal regimes that could ensure a fair distribution of mining revenues.

Sustainability solutions can be provided by the mining industry. Renewable energy has a vital role in the mining industry and the final chapter confirms the contribution of the mining industry to the global society. The concept of shared used infrastructure is a novel concept that suggests that mining companies can contribute positively towards building sustainable societies as envisioned by global bodies such as the United Nations.

This book provides a mere snapshot of current issues in mining and sustainable development. Addressing all possible matters in relation to mining and sustainable development goes beyond the scope of a book and may not even be achieved in an entire volume. However, there are other areas that could be developed in future publications on mining and sustainable development.

There is a need for further work to highlight the extent to which the mining industry is recognising the importance of sustainability. Publications such as Franks (2015) and Bice (2016) can be complemented by other specific studies that look at sustainable mining in particular contexts. Both the successes and the failures need to be explored in order to establish the key success factors and impediments to mining and sustainable development.

The concept of due diligence has been discussed in depth in this book. A particular emphasis on human rights has also been highlighted. There is a need for further examination of due diligence in practice, enabling an understanding of the specific sustainability issues that are addressed by mechanisms such as environmental and social impact assessments. The processes uses to initiate these assessments, the outcomes and the responsiveness of mining stakeholders to the outcomes are worthy of further investigation.

There are a number of contemporary challenges in relation to the mining industry. For instance, the tension between benefits of mining such as royalties and employment of locals, and depletion of resources and destruction of the pristine environment, is a complex issue that requires an in-depth analysis. Identification of other contemporary challenges (including those specific to particular regions), their impact on the mining industry and the approaches to address these would provide updated knowledge on the current situation in the mining industry.

Sustainability accounting and reporting research is quite extensive and there are a number of further areas that can be explored within the mining industry (see Lodhia and Hess, 2014 for specific details). Whilst this book has focused on sustainability reporting, subject matter such as carbon accounting and pricing, environmental management systems, and occupational health and safety would provide viable areas of investigation within the context of the mining industry. Taxation is also fundamental to ensuring a fair and equitable distribution of minerals wealth and there is a need to examine the existing approaches used in various countries in relation to taxation of mining revenues and the resulting impact on relevant stakeholders.

Finally, there is a need to document and publicise the various sustainability solutions in the mining industry. This would provide insights into mining's contribution to sustainable development and facilitate the sharing of knowledge across the entire industry.

References

Bice, S. (2016) *Responsible Mining: Key Principles for Industry Integrity.* Routledge, London and New York.

Franks, D.M. (2015) *Mountain Movers: Mining, Sustainability and the Agents of Change.* Routledge, London and New York.

Garcia, L.C, Ribeiro, D.B, Roque, F.O, Ochoa-Quintero, J.M. and Laurance, W.F. (2017) 'Brazil's Worst Mining Disaster: Corporations must be Compelled to Pay the Actual Environmental Costs'. *Ecological Applications 27, 1*, 5–9.

Lodhia, S. (2007) 'Corporations and the Environment: Australian Evidence'. *International Journal of Environmental, Cultural, Economic and Social Sustainability 3, 3*, 183–193.

Lodhia, S. and Hess, N. (2014) 'Sustainability Accounting and Reporting in the Mining Industry: Current Literature and Directions for Future Research'. *Journal of Cleaner Production 84*, 43–50.

Moran, C., Lodhia, S., Kunz, N. and Huisingh, D. (2014) 'Sustainability in Mining, Minerals and Energy: New Processes, Pathways and Human Interactions for a Cautiously Optimistic Future'. *Journal of Cleaner Production 84*, 1–15.

Part I

Importance of sustainability in mining

2 The changing role of minerals in society

Managing a shift in paradigms

Saleem H. Ali

Introduction

All too often the key argument from environmentalists regarding the sustainability of mineral extraction is linked to their ostensible "non-renewability" on human timescales. Yet from a chemical perspective elements are renewable if we are able to harness them back from their higher state of entropy in manufactured systems. This fundamental recognition has begun to percolate in designing products that are better suited towards the use of minerals to maximize economic and ecological efficiency. Improved metrics that link biophysical constraints to mineral usage are also assisting with better design of green technologies so minerals are considered as part of the broader "sustainability landscape" of energy and material infrastructure planning (Ali, 2010).

Mining extracts minerals from higher states of entropy in geological environments. However, manufactured uses of these elements raise their entropy again. Energy in the form of extraction technologies as well as labor are then required to extract the metals back from their product use at the end of the product cycle. The viability of reuse and recycling of minerals in the stockpile of products is dependent on the durability of the product itself and the recoverability of the material. From a purely resource use minimization perspective it would be more sustainable to have a durable product than having to remanufacture disposable products. However, if one considers the broader systems ecology of material usage, calibrating stocks and flows of minerals with rising demand, based on population or development, one has to consider whether durability of the product would necessitate more mining at the expense of recycling. For example, if we make more durable aircraft but there is still a greater demand for them, the metal locked in their existing stock would not be available for recycling, and hence mining of the metal would become necessary.

Energy use calculations as well as the social and environmental trade-offs of mining versus recycling are needed in more detail to ascertain the optimal profile of recycled versus mined material sourcing. This chapter will consider the aforementioned hybridity of mineral supply and its implications for dynamic modern societies.

Minerals will need to be considered from multiple supply sources and mining companies would need to reinvent themselves as material service providers from multiple sources rather than just mining itself. This may also involve the advent of new companies and players that form a new kind of industrial ecosystem. A potential win–win outcome related to mineral supply flows in this context is the use of minerals in green technologies, particularly for cleaner energy production that could in turn help to harness minerals more sustainably. The key to such an approach would be to track the overall impact reduction of the extractive process as more use of those minerals in green technologies could also lead to greater aggregate ecological impacts. It is also essential to track the energy–material flow relationship. Substituting certain minerals for use in green technologies will likely have impact on energy consumption that is an important metric for systems-wide aggregate impacts. Furthermore, we need to consider the role of recycling within a "circular economy" paradigm with greater technical complexity (World Economic Forum, 2014). Postconsumer resource usage is also changing in ways to consider aggregate composites of metals and plastic or glass materials collectively for different uses. Thus the conventional view of recycling metals through their disaggregated waste streams is also shifting (Sahajwalla, 2015). This chapter navigates the history of this transition; recent methodological trends in measuring and monitoring these shifts; and how management professionals in the industry and government can best adapt to the change.

Prerequisites of transition

The industrial revolution, which began in Britain in the late eighteenth century, marked a fundamental distancing of human society from the natural system because it was characterized by a transition from a primarily agricultural economy to one based on manufactured goods. In other words, economic reliance on natural systems as the primary means of production was shifted to mechanized systems of production that were self-perpetuating. Technology gave us the ability to produce finished goods in great numbers and supply them to consumers who were consequently less aware of how the finished product had been manufactured. For example, instead of buying wheat from a farmer or even flour from a mill, you could simply buy large quantities of finished confectionery products and often be quiet oblivious of the manufacturing process.

The population began to depend more directly on the firm that supplied the goods rather than the natural system that latently supported the actual enterprise. At the same time the firm too focused more on the needs of the consumer and took for granted the natural resource base on which it fundamentally depended. The environment was thus short-circuited out of the circle of affluence and prosperity, so long as the resource was available within the desired profit margin. The impact on the natural resource base thus became an "externality" so long as there was a perceived abundance of the resource.

Around the same time as the boom in coal mining and industrial expansion across Europe, the term "ecology" was conceived by the German naturalist Ernst Heinrich Haeckel in 1869 as the study of the interactions between organisms and their environment. It soon became apparent that organisms and their environment have more than just a biological interaction and thus by its very nature ecology was forced to depart from reductionism and offer a more holistic spectrum of inquiry. The concept of an "ecosystem", introduced by the British biologist Alfred Tansley in 1935, played a major role in giving structure and coherence to this field. According to ecological historian Frank Golley (1996, p. 8) "the ecosystem referred to a holistic and integrative ecological concept that combined living organisms and the physical environment into a system." This concept heralded an important realignment in academia from reductionism to holism. Ecology, and more specifically the concept of an ecosystem, were thus obliged to consider industrial processes, keeping in line with the holistic – all-encompassing worldview – which they espoused. The field of *cybernetics* emerged embracing this holistic world-view from a computational perspective under the direction of the great mathematician Norbert Weiner. Central to the success of computer science has been the significance of feedback loops and networks which can be traced back to cybernetics (Weiner, 1948; Andrews, 1974). Cybernetics is now an interdisciplinary science dealing with communication and control systems in living organisms, machines and organizations.

These concepts were further reinforced by the publication in 1971 of Barry Commoner's classic work *The Closing Circle* (1971) which argued for a stronger relationship between modern industrial activity and ecology. The same year the Japanese Ministry of International Trade and Industry (MITI) started a program which promoted "principles of industry-ecology", believed by many to be the first formal usage of the concept. This program recognized systems boundaries for industrial activities, and emphasized the development of mechanisms to control human impact on ecosystems and promote ecological equilibrium. This was in sharp contrast to the common modes of engineering discourse that isolated human endeavor and nature as different components with little or no interactions.

The trend towards holistic thought since then has come about largely due to humanity's growing ability to effectively manage large amounts of information. Advances in quantitative analysis and computing are perhaps the most salient developments to facilitate the reemergence of comprehensive rationality. The potential for using quantitative methods for multiple-criteria decision analysis and other tools of operations research in ecological systems is immense. Accessibility to data and learning through electronic means such as the Internet and computerized databases has also transformed the information processing abilities of society, thereby facilitating the development of holistic approaches to industrial management.

Braden Allenby and Thomas Graedel were among the pioneers who first enunciated the term "industrial ecology" within the American corporate realm to harmonize various strands of research into practice. While employed at American Telephone and Telegraph (AT&T) in two different divisions, Allenby and Graedel brought environmental reform to the forefront within the corporation. The difference in their academic background is an important illustration of the breadth which industrial ecology aims to cover. Allenby is a lawyer by training and also has a doctorate in engineering. Graedel is an atmospheric chemist, who had spent most of his career at Bell Laboratories. Their work has greatly helped in bringing industrial ecology into the limelight of government policy and educational discourse. Allenby and Graedel are authors of a comprehensive textbook on Industrial Ecology which was sponsored by AT&T (Graedel and Allenby, 2002; McDonough and Braungart, 2002).

For some purists the term "industrial ecology" may seem to be an oxymoron. How could industrial processes, which had distanced humans from their natural environment, be married to the very natural science of ecology? Part of the answer to this question lies in the realization that whether we liked it or not industrial processes were inevitably impacting the natural system and vice versa. Humankind had removed itself from managing these latent interactions because it was too busy managing the production and consumption of goods and services. Second, the permanence of industrial processes began to dawn upon scientists and engineers alike. There was no plausible turning back from the lifestyles of comfort and convenience which we had come to accept – and thus natural science would inexorably need to accommodate the industrial system.

Robert Ayres, an eclectic engineer who spent most of his career at a business school in France, developed the concept of *industrial metabolism* which aims to describe industries as "mega-organisms," consuming low-entropy resources to provide for their own sustenance while allowing for growth and reproduction. Ayres argues that the analogy between biological organisms and industrial activities is compelling since "both are examples of self-organizing, dissipate systems in a stable state, far from thermodynamic equilibrium" (Ayres and Simonis, 1994). While interdisciplinary engineers such as Ayres were considering industrial metabolism, input-output analysts revolutionized how we consider materials flow in our economy and helped to bridge engineering and economics (Piluso *et al.*, 2008).

Combining concerns about energy usage and entropy leads to another useful concept, called "exergy," which is being explored increasingly as a metric for understanding the irreversibility of certain kinds of resource extractions. Originally developed by the great physicist J. Willard Gibbs in 1873, the concept has been refined as physicists, ecologists and some economists joined forces to understand resource depletion. The term itself was first used by Slovenian engineer Zoran Rant in 1956. The exergy of a material can be defined by its ability to do useful work in achieving thermal equilibrium with its environment. While energy can neither be created nor destroyed under normal circumstances, a material's exergy can be destroyed based on an increase in entropy through mixing and dispersal. Both energy and exergy have the same measurement units (Joules), but for understanding material usage and sustainability, exergy is a more useful concept to be further developed (Dincer and Rosen, 2007).

For if the industrial sector is to be considered a pseudo-organism we must also relate that entity to the broader environment in which it subsists: hence the idea of *industrial ecosystems*. The interrelationships between the environment and industry extend to biotic as well as societal factors. It is no wonder, therefore, that economics, ethics and anthropology are often invoked in discourse pertaining to industrial ecology. However, the most consequential disciplines in applying these principles are either business administration or public administration.

Since industrial ecology has emerged as a synthesis of several different disciplinary efforts, the task of implementing its principles must take place at all conceivable echelons of society. First, it is evident that we need to somehow integrate regulatory systems, so that they do not look at each medium of pollution separately but try to understand how various input/output channels are interconnected. This does not necessarily mean that we integrate all statutes but rather that the licensing procedure for pollution control should be integrated, as is the case in many European countries. This saves tremendous transaction costs on separate permitting procedures and also encourages companies to think about synergies in pollution prevention initiatives, for example, reusing wastes from one process for another usage. However, to further the aims of industrial ecology inter-industry cooperation needs to be facilitated through corporate initiatives as well such as *Responsible Care* (initiated by the American Chemical Manufacturers' Association and now part of the International Council of Chemical Associations), and *The Global Environmental Management Initiative* (initiated by the International Chamber of Commerce), as well as government involvement to ensure that such efforts have meaningful results are not an attempt at "greenwash." One does, however, need to be careful in knowing the limits of this approach, because a very large-scale interdependence of industries can make all vulnerable to a slight malfunction of their symbiotic components. Therefore, we must have appropriate contingency alternatives for "industrially symbiotic" systems which should be part of the engineering designs for such efforts.

A lot of the win–win options of being green are now taken. Certain choices will have to be made that may be costly in the short run but whose far-reaching benefits (for example, with the use of naturally derived pesticides, that are initially more expensive) will be significant enough to warrant the investment. A good example of this long-term approach to competitive advantage is exemplified by the Japanese car industry which anticipated fuel shortages and designed smaller cars in the 1960s. They were thus at a strong advantage against their American competitors that did not take into account such contingencies. Appreciating the importance of material cycles will give corporations and individuals alike an opportunity to take into account such long-term considerations by providing a means for looking at the interconnections within systems from energy supply to waste removal. It is important to note that merely reducing materials throughput does not necessarily render the system ecologically sustainable. Processes which transform high entropy wastes into even higher entropy feedstocks can in fact inhibit the industrial ecology goal of achieving closed materials cycles. Critics of the approach contend that an effort to holistically consider all the environmental implications of a product or process "would generate a barrage of formidable tradeoffs between uncertain and widely disparate outcomes that must ultimately be reduced to social value judgments" (O'Rourke, 1996).

Yet, the advancement in computational means of information management and prioritization regimes that can also involve communities effectively as part of the planning process can assuage such concerns (van den Belt, 2004). Industries need to plan such ventures to ensure that they find the separation and reprocessing technologies to refine the wastes so that high entropy wastes can be converted to low entropy feedstock. This process would of course require energy usage and a detailed assessment of costs and benefits would need to be carried out to assess the environmental impact of this extra energy usage (Brodyansky *et al.*, 1994).

Some have even argued that "industrial ecology" is an oxymoron because industry is by its very existence a non-natural phenomenon and hence exogenous to the ecosystem approach. However, what matters most is a realization that industry does indeed have effects on ecosystems and shares many similarities of process with them. Hence anthropogenic ecosystems, such as industries, may indeed gain from a more harmonious interaction with nature. To reaffirm the essential linkages between industry and nature, it has even been suggested that we use the term "earth systems ecology" instead of "industrial ecology." Whatever the choice of words, it is important to keep in mind the concepts which we need to implement a systems approach to environmental management.

Managing industrial change

The American statistician W. Edward Deming studied Japan's tremendous business success in the aftermath of World War II and proposed a much celebrated concept in business circles called "Total Quality Management" (TQM). For his work Deming was celebrated in both his homeland and in Japan which awarded him an "Order of the Sacred Treasure," in 1960.

Deming proposed that Total Quality Management entails looking at all stakeholders involved in the process of production and consumption of a product. Expanding on this concept in the 1990s, environmental managers suggested adding an 'E' to the acronym and expanding its scope to include all environmental flows in the production process. TQEM lays a lot of emphasis on the measurement of performance, continued change and innovation. Decision-making should be data-driven and there should be an emphasis on continuous improvement. Design should be geared toward quality and must anticipate problems as opposed to reacting to mistakes. From an environmental standpoint, this may be achieved through management changes, technological improvements and the establishment of self-correction mechanisms. There is a need for corporations to institute this management mechanism and for government to encourage its establishment, through institutional cooperation. TQEM programs require greater communication between various departments of a corporation so that environmental concerns can be tackled collectively. For example, the manufacturing and sourcing department needs to coordinate modular design for easy recyclability with the research and development (R&D) department of a company. Most large American corporations have developed TQEM programs which have also been embraced by the larger mining companies. Yet, change management within the mining sector has met with certain structural limitations around the way material flows are considered by the business environment. Although social and environmental performance of the sector has shown a remarkable shift from the two-decades period of 1995 to 2015 (Franks, 2015), the broader structural incentives for change need to be realigned with nonlinear material flows.

An important way forward to appreciate the changing role of minerals in society is to consider the implementation of the concept of "Life Cycle Analysis" (LCA). The concept emerged in product engineering on account of the realization that a product may affect the environment in adverse ways, before and after it is consumed. It underscores the importance of manufacturing processes and disposal processes that were previously sidelined by the most palpable aspects of consumption (Santero and Henry, 2016). Detailed LCAs are often expensive to conduct, but with computer modelling and increased skills, they may become much more efficient. LCA is a means of environmental accounting that helps to prevent post-facto remediation efforts and offers a means of achieving long-term efficiency. There is now an evolving international standard for Life Cycle Analysis under the ISO 14000 series of international standards. This standard was promulgated in 1998 and has gained considerable acceptance within the past decade.

Industrial ecologists believe that a product remains the responsibility of the producer until it is actually absorbed by the system in which it enters. Therefore, food products that are digested by organisms no longer remain the responsibility of the producers. However, products containing materials such as steel and plastics do indeed remain the responsibility of the producer since they are not permanently digested or "metabolized" by any entity and become a liability on the system after usage. This is particularly a problem with obsolescent technology items such as cars, computers and photocopiers. Increasingly there is a trend to have product-takeback schemes, where the producer must take back the product after use and is responsible for either refurbishing it or disposing of it in an environmentally appropriate manner. Such schemes have been especially successful with photocopiers and laser printers in the United States.

A few attempts have been made in the management literature to examine various ways of implementing the principles of industrial ecology in the corporate world, most notably in the writings of Paul Shrivastava who believes that industrial societies have traditionally led managers to focus their efforts on the creation of wealth through technological expansion, whereas managers in postindustrial societies must shift their efforts towards managing risks which accrue from the creation and distribution of wealth (Shrivastava, 1995). His analysis emanates from a study of major industrial accidents, such as the methyl isocyanate leakage from a Union Carbide plant in Bhopal, India. Risk, he proposes, is thus the primary motivating force behind the adoption of industrial ecological principles by managers in the modern corporation.

While Shrivastava's model of "ecocentric management" is useful from a macroscopic perspective, he does not offer suggestions for how the business administration of the corporation should change in tangible ways. What follows is a brief set of recommendations in nine significant sectors of a modern corporation which would follow the paradigm of industrial ecology. It is important to appreciate that 70 percent of our economy is now in the service sector and hence many of the changes which are being recommended for the manufacturing sector will inexorably need to be reinforced in the service sector.

1 Strategic Planning Division
   - Plan to integrate vertically rather than horizontally in order to minimize transactional impact on natural resources that are to be used in the production process.
   - Avoid large transportation costs and resulting pollution by geographically locating facilities in closer proximity to each other.
   - Look for synergies in energy and waste utilization with nearby industries through the establishment of eco-industrial parks. Share best practices with industries to achieve better cooperation.

2 Government and Community Relations Department
   - Lobbying efforts of the industry should focus on long-term voluntary compliance initiatives which could reduce the infrastructure required for compliance-centered government agencies. However, the voluntary compliance must be effectively enforced internally.

- Favor integrated environmental regulations rather than the conventional air, water and waste mode of incremental regulations.
- Dispute resolution and negotiation strategies should be favored over legal action to reduce transaction costs of litigation, unless it is important to set an institutional precedent with a case.

3 Research and Development Division
- Utilize industrial ecology concepts of Design For Environment and Dematerialization to develop more eco-friendly products.

4 Manufacturing/Sourcing Division
- Coordinate activities with R&D sector to ensure manufacturing processes optimize energy usage for product manufacturing.
- Choose suppliers that are in close proximity to the manufacturing location to reduce transportation costs and risks of environmental accidents.

5 Environmental Health and Safety (EHS) Department
- Move from compliance-oriented EHS management to proactive pollution prevention.
- Work with R&D department to see if emissions can somehow be reused in the manufacturing process in your company or in other nearby companies.

6 Financial Management and Accounting Departments
- Use a low discount rate for evaluating the future benefits of environmental projects in order to ensure that the long-term benefits are accounted for. Consider reporting performance over longer time horizons as well.
- Include the cost of resource depletion or resource amelioration when calculating company's profitability.

7 Human Resources Department
- Provide training for all employees on environmental issues so that company initiatives are appreciated and taken in context (an ecoliteracy requirement across the company).
- Encourage employees to live near the company's location and provide incentives for use of collective or public transportation.

8 Marketing Department
- Reduce advertising through paper-based or other disposable media.
- Persuade industry competitors to produce and market items with ecological impact data and benchmarks on product labels to encourage positive competition on environmental performance.

9 Customer Service Department
- Encourage customers to participate in product-takeback by offering incentives for recycling and return of products.
- Provide services for product repair or telephonic guidance for home-repairs, with modest fees as a revenue stream rather than encouraging obsolescence.

The measures described above are by no means an exhaustive listing but provide a skeletal set of points to consider in the context of reconfiguring a corporation to account for material cycles. These measures also attempt to keep in view the fact that manufacturing does indeed provide lots of jobs but that services associated with product repair and recycling can provide comparable impacts which can be evaluated through life cycle analysis.

Critics of this approach summarily argue that structured management leads to centralized planning which failed in history starting with the Greeks, the Romans, and more recently with the Soviet Union. It is important not to confuse thought and process at this juncture. The vision of industrial ecology, though stressing the intrinsic interrelationships between various biotic and abiotic processes, does not necessarily imply that we centralize efforts to deal with all material problems. We need to be far more discerning than to simply propose a single set of solutions. Where do we draw the line between integrating holistic ideals (that are implicit in a systems approach) on the one side and practical implementation in segmented form on the other? The best way to approach this question is to first try the integrative or holistic approach at the communication and networking level, without instituting widespread organizational change. Once successful interdepartmental and interdisciplinary programs have been implemented, then organizational change to integrate synergistic systems may be implemented more effectively as well.

Conclusion: extractive industries and the shift to sustainability

There are specific features of the non-renewable sector which make it a particular challenge for CSR and for environmental management and which also render it a particularly interesting arena for the analysis of CSR. Some of these features include the physically irreversible impact of many mining operations on topography, their potential for adversely affecting the environment, and more specifically the use of processes (for instance, river disposal of wastes) and inputs (for example, cyanide) that can quickly destroy ecosystems (see next section). They also include the large scale of modern operations relative to adjacent communities and their consequent tendency to generate major social impacts; and the cyclical nature of metal markets and the potential social disruption associated with downsizing and closure (Bridge, 2004; Hilson and Haselip, 2004; Rajaram *et al.*, 2005). On the other hand extractive industries have the potential to create considerable wealth because of the economic rents they can generate, and may be able to fund social and economic development initiatives that few other industries could support (Mitchell, 2006; Richards, 2005). An additional point that render extractive industries a fruitful case for analyzing CSR is that in most cases they are exploiting publicly-owned (i.e., "social") minerals which are a wasting asset, raising important questions regarding distribution of economic benefits both in the current period and across generations.

Thus at the core of the CSR challenge for the extractive industries lies the inherent non-renewability of minerals, on the one hand, and the expansive definition of sustainability, which includes social and economic variables, on the other. Key to addressing this challenge is that a physically non-renewable resource may be deemed "sustainable" if there is an effective conversion of the natural capital, represented by the resource, to social capital that would allow for long-term livelihoods. This assumes that the resilience of the natural environment is not compromised,[1] undermining social and economic sustainability. Against this background it is both critical to disaggregate sustainability into its environmental, social and economic dimensions, but also to recognize the links between them.

Nonrenewable resource extraction has been anathema to environmentalists because extraction of such a resource is, by definition, irreversible and leaves an indelible impression on the ecology of a region. However, extracting some nonrenewable resources, particularly metals, is often defended on the grounds that they are recyclable. Hence even though the extraction from the Earth is nonrenewable, the material itself is still more worthwhile than a non-recyclable substitute such as a composite plastic. This argument, nevertheless, ignores the fact that metals can also be oxidized and decay into forms that are not economically reusable, and it certainly does not apply to energy minerals such as coal and uranium. Furthermore, the energy required for recycling must also be considered in any systematic analysis of impact. Perhaps more research on this issue is needed from an industrial ecology perspective to fully understand the life cycle impact of different materials for specific uses (Gordon *et al.*, 2006).

There is also a continuing perception among Cornucopian researchers[2] that innovation, spurred by scarcity, will self-correct any potential depletion of the resource.[3] Modern technology has already led to the substitution of copper by fiber optics (produced from sand), and the substitution of iron by ceramic materials and composites. In some cases materials technology has been advancing very rapidly in response to supply limitations signaled by rising prices for individual minerals. Moreover, the potential for recycling and conservation of less abundant minerals is enormous. The late economist Julian Simon extended this reasoning, perhaps too optimistically, to declare that even with the finite resources of minerals at our disposal, we can still say that the supply is infinite because we do not know the full potential of reserves and how they can be utilized. He compared the situation to a straight line segment which has a finite length, but which has an infinite number of points contained within it (Simon, 1999).

The question of non-renewability and the wider issue of sustainability has been approached from diametrically different perspectives with reference to the mineral sector. Pro-mining forces tend to frame the issue as one of livelihoods, while anti-mining activists have framed it as an issue of resource depletion. The debate has thus been markedly polarized and reconciling these differences has been a challenge for policy-makers and planners. Table 2.1 is an attempt to dissect the arguments on both sides.

Both sets of arguments are plausible, but often the result of any effort at planning for a mining venture results in positional entrenchment. Given the analysis in Table 2.1, it appears that nonrenewability of minerals is only an issue vis-à-vis sustainability if we believe that:

1 Keeping the resource in the ground is inherently valuable, and analogous to the preservation of biodiversity. However, since the resource in this case is inanimate and perhaps less consequential to food chains and other biological processes, the argument is often considered less convincing.
2 The environmental damage of the extraction process itself will cause irreversible damage and hence is contrary to any vision of sustainable development. In this case, the nonrenewability is a derivative issue and the irreversible environmental impact is the primary issue. In this case, the damage should be compared to renewable resource extraction.
3 The dependence on the use of mined resources will lead to severe economic and social problems when they are eventually depleted, since there will be a paucity of production opportunities for alternatives.
4 The dependence of remote communities on a resource extraction as a sole means of livelihood will lead to economic stagnation after mine closure and is thus not sustainable without a plan for subsequent development.

However, if we evaluate mineral usage from a systems perspective whereby minerals are considered in their broader role of converting natural capital to economic and social capital, while accounting for any diminution of ecological capital, a very different role emerges. We then see minerals as an essential catalytic commodity, both literally and figuratively, for the functioning of modern society. Such a systems approach also broadens our supply horizon to meeting mineral demand by evaluating the cost of extraction in terms of land degradation versus energy usage for retrieval from "urban mining" of infrastructure and post-consumer product "wastes." Product design also shifts to consider ease of disaggregation to allow for such post-consumer usage. With such an approach, green technology producers such as solar and wind energy generators also begin to consider mineral supply constraints in their innovation investment (Alonso *et al.*, 2012). This does not mean that geological exploration should abate for minerals because demand would need multiple supply streams to be met effectively and efficiently. For example, copper has major recycling potential, but its End of Life Recycling Efficiency Rate is currently only ~60 percent and, due to delays between manufacturing and scrapping, the Recycling Input Rate is only 33 percent (the best statistical measure of raw material availability).[4]

Table 2.1 Divergent arguments on non-renewability and sustainability of mineral extraction activities

Cassandran	*Cornucopian*	*Evaluative notes*
Non-renewable resource extraction Mineral ores cannot be replenished in the earth's surface over human time-scales and thus reliance on them is risky and unsustainable. Energy needed to harness abundant minerals such as aluminum must also be considered.	*Non-renewable but recyclable (at least metals)* Metals are elements and hence irreduceable low entropy products that can be recycled rather than being "regrown." Green technologies such as wind and solar power require minerals for their infrastructure.	Highly dependent on type of mineral; e.g. aluminium is both very abundant and easily recyclable, whereas nickel is much less abundant and requires complex product disaggregation for recycling. Also, is there intrinsic value to keeping minerals in ground?
Land degradation is irreversible Common forms of mining and beneficiation effluents scar the landscape in ways that leave it unproductive for future uses.	*Economic output per land acreage is high* While open-pit mining can leave permanent landscape scars, much of the use area is underground and productive land used is relatively small.	Underground mining and leaching techniques may reduce need for large-scale land degradation, though still require reclamation and monitoring after closure to prevent pollution and subsidence risks.
Supply creating demand Corporate marketing is creating "wants" of consumers. Such "wants," rather than needs of society, are spurring investment in mining.	*Demand creating supply* Needs of remote communities and traditional demands of consumers are spurring investment in mining. Few alternative development trajectories for remote communities.	Diamond and gem-stone demand may have been spurred by marketing. Gold demand can easily be met through recycling and bullion reserves, though the subsistence "needs" of artisanal gold miners and "traditional" users of gold are prescient.
Ephemeral employment Mines usually have a life of a few decades and hence employment is not continuous and leads to deceptive economic indicators.	*Evanescent but catalytic* While mining operations may fold, satellite industries which they spawn can continue and perpetuate economic development	Mining planners need to consider whether a new "mining town" is viable following closure or a fly-in operation makes more sense. Highly dependent on derivative industries that could potentially evolve.
Negative impacts outlast closure Large financial investment is required to reclaim land after mining, as well as rebuild economic and social capital of communities.	*Positive impacts also outlast closure* Infrastructure development, service sector jobs and educated workforce are also a byproduct of mining that outlive the life of the mine.	Closure planning must be part of the initial environmental impact assessment before the project commences, in order to ensure long-term viability of land-use.
Sustainability of natural capital guides development of economic and social capital.	*Conversion of natural capital into human capital is a means of attaining economic and social sustainability.*	Both views necessitate the viability of natural capital – whether for ornamental or instrumental purposes.

Source: adapted from O'Faircheallaigh and Ali, 2008.

To avoid disruptive volatility in prices and supply, broader discussion of current and future mineral supply will also be needed, particularly with reference to infrastructure to managing climate change (DeKoning *et al.*, 2015). Given the rising pressures on the planet in terms of demographic intensity (both actual population increase as well as resource usage per capita increasing with improved standards of living), we will need to follow such an approach to shift the role of minerals in society. The concept of a "circular economy" posits such a definitive paradigm shift in the way industrial processes relate to the modern economy and mineral resource planning will need to eventually follow such a path. The conventional economic model has been focused on linear material flows from mines to markets (World Economic Forum, 2014). As noted in this chapter, a paradigm shift has been underway for some time around industrial ecological systems. However, the mining industry has only recently begun to realize the implications of such a shift for mineral demand and supply. Researchers and practitioners will need to assist in this industrial transformation through a deliberate process of engagement and innovation to ensure that mining is recognized for its contributions to reaching sustainable development targets.

Notes

1 There is a vast literature on "weak" versus "strong" sustainability in this context. In our quest for sustainability we are faced with two options. First, we could try to ensure that all natural resources are maintained at adequate levels to provide for an indefinite supply (also known as the strong sustainability argument). In this case, we would try our utmost to focus on renewable resources that can be grown on human timescales – essentially vegetal and animal materials. The second option is to focus not on the resource quantity itself but rather on the aggregate stock of natural and human capital (also known as the weak sustainability argument). In this case consumption of a non-renewable resource is not problematic as long as its use leads to an equivalent increase in the human capital.

2 The term "Cornucopian" is used to describe those scholars who are very optimistic about the abundance of resource availability and technological solutions to scarcity. In contrast "Cassandran" perspectives are those which tend to be more pessimistic about human-induced environmental change. The terms are widely used in American environmental discourse.

3 For an excellent review of the debate among resource economists about the market mechanisms for dealing with resource depletion concerns, see Auty, 2001.

4 The *World Copper Fact Book 2015*, published by the International Copper Study Group, available from www.icsg.org/index.php/component/jdownloads/viewdownload/170/2092.

The *End of Life Recycling Efficiency Rate* refers to the percentage of metal that ultimately gets recycled when the product is scrapped at the end of its life. The *Recycling Input Rate* refers to the ratio between the current amount of recycled metal entering the system versus overall current total metal consumption rate.

References

Ali, Saleem H. *Treasures of the Earth: Need, Greed and a Sustainable Future* (New Haven: Yale University Press, 2010).

Alonso, E., A.M. Sherman, T.J. Wallington, M.P. Everson, F.R. Field, R. Roth and R.E. Kirchain. "Evaluating Rare Earth Element Availability: A Case with Revolutionary Demand from Clean Technologies." *Environmental Science and Technology* 46(6): 3406–3414 (2012).

Andrews, A.M. "Ecofeedback and Significance Feedback in Neural Nets and in Society." *Journal of Cybernetics* 4(3): 61–72 (1974).

Auty, R.M., ed. *Resource Abundance and Economic Development* (Oxford: Oxford University Press, 2001).

Ayres, R.U. and U.E. Simonis, eds. *Industrial metabolism* (Tokyo: United Nations University Press, 1994).

Bridge, G. "Contested Terrain: Mining and the Environment." *Annual Review of Environment and Resources* 29: 205–259 (2004).

Brodyansky, V., M.V. Sorin, T.J.A. Le Goff and P.A. Pilavachi. *The Efficiency of Industrial Processes: Exergy Analysis and Optimization* (Amsterdam: Elsevier, 1994).

Burchart-Korol, D., A. Fugiel, K. Czaplicka-Kolarz and M. Turek. "Model of Environmental Life Cycle Assessment for Coal Mining Operations." *Science of the Total Environment* 562: 61–72 (2016).

De Koning, A., R. Kleijn, G. van Engelen and G. Huppes. *Resource constraints in successful climate policy* (Leiden University, CECILIA 2050 Publication, 2015).

Dincer, Ibrahim and Marc A. Rosen. *Exergy: Energy, Environment and Sustainable Development* (Amsterdam: Elsevier Science, 2007).

Franks, Daniel. *Mountain Movers: Mining, Sustainability and the Agents of Change*. (London: Routledge, 2015).

Golley, Frank B. *A History of the Ecosystem Concept in Ecology: More than the Sum of the Parts* (New Haven: Yale University Press, 1996).

Gordon, R.B., M. Bertram and T.E. Graedel. "Metal Stocks and Sustainability." *Proceedings of the National Academy of Sciences* 103.5(1): 209–214 (2006).

Graedel, Thomas E. and Braden R. Allenby. *Industrial Ecology* (Englewood Cliffs, NJ: Prentice Hall, 2002).

Heeres, R.R. and W.J.V. Vermeulen. "Eco-industrial Park Initiatives in the USA and the Netherlands: First Lessons." *Journal of Cleaner Production* 12(8–10): 985–995 (December 2004).

Hendrickson, Chris, Lester Lave and H. Scott Matthews. *Environmental Life Cycle Assessment of Goods and Services: An Input-Output Approach* (Washington, D.C.: Resources for the Future, 2006).

Hilson, G. and Haselip, J.A. "The Environmental and Socioeconomic Performance of Multinational Mining Companies in the Developing World Economy." *Minerals and Energy – Raw Materials Report* 19: 25–47 (2004).

McDonough, William and Michael Braungart. *Cradle to Cradle: Remaking the Way We Make Things* (New York: North Point Press, 2002).

Mitchell, P. "Giving Practical Meaning to CSR in the Mining Industry." Paper presented at the Globe 2006 Conference, Vancouver, Canada, 2006.

Piluso, C., Y. Huang and H.H. Lou. "Ecological Input-Output Analysis-Based Sustainability Analysis of Industrial Systems." *Industrial and Engineering Chemistry Research* 47(6): 1955–1966 (March 19, 2008).

O'Rourke, Dara. "Industrial Ecology: A Critical Review." *International Journal of Environment and Pollution* 6(2/3): 89–112 (1996).

Rajaram, V., S. Dutta and K. Parameswaran. *Sustainable Mining Practices: A Global Perspective* (London: Taylor & Francis, 2005).

Richards, J.P. "The Role of Minerals in Sustainable Human Development," in B.R. Marker, M.G. Peterson, F. McEvoy and M.H. Stephenson (eds.), *Sustainable Minerals Operations in the Developing World* (London: Geological Society, 2005), 25–34.

Sahajwalla V., R. Cayumil, R. Khanna, M. Ikram-Ul-Haq, R. Rajarao, P.S. Mukherjee and A. Hill. "Recycling Polymer-Rich Waste Printed Circuit Boards at High Temperatures: Recovery of Value-Added Carbon Resources." *Journal of Sustainable Metallurgy*, 1(1): 75–84 (2015).

Santero, Nicholas and Josh Henry. "Harmonization of LCA Methodologies for the Metal and Mining Industry." *International Journal of Life Cycle Assessment.* doi: 10.1007/s11367–015–1022–4 (published online January 26, 2016).

Shrivastava, Paul. "Ecocentric Management in Industrial Ecosystems: Management Paradigms for a Risk Society." *Academy of Management Review* 20(1): 118–127 (1995).

Simon, J. *The Ultimate Resource 2* (Princeton, NJ: Princeton University Press, 1999).

van den Belt, Marjan. *Mediated Modeling: A System Dynamics Approach To Environmental Consensus Building* (Washington, D.C.: Island Press, 2004).

Weiner, Norbert. *Cybernetics: Or the Control and Communication in the Animal and the Machine* (Cambridge, MA: MIT Press, 1948).

Weiss, J. "Sweden Solving the Four E's: Economics, Employment, Environment, Energy." *Europe* 349: 6–9 (1995).

World Economic Forum. *Towards the Circular Economy: Accelerating the Scale Up across Global Supply Chains* (Geneva: World Economic Forum, 2014).

3 Understanding the social acceptance of mining

Kieren Moffat, Justine Lacey, Naomi Boughen, Simone Carr-Cornish and Michelle Rodriguez

Introduction

Fifteen years on from the Mining, Metals and Sustainable Development (MMSD) process (MMSD, 2002), the imperative to directly engage citizens of resource intensive countries remains. Increasingly, community concerns strongly influence the way the minerals industry operates, how governments regulate it, and the manner in which broader development responsibilities are met. It is now increasingly understood that the voice of citizens must be heard if mining developments are to achieve broad social acceptance. This has largely been brought about by changing societal expectations over recent decades, which have fundamentally influenced the way the minerals industry conducts its operations around the world.

The shift toward more socially acceptable mining development has emerged, in part, as a result of the increasing pressure and scrutiny the minerals industry was coming under in terms of its environmental impacts and social performance. For example, throughout the 1990s, there was a fundamental shift in the way that the environmental and social impacts of this industry were perceived, with highly publicised tailings dam failures, chemical spills and conflicts with communities impacting negatively on the industry's reputation (Schloss, 2002; Thomson and Boutilier, 2011). At the same time, societal values and attitudes toward the natural environment and the industries impacting negatively on it were changing (Joyce and Thomson, 2000). Increasingly, the concerns of society were also being translated into direct action against mining projects at a local level. Such conflict with communities has been shown to have high financial, opportunity and personal costs to mining companies and their personnel (Franks *et al.*, 2014).

These pressures on industry also signalled that communities were becoming more active in challenging the nature and fairness of the impacts and benefits associated with mining developments (ICMM, 2012). This was further reflected in communities demanding more involvement in decision-making around such operations, having clear expectations about receiving a greater share of the benefits from these operations, and requiring assurances that the industries involved were being appropriately regulated (Prno, 2013). Thus, not only have community expectations about the performance of the minerals industry increased over time, so too has the direct involvement of citizens in decision-making about industry development (Harvey and Brereton, 2005). This has seen community relations and participation now recognised as a strategic part of managing risk and opportunity (Humphreys, 2000). This combination of increasing pressures on industry performance and the associated social acceptance of mining operations has been widely referred to as the industry's 'social licence to operate'. However, the drivers of acceptance are complex and operate across scales.

Social acceptance at multiple scales

At the local scale, a mining operation is said to have a social licence when it achieves ongoing acceptance or approval from the local community and other stakeholders who can affect its profitability (Graafland, 2002). Without this social acceptance, it is very difficult for a mine to operate effectively or profitably. At this local scale, it is well understood that social (or community) acceptance of a mining operation is a reflection of the quality of the relationship a company has with their host community (Thomson and Boutilier, 2011; Lacey and Lamont, 2014; Parsons *et al.*, 2014; Moffat *et al.*, 2015a; Cooney, 2017). Community relations are an integral part of successful mining operations and where these interactions are effective, they tend to foster mutual understanding, trust and support between a company and the host community (Kemp *et al.*, 2006; Holley and Mitcham, 2016). Research further demonstrates that where such interactions are perceived to be procedurally fair, the increased trust created in these company–community interactions tends to lead to higher levels of acceptance of mining operations (Moffat and Zhang, 2014; Lacey *et al.*, 2017).

Similarly, at a national scale, social acceptance of the mining industry reflects the distribution, and perception of distribution of risks and benefits arising from the industry's activities. Frequently, the acceptability of operations at the local and regional scales can be affected by what happens at national or even international scales. For instance, local rejection of some mining projects has been fundamentally strengthened by the involvement of 'outsiders' or distal communities across national and even international boundaries, leading to the loss of support in a number of mining projects (e.g. Kirsch, 2007; Prno and Slocombe, 2014). Hence, local acceptance of a mining project cannot be obtained and maintained in isolation from what happens at national and international scales (Zhang *et al.*, 2015). Similarly, what takes place at the local scale can also impact perceptions of and attitudes toward mining at the national and international scales. The performance of a particular mining project, either positive or negative, can affect the reputation of the industry and shape the general public's perceptions of and attitudes toward mining.

In many ways, the drivers of social acceptance of mining across these scales reflects the evolving nature of the relationships between industries and their communities and other stakeholders. The variables operating at these multiple scales are intertwined, effectively influencing both the acceptance of mining projects at the local scale and of the mining industry at the national scale. Hence, there is real value in understanding how the general public's attitudes toward mining can influence the local conditions for acceptance of a mining operation, and how local issues influence decision-making by companies and governments at the national scale. It is also critical to be able to bring citizen voice into decision-making about minerals resource development, which has traditionally been the domain of industry and government alone.

Applied research to identify the drivers of social acceptance

Applied research can play a critical role in developing the evidence-base for a detailed knowledge of the drivers of trust and social acceptance of mining across scales and how they operate. For example, research to date has quantified the critical role of trust for social acceptance including how the relational aspects of stakeholder interactions can influence this. Key findings to date have already identified that:

- as stakeholder expectations and experiences of mining impacts converge, acceptance and approval of an operation increases (i.e. when companies do what they say they will do acceptance is high);
- procedural fairness (i.e. influence over decisions made by company, respect shown to community) is a strong predictor of trust;
- relationship quality rather than the amount of contact with company personnel is key to building trust.

Such insights can assist industry, communities and governments understand what drives increased trust and, in turn, support stronger relationships between these stakeholders that will lead to better outcomes for all parties and a more sustainable and efficient industry. Drawing on surveys of more than 14,000 community members conducted in eight countries, this chapter summarises recent applied research to measure and model the drivers of trust and social acceptance of mining across scales, describes how these variables interact and identifies implications for improved practice.

The drivers of social acceptance of mining

There is significant qualitative research documenting processes of community relations practice and the successes and failures of citizen engagement around mine sites. Such failures can arise even where communities are explicitly involved in consultation processes around new or existing resource development, where the potential for mismatched expectations among the stakeholders in these operations is high (Kapelus, 2002; Prno and Slocombe, 2012; Bice, 2013; Kemp and Owen, 2013). For example, in a study of mining-affected communities in Australia, Cheney *et al.* (2001) found that local communities often felt marginalised in what was perceived to be a predetermined development trajectory defined together by government and mining companies.

Community members have also reflected that companies and communities tend to hold distinctly different value sets and worldviews. This is even more likely in the context of negotiations with Indigenous peoples on whose land minerals development may be taking place (Banerjee, 2000), particularly where a stakeholder approach which involves 'providing a seat at the table' may reduce a radically distinct and prior historical claim to one among a series of other interests to be traded off, effectively limiting the possibility of reaching understanding with key cultural and community groups. This difference in values and worldviews between companies, communities and government may also lead to fundamental misalignment of expectations regarding the terms of their relationship with each other and what is deemed socially acceptable to each party (Thomson and Joyce, 2006). While Nelsen and Scoble (2006) see the path to social acceptance through industry maintaining positive corporate reputation and educating local stakeholders about a project, Thomson and Joyce (2006) point out that community members, in their experience, tend to be more concerned about whether they are respected, listened to and allowed to participate in the development of an operation. These criteria summarise the distinctly relational aspects of procedural fairness in company–community interactions but these differences also bear out the powerlessness that Cheney *et al.* (2001) observed among community members, and reflect a more general disconnect between a key company driver to 'make a deal' and that of community to establish an equitable relationship of exchange (Joyce and Thomson, 2000).

Thus, even when all key stakeholders are explicitly invited into a conversation regarding the nature and shape of minerals development, asymmetric power relations between parties, and differences in values, worldviews and perspectives are still likely to create opportunity for mistrust and conflict. As Swain and Tait (2007) observe, creating and sustaining trust among parties with conflicting goals and deeply different underlying values remains one of the major challenges of effective participatory processes, and this equally relates to the engagement and dialogue that underpins the social acceptance of minerals development. What emerges from this is that it is most often the relational factors that play a critical role in determining the quality of the interactions and relationships between companies, communities and other stakeholders in minerals development. The importance of these relationships underpins how communication take place and how negotiations can be reached.

There is little doubt that mines and communities vary widely across contexts. This means that the nature of those stakeholder interactions can also look very different based on differences in local priorities (for a company, a community or both), the nature of the mining activity and its history in a place, or even the demographic profile of a community and the mix of other industries comprising the economy. For example at the local scale of impact, mining developments can create adverse environmental and amenity impacts associated with increased noise, dust, pollution or other disturbances. While these negative impacts are often managed through formal instruments such as Environmental and Social Impact Assessments or other regulatory instruments, it has been demonstrated that a community's experience of those localised social, environmental and economic impacts of mining and a company's ability to reduce those impacts voluntarily in response to community feedback plays a role in determining their acceptance of mining operations (Moffat and Zhang, 2014).

Similarly, these contextual differences can influence how mining operations are perceived at the national scale. For example, mining tends to be associated with a ranges of costs and benefits. The nature and extent of these costs and benefits play in a role in the level of acceptance of mining. For example, in a national survey of Australian citizens' attitudes to mining (Moffat *et al.*, 2014a), the three main impact and benefit areas were found to be:

- impacts on the environment (including climate change), costs of living and negative impacts on other sectors (including manufacturing, agriculture and tourism);
- employment and other regional benefits, general economic benefits (personal, family and national wealth) and development of regional infrastructure.

Routinely, similar research in different contexts around the world tends to find similar patterns in how citizens assess the impacts and benefits of the minerals industry (Moffat *et al.*, 2014b; Zhang *et al.*, 2015) (i.e. environmental impacts are routinely perceived as the most negative impact associated with mining whereas the economic contributions of the sector are considered to be the most positive benefit).

The way citizens perceive these impacts and benefits does influence their acceptance of mining, such that the more negative citizens believe the impacts are, the less inclined they are to accept the industry; and the more positive citizens perceive the benefits to be, the higher their acceptance of the industry. While these large-scale surveys of citizen attitudes provide an evidence base for confirming how such impacts and benefits are perceived, what tends to be more revealing is assessing the strength of the relationships between them. For example, in the Australian national survey, citizens were also asked to consider whether they felt the benefits of mining outweighed the impacts (i.e. was it worthwhile having a mining industry in Australia?), in order to understand how this influenced their acceptance of the industry. The results from this analysis revealed that weighing up the impacts and benefits was a strong positive predictor of social acceptance over and above the other individual impact and benefit measures. This suggests that citizens hold nuanced view of the impacts and benefits of mining and that where the balance of benefits is seen to outweigh the impacts, acceptance will likely be higher (Moffat *et al.*, 2014a, 2014b; Lacey *et al.*, 2017).

However, what is more interesting is that the most significant predictors of trust in the industry and acceptance of the industry have tended not to be related to impacts and benefits. Rather, at both the local and national scales and in diverse mining contexts around the world what has emerged is that strong acceptance tends to be about building trust between industry, government and society. There is a growing understanding that the way people are treated in decision-making processes, the ways that benefits are distributed from mining and the role of governance in setting the rules for mining, are most important for developing strong trust and acceptance (Moffat *et al.*, 2014a; Zhang *et al.*, 2015). This confirms the observations of Joyce and Thomson (2000). Despite differences in the experiences and conditions of mining around the world, research conducted over several years has now identified a common set of relational variables that underpin social acceptance at local and national scales. These critical relational variables (i.e. focusing on stakeholder interactions) include: (1) contact quality between company personnel and community members, at the local scale; (2) distributional fairness (particularly in relation to benefits), across scales; (3) procedural fairness, across scales; and (4) citizen confidence in the governance arrangements around mining, at the national scale. Each of these variables is summarised below.

Contact quality between company and community members

At the local scale, the quality of contact between company personnel and community members can have a significant influence on the quality of company–community interactions. Extensive research demonstrates that positive contact or interactions between groups can improve intergroup relations and increase trust between those groups (Pettigrew and Tropp, 2006; Tam *et al.*, 2009; Hewstone and Swart, 2011). This has been shown to be equally true when tested in mining contexts. For example, in a longitudinal survey of community attitudes to mining, Moffat and Zhang (2014) found that the quality of contact between mining company personnel and community members was a significant predictor of trust in the company and acceptance of its operation. What made no difference to trust and acceptance was the amount of contact between the company and community.

Their findings corroborate those of Kemp *et al.* (2011) who also found that the nature and quality of the interface between individuals plays a key role in mitigating social conflict in mining contexts.

Distributional fairness

Distributional fairness refers to the extent to which the benefits of a mining operation are perceived to be distributed fairly within a community or society, more broadly (Kemp *et al.*, 2011; Zhang *et al.*, 2015). Empirical studies have also shown that people express greater satisfaction when they believe that they receive a fair share of the benefits in a given situation, or they will tend to reject the arrangement (McComas and Besley, 2011; Siegrist *et al.*, 2012). In the mining context, the fair distribution of mining-related benefits has been shown to be a significant predictor of trust and acceptance of both local operations and the industry, more broadly (Moffat *et al.*, 2014a). For example, communities may benefit through direct compensation, royalty payments or participation in joint ventures (O'Faircheallaigh, 2002). Other benefits may include the industry's contribution to employment and training opportunities (Measham and Fleming, 2014) or investment in local and regional infrastructure (Michaels, 2011). At the national scale, such benefits may be reflected in macroeconomic consequences such as increased revenues resulting from export markets or taxation regimes (Battelino, 2010).

Procedural fairness

Procedural fairness can be achieved in many ways but it routinely requires the implementation of processes that are considered to be fair by all involved, are transparent and inclusive of diverse perspectives and priorities, allow the public to access information and debate, and to feel respected and listened to in that process (Lacey *et al.*, 2017). Procedural fairness also refers to whether individuals believe that they have had a reasonable voice in decision-making processes (Tyler, 2000; Besley, 2010). Perceptions of fairness in processes leading to decision outcomes increase trust between those who are involved in negotiating decisions and, ultimately, the acceptance of the outcomes of those decisions, even among those who may be disadvantaged by such outcomes (Lind and Tyler, 1988; Tyler, 2015). Given the increased participation of communities in decision-making about how mining operations will be developed, designing and implementing fair processes has become a critical part of creating equitable participation, creating meaningful dialogue among stakeholders, diffusing conflict and achieving sustainable resource management decisions (Kemp *et al.*, 2011; Holley and Mitcham, 2016; Lacey *et al.*, 2016).

Governance

At the national scale, governments around the world play a major role in regulating the mining industry and stipulating how mining activities should be conducted in their jurisdiction. The regulations are often introduced in the form of legislation, and approval and reporting processes. This also includes regional and national laws governing environmental assessment and public participation processes (MMSD, 2002; Solomon *et al.*, 2008). From the public's perspective, these are the major formal mechanisms for managing the social and environmental impacts of mining activities. When the public believe that the governance arrangements in place are not capable of ensuring responsible mining development, their attitudes toward mining tend to be less favourable. Indeed, research has shown that public perceptions of the governance arrangements around mining moderate the relationship between their concerns over environmental impacts and their acceptance of the industry (Zhang and Moffat, 2015). More specifically, when citizens strongly believe that existing regulation and legislation has the capacity to hold the mining industry to account for its actions (i.e. strong governance), there is an increased likelihood to accept mining compared to those who perceive governance arrangements as being weak, irrespective of their views on the environmental impacts of the mining industry (Zhang *et al.*, 2015).

How the drivers of social acceptance interact in practice

There is clear evidence that the interactions between these relational drivers of social acceptance can be systematically modelled and measured at local and national scales by conducting large-scale surveys of citizen attitudes (Moffat and Zhang, 2014; Moffat *et al.*, 2015b; Zhang *et al.*, 2015).

Social acceptance at the local scale

At the local operational level, for example, Moffat and Zhang (2014) have developed an integrative, quantitative model to understand the paths to community acceptance of mining operations. Their analysis reveals that building trust with local communities is crucial for mining companies to obtain and maintain support and acceptance of those operations. This trust is fundamentally shaped by the contact quality (but not quantity) and procedural fairness through which mining companies deal with communities, as well as perceptions of how fairly the benefits of mining are distributed in the community.

Figure 3.1 illustrates how these relational variables interact in practice at the local scale, with positive relationships between the three relational variables indicating that the more distributional fairness, contact quality and procedural fairness perceived by communities, the greater the level of

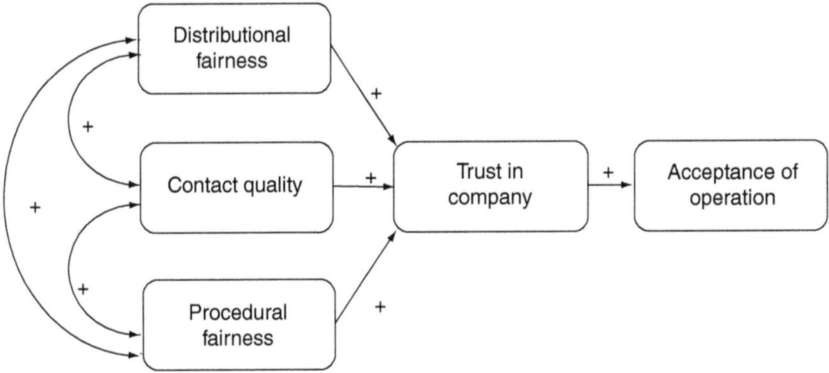

Figure 3.1 Conceptual model of the drivers of trust and acceptance of local mining operations.

trust in and acceptance of operations is realised. The model and the relationships illustrated in Figure 3.1 have been developed based on a range of theoretical and applied research (e.g. Kemp *et al.*, 2006, 2011; Thomson and Boutilier, 2011; Kemp and Owen, 2013; Lacey and Lamont, 2014; Moffat *et al.*, 2014a, 2015a; Moffat and Zhang, 2014; Zhang *et al.*, 2015; Lacey *et al.*, 2017) and empirically validated in multiple contexts including Australia, New Zealand and South Africa. The arrows represent the predicted interactions between the variables that can be measured and modelled using structural equation modelling. A positive symbol indicates that more of one variable is expected to lead to more of another (e.g. increased procedural fairness predicts increased trust). The strength of these predictive relationships often varies between contexts but the elements themselves have been found to remain unchanged across highly differentiated contexts. These three relational variables were also found to be strongly correlated with each other suggesting that increased procedural fairness can positively influence perceptions of contact quality and distributional fairness, and vice versa.

This model challenges some key assumptions about the drivers of trust in company–community relations. For example, all communities surveyed tend to express the view that the environmental and social impacts of mining matter a great deal to them. However, even though these concerns are important across all contexts, they are rarely found to be the main predictors of trust or acceptance of a company or its operations. This is significant because it highlights that the relationships between the stakeholders needs to be strong and supported to enable effective negotiations around matters such as the social and environmental impacts of mining operations.

Social acceptance at the national scale

Similarly, large-scale survey research at the national scale assessing citizen attitudes towards the mining industry (as opposed to localised impacts) also reveal the key predictors of trust in the mining industry, and in turn, the drivers of social acceptance of the industry. Figure 3.2 illustrates an empirically validated model of social acceptance that highlights procedural fairness, distributional fairness and confidence in governance as the three most significant predictors of trust, and in turn acceptance of the industry (Zhang *et al.*, 2015). This model was developed based on over 14,000 citizen responses testing attitudes to the mining sector collected in Australia, Chile, China and Zambia over a two-year period.

At this scale, a measure such as contact quality ceases to become relevant (i.e. most citizens in a nation do not live near mines) but the citizenry's expectations of government tend to come to the fore more strongly as the drivers of trust in and acceptance of the industry. Research like this demonstrates the power of quantitative methods when applied to large and systematic datasets, in particular for teasing apart the complexity of the manifold relationships between resource development industries and society more broadly. It also demonstrates the capacity to understand and model the nuance that exists within those relationships, as well as measure and benchmark changes over time. Consistent and well defined measures will help assist industry, communities and governments to understand what underpins social acceptance and what supports relationships between these stakeholders leading to better outcomes for all parties.

Implications of these findings for practice

There are three key ways in which these findings can be used to improve minerals industry practice. These are:

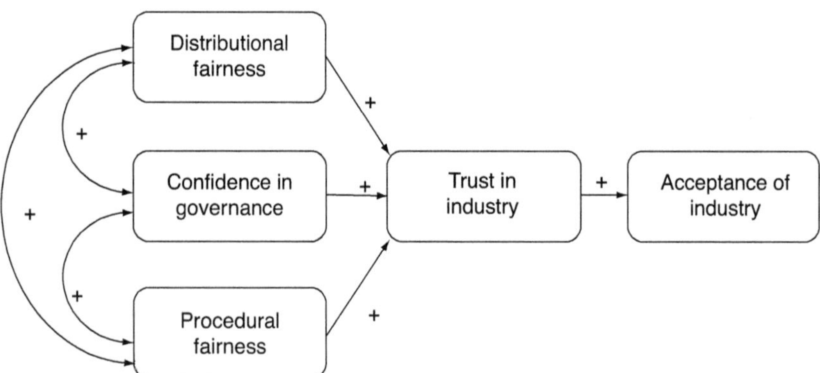

Figure 3.2 Conceptual model of the drivers of trust and acceptance of national scale mining industry.

- benchmarking and improving the operational performance of mining operations at the local scale;
- measuring and modelling the drivers of trust and acceptance to provide an evidence-base of citizen preference and views;
- bringing citizen voice to decision-making about minerals development.

Benchmarking and improving operational performance

Effective community engagement is a critical element of local social acceptance of mining operations. For example, recent research in Australia to review community engagement approaches and practices has been successful in determining how and why the social licence of an operation may become threatened and what is required to strengthen company–community engagement (Parsons *et al.*, 2013). For example, an audit of company practice against industry best-practice standards is one mechanism for identifying issues that may require early intervention to avoid further escalation of existing social conflict. In some cases, findings in these contexts have lead to the development of a series of recommendations for both short-term actions to reduce current tensions, as well as medium- to long-term actions for operationalising a more dialogic and inclusive approach to community engagement, and included:

- reviewing current practices around the use of communication channels and message framing;
- understanding how to use the company data on community attitudes and perceptions more effectively to build a positive company–community relationship;
- developing context relevant impact metrics;
- supporting dialogic relations with community through augmenting the community relations plan;
- the potential development of a diagnostic tool for ongoing monitoring and 'health checking' of the operation's social licence.

Similarly, work with global companies has revealed the use of evidence-based approaches to engagement such as the use of research, polling and developing a systematic understanding of communities and their perspectives is a critical foundation for developing engagement approaches that are appropriate to context. For example, in a case study examining a potentially controversial mine site extension where trust and general acceptance of the company were already known to be high, procedural fairness was maintained through challenging negotiations by adopting a multi-stakeholder approach that brought community, government, company and other stakeholders together in a participatory and collaborative engagement. This resulted in new decision-making processes being jointly developed and implemented by those stakeholders (Lacey *et al.*,

2017). Such research not only validates the theoretical and applied research about the drivers of social acceptance, it also affords opportunity to closely examine the collaborative arrangements that draw on multiple stakeholder perspectives to operationalise procedural fairness, distributional fairness and contact quality in ways that will meaningfully enhance trust in company–community interactions.

Measuring and modelling social acceptance

By successfully measuring and modelling the critical elements leading to social acceptance, companies can also prioritise their activities and investment in a way that maximises the creation of trust between the operation and its community. This also allows communities, companies and government stakeholders to engage with each other on the issues that matter before they reach a critical point and lead to conflict.

For example, at the local scale, this research not only identifies the strongest predictors of acceptance from the perspective of communities, it also importantly reveals that this acceptance is mediated by trust. This reveals that increasing the level of trust a community has in a mining company tends to lead to increases in the community's level of social acceptance of the company's operations. The research also reveals the importance of fair treatment and high-quality engagement of companies with communities, which needs to exist alongside the mitigation of its operational impacts. The value of measuring the strength of these interactions and relationships in these contexts also allows for consistent and robust benchmarking of social performance across time as an operation develops. This, in turn, allows mining companies to understand the separate and proportional influence that operational impacts and community engagement activities have on the level of trust in companies, and the resulting acceptance and approval of their operations.

Similarly, in assessing the level of social acceptance of mining around the world, Zhang *et al.* (2015b) have found that societies with different social, cultural and political backgrounds may have different views on what is most important in determining trust and, in turn, acceptance of mining activities. This can be reflected at the national scale in the high-level differences between the drivers of trust and acceptance that exist in Australia, Chile and China, for example. Alternatively, such data can also reveal the differences that exist among communities within these nations, such as variations in the perceptions of communities living alongside mining operations and those of urban communities, for example. Such a model can help us to understand the strengths in these relationships and also the weaknesses. By modelling the critical elements of social acceptance, it can be determined what is needed in order to ensure how fairer processes can be prioritised, how industry and government can work more effectively to promote fair sharing of the benefits of resource development for citizens, or even how governance of the industry can be improved.

Bringing citizen voice to decision-making about minerals development

The ultimate aim of identifying the drivers of social acceptance of mining is invariably to understand the priorities and expectations of communities and citizens so that minerals development is representative of a range of social needs and priorities. There is already a recognition of the rights of communities and the need for communities to participate in decision-making about minerals development at the local scale (MMSD, 2002) but the pathways to achieving this participation and benefit sharing arrangements have not always been clear. Similarly, citizens of resource-rich countries should also have the opportunity to shape how these resources are developed on their behalf.

In national and international dialogues regarding resource development, the voice of citizens are often mediated through institutional mechanisms that are exclusive and/or interest groups that do not represent broader perspectives, or are absent altogether. There is a need to capture the perspectives and experiences of citizens in resource-intensive countries around the globe in a systematic way. Such efforts capture comprehensive and comparable data with which to establish the level of social acceptance or resistance that exists in differing resource-rich countries. This has been demonstrated to date through national-scale work already undertaken in Australia, China, Chile and Zambia. It also indicates the potential to make international comparisons of social acceptance around the globe. Given that many mining industry entities are global, multinational companies, finding ways of systematically bringing citizen voice to decision-making around the world has the potential to influence more potive and inclusive minerals development, and may shape standards of professional practice in citizen engagement. For example, understanding citizen priorities through large-scale surveys and dialogues has the capacity to:

- shape policy at a national level to support a socially sustainable mining industry;
- support conversations between key stakeholders in the mining industry through public presentation of findings, briefings to key stakeholders (including senior government and major mining companies) to make such data transparent and accessible;
- identify those actions that will strengthen social acceptance of the industry and assist in developing constructive dialogue between stakeholders;
- provide trusted datasets to benchmark public attitudes to enable progress against social sustainability goals to be measured, monitored and evaluated.

Conclusion

Controversial cases of minerals development will always give rise to persistent political and moral disagreement among diverse stakeholders with competing priorities and perspectives. In this environment of conflict, social acceptance is a way of framing how mineral resources are used and developed, and the expectations that communities and the public have of industry and government in this domain. However, the role of communities and the public in shaping how minerals have been developed in the past has been less certain. The mere participation of stakeholders and the public does not solve this disagreement and can, in poorly managed cases, exacerbate it. It will never be the case that all citizens will agree on the outcomes of these decisions but more effort is clearly needed to improve the interactions between expertise, policy-making and public debate in order to be able to justify those decisions. A deeper understanding of the role of relational variables in those interactions is critical. The research summarised in this chapter aims to assist industry, communities and government to understand the drivers of trust and social acceptance of mining so as to support relationships between these stakeholders that lead to better outcomes for all parties, and a more sustainable and efficient industry.

References

Banerjee, S.B. 2000. Whose land is it anyway? National interest, Indigenous stakeholders, and colonial discourses: The case of the Jabiluka uranium mine. *Organization and Environment* 13, 3–38.

Battelino, R. 2010. Mining, booms and the Australian economy: Address to the Sydney Institute. In: *Reserve Bank Bulletin*, March Quarter, 63–69.

Besley, J.C. 2010. Public engagement and the impact of fairness perceptions on decision favorability and acceptance. *Science Communication* 32, 256–280.

Bice, S. 2013. No more sunshades please: Experiences of corporate social responsibility in remote Australian mining communities. *Rural Society* 22(2), 138–152.

Cheney, H., Lovel, R. and Solomon, F. 2001. 'I'm not anti-mining but ...': Community perspectives of mining in Victoria. Paper presented at MCA Environment Workshop, October, Adelaide, Australia.

Cooney. J. 2017. Reflections on the 20th anniversary of the term 'social licence'. *Journal of Energy and Natural Resources Law* 35, 197–200.

Franks, D., Davis, R., Bebbington, A.J., Ali, S.H., Kemp, D. and Scurrah, M. 2014. Conflict translates environmental and social risk into business costs. *Procedings of the National Academy of Sciences* 111, 7576–7581.

Graafland, J. 2002. Profits and principles: Four perspectives. *Journal of Business Ethics* 35, 293–305.

Harvey, B. and Brereton, D. 2005. Emerging models of community engagement in the Australian minerals industry. Paper presented to the International Conference on Engaging Communities, 14–17 August, Brisbane, Australia.

Hewstone, M. and Swart, H. 2011. Fifty-odd years of inter-group contact: From hypothesis to integrated theory. *British Journal of Social Psychology* 50, 374–386.

Holley, E.A. and Mitcham, C. 2016. The Pebble Mine Dialogue: A case study in public engagement and the social license to operate. *Resources Policy* 47, 18–27.

Humphreys, D. 2000. A business perspective on community relations in mining. *Resources Policy* 26, 127–131.

ICMM (International Council on Mining and Metals). 2012. *Mining's contribution to sustainable development: An overview*. London.

Joyce, S. and Thomson, I. 2000. Earning a social licence to operate: Social acceptability and resource development in Latin America. *Canadian Mining and Metallurgical Bulletin* 93, 49–53.

Kapelus, P. 2002. Mining, corporate social responsibility and the 'community': The case of Rio Tinto, Richards Bay Minerals and the Mbonambi. *Journal of Business Ethics* 39(3), 275–296.

Kemp, D. and Owen, J. 2013. Community relations and mining: Core to business but not 'core business'. *Resources Policy* 38(4), 523–531.

Kemp. D., Boele, R. and Brereton, D. 2006. Community relations management systems in the minerals industry: Combining conventional and stakeholder-driven approaches. *International Journal of Stakeholder Development* 9(4), 390–403.

Kemp, D., Owen, J., Gotzmann, N. and Bond, C.J. 2011. Just relations and company-community conflict in mining. *Journal of Business Ethics* 101, 93–109.

Kirsch, S. 2007. Indigenous movements and the risks of counterglobalization: Tracking the campaign against Papua New Guinea's Ok Tedi mine. *American Ethnologist* 34, 303–321.

Lacey, J. and Lamont, J. 2014. Using social contract to inform social licence to operate: An application in the Australian coal seam gas industry. *Journal of Cleaner Production* 84, 831–839.

Lacey, J., Carr-Cornish, S., Zhang, A., Eglinton, K. and Moffat, K. 2017. The art and science of community relations: Procedural fairness at Newmont's Waihi Gold Operations, New Zealand. *Resources Policy* 52, 245–254.

Lacey, J., Edwards, P. and Lamont, J. 2016. Social licence as social contract: Procedural fairness and forest agreement-making in Australia. *Forestry: An International Journal of Forest Research* 89(5).

Lind, E.A. and Tyler, T.R. 1988. *The social psychology of procedural justice*. New York, Plenum Press.

McComas, K.A. and Besley, J.C. 2011. Fairness and nanotechnology concern. *Risk Analysis* 31, 1749–1761.

Measham, T. and Fleming, D. 2014. Impacts of unconventional gas development on rural community decline. *Journal of Rural Studies* 36, 376–385.

Michaels, G. 2011. The long-term consequences of resource-based specialisation. *The Economic Journal* 121, 31–57.

MMSD (Mining, Minerals and Sustainable Development Project). 2002. *Breaking new ground: Mining, minerals, and sustainable development. Report of the MMSD project*. London, Earthscan Publications.

Moffat, K. and Zhang, A. 2014. The paths to social licence to operate: An integrative model explaining community acceptance of mining. *Resources Policy* 39, 61–70.

Moffat, K., Boughen, N., Zhang, A., Lacey, J., Fleming, D. and Uribe, K. 2014b. *Chilean attitudes toward mining: Citizen Survey, 2014 results*. Australia, CSIRO.

Moffat, K., Lacey, J., Carr-Cornish, S., Zhang, A. and Boughen, N. 2015b. *Stakeholder Research Toolkit: Best practice guidelines for measuring and monitoring stakeholder relationships in the mining and metals industry resources sectors*. London, International Council on Mining and Metals.

Moffat, K., Lacey, J., Zhang, A. and Leipold, S. 2015a. The social licence to operate: A critical review. *Forestry: An International Journal of Forest Research* 89(5), 477–488.

Moffat, K., Zhang, A. and Boughen, N. 2014a. *Australian attitudes toward mining: Citizen Survey, 2014 results*. Australia, CSIRO.

Nelsen, J. and Scoble, M. 2006. *Social license to operate mines: Issues of situational analysis and process*. Vancouver, University of British Columbia, Department of Mining Engineering.

O'Faircheallaigh, C. 2002. *A new approach to policy evaluation: Indigenous people and mining*. Aldershot, Ashgate.

Parsons, R., Lacey, J. and Moffat, K. 2014. Maintaining legitimacy of a contested practice: How the minerals industry understands its 'social licence to operate'. *Resources Policy* 41, 83–90.

Parsons, R., Lederwasch, A. and Moffat, K. 2013. Clermont preferred future: Stakeholder reflections on a community foresight and planning initiative. *Resources* 2, 528–554.

Pettigrew, T.F. and Tropp, L.R. 2006. A meta-analytic test of intergroup contact theory. *Journal of Personality and Social Psychology* 90, 751–783.

Prno, J. 2013. An analysis of factors leading to the establishment of a social licence to operate in the mining industry. *Resources Policy* 38, 577–590.

Prno, J. and Slocombe, D.S. 2012. Exploring the origins of 'social license to operate' in the mining sector: Perspectives from governance and sustainability theories. *Resources Policy* 37, 346–375.

Prno, J. and Slocombe, D.S. 2014. A system-based conceptual framework for assessing the determinants of a social licence to operate in the mining industry. *Environmental Management* 53, 672–689.

Schloss, M. 2002. *Transparency, governance and government in the management of mineral wealth*. Toronto, World Mines Ministries Forum.

Siegrist, M., Connor, M. and Keller, C. 2012. Trust, confidence, procedural fairness, outcome fairness, moral conviction, and the acceptance of GM field experiences. *Risk Analysis* 32, 1394–1403.

Solomon, F., Katz, E. and Lovel, R. 2008. Social dimensions of mining: Research, policy and practice challenges for the minerals industry in Australia. *Resources Policy* 33, 142–149.

Swain, M. and Tait, C. 2007. The crisis of trust and planning. *Planning Theory and Practice* 8, 229–247.

Tam, T., Hewstone, M., Kenworthy, J. and Cairns, A. 2009. Intergroup trust in Northern Ireland. *Personality and Social Psychology Bulletin* 35, 45–59.

Thomson, I. and Boutilier, R. 2011. Social licence to operate. In: P. Darling (Ed.), *SME mining engineering handbook*, third edn (pp. 1779–1796). Englewood, Society for Mining, Metallurgy and Exploration.

Thomson, I. and Joyce, S. 2006. Changing mineral exploration industry approaches to sustainability. In: Michael D. Doggett and John R. Parry (Eds.), *Wealth creation in the minerals industry: Integrating science, business and education* (pp. 149–169). Littleton, Society of Economic Geologists.

Tyler, T.R. 2000. Social justice: Outcome and procedure. *International Journal of Psychology* 35, 117–125.

Tyler, T.R. 2015. Social justice. In: M. Mikulincer, P.R. Shaver, J.F. Dovidio and J.A. Simpson (Eds.), *Group processes* (pp. 95–122). Washington, D.C., American Psychological Association.

Zhang, A. and Moffat, K. 2015. A balancing act: The role of benefits, impacts and confidence in governance in predicting acceptance of mining in Australia. *Resources Policy* 44, 25–44.

Zhang, A., Moffat, K., Lacey, J., Wang, J., González, R., Uribe, K., Cui, L. and Dai, Y. 2015. Understanding the social licence to operate of mining at the national scale: A comparative study of Australia, China and Chile. *Journal of Cleaner Production* 108, 1063–1072.

Part II

Due diligence

4 Environmental impact assessment and the quest for sustainable mining

Alan Bond and Angus Morrison-Saunders

Introduction

Environmental impact assessment (EIA) is arguably the most well known and widespread environmental management instrument in use, with virtually all nation states having formal procedures in place (Morgan, 2012), not to mention processes implemented by other tiers of government, and by other agencies such as NGOs and the development banks. EIA is applied to new development proposals, including mining activity, from the early design stages through to the approval decision stage, with some practice extending to implementation and decommissioning. Through considering the likely environmental consequences of proposed development, appropriate mitigation measures can be put in place to avoid or minimise adverse effects and maximise positive outcomes.

Despite the emphasis on 'environment', Sheate (2009) argues that all environmental assessment and management tools share the common cause of sustainability even if they did not originally have that as the underlying purpose. This argument is based on a change in the global rhetoric away from environmental conservation and towards sustainability as the desired goal (as enshrined in the Sustainable Development Goals; United Nations, 2015) at a time when EIA was already the decision-tool of choice in many jurisdictions. As a result, the process of EIA has remained largely unchanged, but the articulated goals are now the achievement of, or contribution to, sustainable development.

EIA was established on the basis that it was appropriate for decision makers to be fully aware of the potential for significant impacts caused by any proposed development action (Glasson *et al.*, 2012). Whereas the link between EIA and sustainable development may be relatively easy to make, for many people so far as mining is concerned – i.e. an activity of extraction of material from the Earth's crust – the link with sustainable development is less clear. For example Young and Septoff (undated) stated that 'Mining is inherently unsustainable "because" it requires the depletion of non-renewable natural and cultural resources' (p. 1), and numerous other authors have debated the notion that 'sustainable mining is an oxymoron' (e.g. Horowitz, 2006; Mudd, 2007; Laurence, 2011; Worrall *et al.*, 2009; Franks, 2015). Given that all major new mining proposals can be expected to trigger EIA, the sustainability credentials of mining warrant some attention.

The purpose of this chapter is to explore the EIA and mining interface in the context of sustainable development. We do this in four main ways. First, we define and explain the EIA concept with respect to sustainable development. Second, we introduce sustainable development so that the plural nature of this concept is clear. Third, we posit that sustainable mining must be feasible fundamentally and introduce the long history of understanding of the sustainability implications of this industry. Fourth, we introduce the best-practice EIA principles that should be integrated into any EIA associated with mine planning, implementation and closure to ensure optimum sustainability outcomes, before briefly concluding.

The practice of environmental impact assessment

Whilst EIA is a relatively ubiquitous process practised globally, recently we identified over 40 different specialist types of impact assessment (Morrison-Saunders *et al.*, 2015) that focus on different elements of the environment, or the socio-economic environment. These include Health Impact Assessment, Social Impact Assessment, Sustainability Assessment, Technology Assessment, Ecological Impact Assessment, to name just a few. Using a broader suite of keywords, Vanclay (2015) identified more than 150 forms of impact assessment. However, for the purposes of this chapter, we focus on Environmental Impact Assessment as: the instrument with a legal basis in most countries in the world (Morgan, 2012); the one that most usually applies to mining development; and the one which we have seen has a goal of sustainable development.

The definition of EIA varies according to the legal context and to the observer. However, the International Association for Impact Assessment employs a simple definition of impact assessment in general (encompassing all forms of assessment including EIA) as 'the process of identifying the future consequences of a current or proposed action'.[1] The purpose of considering future consequences prior to implementation of development is, first, to enable adverse effects to be avoided through good design or by putting in place appropriate mitigation measures to minimise or counterbalance such effects, and, second, to identify and maximise the positive consequences. In this sense EIA is a tool for sustainable development subject to the scope of the effects considered.

The sustainable development purpose of EIA is clearly demonstrated in the world's first legislation establishing the process – the National Environmental Policy Act (NEPA) 1969 of the United States. Included in the statement of overall purposes of NEPA (s2) are the following two aims:

- to declare a national policy which will encourage productive and enjoyable harmony between man and his environment; [and]
- to promote efforts which will prevent or eliminate damage to the environment and biosphere and stimulate the health and welfare or man.

NEPA sets out various mechanisms for advancing such a national environmental policy. EIA was included within Section 102(2)(c) as an action-forcing mechanism to ensure that every federal agency implements the environmental policy act as part of its established responsibilities (Dreyfus and Ingram, 1976) through a requirement to:

> Include in every recommendation or report on proposals for legislation and other major Federal actions significantly affecting the quality of the human environment, a detailed statement by the responsible official on:
>
> i The environmental impact of the proposed action.
> ii Any adverse environmental effects which cannot be avoided should the proposal be implemented.
> iii Alternatives to the proposed action.
> iv The relationship between local short-term uses of man's environment and the maintenance and enhancement of long-term productivity.
> v Any irreversible and irretrievable commitments of resources which would be involved in the proposed action should it be implemented.

While the specific language of 'sustainability' is not employed within NEPA, it is clear that the identified purpose of the act, and point (iv) within section 102(2)(c) especially in the extracts above, clearly align directly with the notion of sustainable development. Sheate (2012) argues that EIA has evolved to have goals of sustainable development rather than environmental conservation in response to international drivers like the Rio Earth Summit of 1992 (United Nations Conference on Environment and Development, 1992). Bond *et al.* (2010) further document the sustainability outcomes expectation underpinning the field of EIA. Whilst we focus on EIA in this chapter, the process we consider and its application to mining could equally apply to any of the other forms of impact assessment that exist. Bond and Morrison-Saunders (2011), for example, define 'sustainability assessment' as 'any process that directs decision-making towards sustainability' (p. 1) which includes, for example, EIA conducted at the scale of singular projects such as individual mine sites. As indicated previously, henceforth in this chapter we focus on EIA, assuming it attempts to deliver sustainable development.

A generic EIA process can be identified that is typical of practice everywhere in the world. While it incorporates the components of section 102(2)(c) of NEPA recorded previously, it comprises the following functions which can be represented as a sequence of steps.

Screening. The decision on whether to apply EIA to a new development proposal is taken based on the likelihood that a significant adverse effect on the socio-economic and physical environment would ensue. Mining on any scale, other than some artisanal activity, is highly likely to cause some significant effect and therefore require EIA to be undertaken. Depending on the legislation, different organisations may have the responsibility to make the screening decision, but it is often the same organisation as that which will ultimately decide whether the project goes ahead. There is usually a requirement for a public notice of the screening decision.

Scoping. Where EIA takes place, there is a need to run the process as cost effectively and efficiently as possible; thus scoping determines which effects fall within the scope of the EIA and which do not. As such, scoping sets out the terms of reference of an EIA study to focus upon the most significant impacts (bearing in mind that consideration of sustainability might include a myriad of ecological, social and economic aspects). Depending on the jurisdiction, regulations might require the proponent to be responsible for their own scoping, or the decision maker, or an environmental authority or EIA agency; and the process may also include public and other stakeholder consultation or review.

Environmental impact statement. The proponent of the development (usually contracting a consultant) will normally be charged with the responsibility of investigating and submitting a formal assessment report on the likely (sustainability) consequences of proceeding with the proposed development activity. The requirement is that the potentially significant impacts are all assessed and then an evaluation of significance for each of them made once the necessary evidence has been gathered. It includes many considerations including an account of:

- *the baseline environment* – which is the expected state of the environment considering all environmental aspects scoped into the assessment at the present day and then forecast into the future in the absence of the proposed development;
- the *nature of the proposed development* and reasonable alternative types or forms of development to the overall preferred option;
- *predictions of impact* arising from the development;
- *proposed mitigation measures* to alleviate or counterbalance the predicted adverse impacts – this may entail design changes to the

original development concept, the addition of particular onsite environmental management strategies to avoid, minimise or repair environmental impacts, or provision of offsets (i.e. offsite actions to compensate for unavoidable adverse effects of significance);
- evaluation of the significance of the mitigated impacts.

Public/stakeholder consultation and reporting. Ideally consultation with relevant parties will occur throughout each step of the EIA process. At the very least there will be disclosure of the environmental impact statement (see next item), although many systems require notifications of screening and engagement with diverse stakeholder groups at the scoping stage. Opportunities for public comments on the overall proposal are generally facilitated once the environmental impact statement has been submitted.

Publication and review of environmental impact statement. The data, methods and significance evaluation, along with descriptions of the engagement processes undertaken and other relevant information (like legal context) must be documented (in an Environmental Impact Statement, or Environmental Impact Report – the name changes depending on jurisdiction) and presented to decision makers along with public comments. In some jurisdictions a separate EIA agency prepares an evaluation report of all this material, including proponent responses to public and other stakeholder inputs and with recommendations of their own regarding any further mitigation measures warranted or suggested approval conditions to be imposed. This allows the decision-maker to make an evidence-based decision.

Evaluation of the environmental impact statement and approval decision-making. Legal contexts vary for how this step takes place, and can include a number of models, the most common of which are as follows.

- Elected decision-makers approve or reject the development proposal based on recommendations made by an EIA or environmental agency.
- Elected decision-makers approve or reject the development proposal based on evidence which includes the environmental impact statement with no EIA agency or environmental agency involved.
- An environmental agency issues or withholds an environmental licence; an additional building permit is separately considered by other decision-makers.

Other variations of these main models are possible and it is always necessary to understand the system in operation in any jurisdiction. Typically approval conditions will be set associated with the permitting processes which require mitigation measures outlined in the environmental impact statement to be implemented, although this is not always a legal requirement.

Monitoring and audit (EIA follow-up). Typically the proponent will be expected to report on implementation progress including compliance with any approval conditions and performance obtained. Some models of EIA follow-up exist that also involve independent auditors, the EIA regulator, the public and other stakeholders in the process of verifying EIA outcomes.

These generic steps deliver the 'consider future consequences' and 'direct decision-making towards sustainability' intention of the environmental impact assessment outlined previously. This explanation of EIA has been necessarily brief. Readers wishing to learn more about the process are referred to Wathern, 1988; Canter, 1996; Petts, 1999a, 1999b; Wood, 2003; Hanna, 2009; Morris and Therivel, 2009; Glasson *et al.*, 2012; Lawrence, 2013.

Sustainable development

Sustainable development as a concept can be traced back to the World Commission on Environment and Development that penned the best known definition: 'development that meets the needs of current generations without compromising the ability of future generations to meet their needs' (World Commission on Environment and Development, 1987, p. 9). However, the Rio Earth Summit in 1992 (United Nations Conference on Environment and Development, 1992) was the main political driver that led governments around the world to develop sustainable development strategies, and to embed them as a key cross-cutting goal across government departments.

Despite its widespread deployment, the nature of 'sustainable development' is highly contested (Williams and Millington, 2004) with O'Riordan (2000, p. 30) arguing that 'there is no clear agreement as to what sustainable development is, every pathway begins and ends at different points ...'. The same debates over the exact meaning of sustainable development occur today with Bond and Morrison-Saunders (2011) detailing specific areas of contention:

Reductionism vs. holism. Sustainability is generally evaluated using indicator sets which break down understanding of the environment into individual measurable variables; but this simplifies understanding of a highly complex socio-ecological system into surrogate measures which, it is argued, cannot fully represent system behaviour.

Time horizons. A pervasive foundation of sustainable development is equity – both intra-generational and inter-generational. For inter-generational equity the expectation is that future generations inherit at least as much capital as the current generation enjoys. There are recurring arguments over how far into the future planning should accommodate – and in mining there are clear parallels with decisions made over the pace of the mining that is appropriate.

Different understandings of sustainability. There are many ways of framing sustainability, but one approach with particular relevance for mining is that based on arguments of weak versus strong sustainability. This framing is based on the 'three-pillars' understanding of sustainable development – that it is based on the aggregate effect of human actions on social, economic and environmental capitals. Some argue that sustainable development should pass on at least as much capital aggregated across social, economic and environmental (this is known as weak sustainability), whereas others argue that at least as much environmental capital should be passed on and not allow it to be offset against gains in economic and social capital. For mining, weak sustainability is the most likely framing.

Increasingly, sustainable development is seen as a goal of convenience for governments because of the plural interpretations that are possible (Bond *et al.*, 2013). This has implications for attempts to achieve approval for mining development given the very diverse understandings that different stakeholders will have of the acceptability of outcomes. As such, failure to engage with the different understandings presents a risk to developers seeking the Social License to Operate for a proposed extractives projects (Prno and Slocombe, 2014; Moffat and Lacey (chapter 3)).

In the next section we look at sustainability specifically in the context of mining, before considering how best EIA can facilitate sustainable mining and act as a vehicle for securing the Social License to Operate (see Bice and Moffatt, 2014).

Sustainable mining

In this section we simply wish to make the case, given the potential for impacts across the three pillars of sustainable development, that fundamentally mining must be capable of being considered a sustainable form of development, and to note the nature of much mining legislation and policy in this regard.

One of the earliest published accounts of the nature of mining in sustainability terms was *De Re Metallica* by Georgius Agricola in 1556, whose approach (in Book 1 of the overall work presented in 12 books) was to compare mining (mainly of metals) as a profession or undertaking with that of agriculture. A key early point is that the metal tools used for agriculture (and all other human undertakings) are themselves a product of mining, and that these have overall increased productivity and the quality of human life. In the Preface of his recent book, Franks (2015, p. ix) makes a similar observation about the intrinsically embedded nature of mining in all aspects of human life as follows:

> The stark reality of modern society is, that of all of the material we use in our daily lives, if it wasn't grown, it was mined or drilled. We are all incredibly reliant on the mining industry. Much of this reliance is hidden. Packaged into products or embedded within the value chain. But for an industry that is so fundamental to most of our lives, it certainly has a bad reputation.

It is primarily for this reason that we reject the notion that mining and sustainable development are incompatible and maintain that fundamentally mining must underpin sustainable development. After all, humans describe and define their own evolution in terms that reflect our mining skills and practices – the Stone Age, Bronze Age, Iron Age, Industrial Revolution etc. If mining cannot form the foundation for sustainable development, then conservation takes precedence over development and 'men would pass a horrible and wretched existence' (Agricola, 1556, p. 71).

Agricola (1556, p. 55) points out that mining is a finite activity and it is of course this aspect of mining that confronts the notion of 'sustaining'. In his reflection on the meaning of sustainable mining, Franks (2015, p. x) writes:

> It is the ecosystems and social systems on the surface of the earth that needed sustaining, not the rocks deep below it.... What mattered to me was not whether minerals were renewable, but whether they could be extracted in a way that did not disturb or degrade the environments and societies above them, and whether we had developed the economic and social systems to equitably distribute those resources, recycle them, and adapt to new resources as stocks waxed and waned.

The environmental impacts of mining are clear and underscore the need for processes such as EIA. The social implications of mining are increasingly a concern for developers, given the potential for conflict which can threaten either the consenting of the mining, or the continued operation. This concern is reflected in the increasing emphasis being placed on efforts to ensure community-sensitive mining which promotes well-being rather than simply impacting communities who happen to be located nearby (see, for example, Lajoie and Bouchard, 2006; Esteves, 2008; Lockie *et al.*, 2009; Sharma, 2010; Esteves and Barclay, 2011; Harvey and Bice, 2014; Ruckstuhl *et al.*, 2014; Nwapi, 2015). This includes economic well-being beyond just provision of jobs for some community members in a local operation, to developing capacity for sustainable livelihoods which will continue in the post-closure stage of mining. Various industry and NGO codes and standards for 'sustainable mining' have been published in the past two decades; some key international sources are MMSD (2002), IFC (2007) and ICMM (2005, 2008).

Sustainable mining is embodied in modern legislation where there is an expectation that mining companies first apply for permission to mine and second 'make good injury'[2] to the surface of the land caused by mining. In the past two decades there has been considerable attention to and advancement in mine closure planning and management, with an expectation that this process is continuous and adaptive throughout the lifecycle of mine planning, implementation, decommissioning and post-closure management (e.g. IFC, 2007; ICMM, 2008; Sánchez *et al.*, 2014). These processes, typically embedded within national and/or state level legislation for mining and associated regulations, policies and guidelines (e.g. DMP and EPA, 2015) mimic or are directly compatible with EIA expectations. For example, Morrison-Saunders *et al.* (2016) demonstrate the parallels between effective mine closure planning and EIA, and sketches out the provisions for each in seven African nations and for the state of Western Australia.

The aspiration in current thinking around sustainable mining is not just to avoid or minimise negative consequences of mining but to actually promote net positive outcomes. For example, the action plan for implementing African Mining Vision (African Union Commission *et al.*, 2012) puts forward several goals for mining that seek to deliver on sustainable development such as:

- to create a mining sector that is knowledge driven and is the engine of an internationally competitive African industrial economy (p. 18);
- to create a sustainable and well governed mining sector that is inclusive and appreciated by all stakeholders and surrounding communities (p. 24); and
- to increase the level of investment flows into mining and infrastructure projects to support broad socio-economic development (p. 37).

Hall and Hall (2015) urge a paradigm shift to thinking about mine closure whereby a closed mine be considered as an asset rather than a financial and environmental liability in light of the millions or possibly billions of dollars that been invested in the site over the operations of the mine. Numerous other authors have called for benefits or net positive outcomes to be realised for all stakeholders from effective mine closure planning, especially affected community members whereby the ideal is to deliver enhanced quality of life or well-being beyond the mine life (Otto, 1997; Downing *et al.*, 2002; Stacey *et al.*, 2010; Davies *et al.*, 2012; Morrison-Saunders *et al.*, 2016).

Using EIA to achieve sustainable mining

In this section we briefly introduce the literature on EIA and mining, which dates back over 20 years (for example, Kobus and Lee, 1993; Pritchard *et al.*, 1995), to illustrate the key issues which researchers have grappled with, or continue to grapple with. We go on to introduce the key principles for EIA that should always be applied for all developments, including mining, before focusing on specific approaches that might help in the quest for sustainable mining.

It needs pointing out that the existence of EIA legislation does not mean that the procedures are necessarily followed. Capacity has to exist in a country in order for the requirements to be reliably and comprehensively implemented (Sankoh, 1996; Innanen, 2004; Van Loon, 2008). There is evidence that EIA in relation to mining projects is not thoroughly implemented in some developing countries (Appiah and Osman, 2014). Legislation can be sector-specific, and so the presence of a mature EIA system in any particular country is no guarantee of effective implementation in the mining sector.

Mining is known to have the potential for a range of different impacts. Table 4.1 from Azapagic (2004) illustrates some of these.

The literature on mining cannot easily be generalised given that the focus of research has covered different extractive industries applied at different scales in different countries. Nevertheless, some of the impacts are likely to be repeated, subject to the management approaches taken and mitigation measures implemented to prevent them. For example, Ogbonna *et al.* (2015) cite key impacts associated with coal mining in Nigeria as health, water, socio-economic, ecological (including extinction of both animal and plant species), and water pollution. These types of impacts are generally interrelated, for example, socio-economic impacts are associated with the loss of tree species that provided income for communities. Positive impacts focus on economic opportunities associated with mine employment.

Social impacts are highlighted by a number of studies (see, for example, Esteves, 2008; Esteves and Vanclay, 2009; Lockie *et al.*, 2009; Holm *et al.*, 2013; Suopajärvi, 2013); and Sharma (2010) refers to gender equality and well-being issues associated with mining communities in Queensland, Australia. Such studies frequently interface with considerations of the social licence to operate in relation to extractive projects (Harvey and Bice, 2014; Martinez and Franks, 2014; Parsons and Moffat, 2014). Thus it is clear that employment opportunities exist in relation to mining projects, but that there are also exists the potential for a number of social impacts on the existing communities. These present a significant risk to the development company where they are not properly identified and managed working with the affected communities.

Health impacts are also commonly researched in relation to mining projects (for example, Kessomboom *et al.*, 2005; Noble and Bronson, 2005;

Table 4.1 Key sustainability issues for mining and the mining sector

Economic issues	*Environmental issues*	*Social issues*
Contribution to GDP and wealth creation	Biodiversity loss	Bribery and corruption
Costs, sales and profits	Emissions to air	Creation of employment
Distribution of revenues and wealth	Energy use	Employee education and skills development
Investments (capital, employees, communities, pollution prevention and mine closure)	Global warming and other environmental impacts	Equal opportunities and non-discrimination
Shareholder value	Land use, management and rehabilitation	Health and safety
Value added	Nuisance	Human rights and business ethics
	Product toxicity	Labour/management relationship
	Resource use and availability	Relationship with local communities
	Solid waste	Stakeholder involvement
	Water use, effluents and leachates (including acid mine drainage)	Wealth distribution

Source: Azapagic, 2004.

Winkler *et al.*, 2010), although the location is important as well as the specific mining process. Extractives projects in the tropics have the effect of bringing workers into contact with a variety of diseases that they would not normally be exposed to.

Thus it is clear that mining can have significant environmental effects where proper anticipation and planning does not take place through an *ex ante* process like EIA. A number of principles exist that provide clarity on appropriate ways forward for EIA, including the principles developed by the International Association for Impact Assessment (IAIA) (1999) which are equally relevant for all sectors, including mining. These are reproduced below.

Environmental Impact Assessment should be:

Purposive. The process should inform decision making and result in appropriate levels of environmental protection and community well-being.

Rigorous. The process should apply "best practicable" science, employing methodologies and techniques appropriate to address the problems being investigated.

Practical. The process should result in information and outputs which assist with problem solving and are acceptable to and able to be implemented by proponents.

Relevant. The process should provide sufficient, reliable and usable information for development planning and decision making.

Cost effective. The process should achieve the objectives of EIA within the limits of available information, time, resources and methodology.

Efficient. The process should impose the minimum cost burdens in terms of time and finance on proponents and participants consistent with meeting accepted requirements and objectives of EIA.

Focused. The process should concentrate on significant environmental effects and key issues; i.e. the matters that need to be taken into account in making decisions.

Adaptive. The process should be adjusted to the realities, issues and circumstances of the proposals under review without compromising the integrity of the process, and be iterative, incorporating lessons learned throughout the proposal's life cycle.

Participative. The process should provide appropriate opportunities to inform and involve the interested and affected publics, and their inputs and concerns should be addressed explicitly in the documentation and decision making.

Interdisciplinary. The process should ensure that the appropriate techniques and experts in the relevant bio-physical and socio-economic disciplines are employed, including use of traditional knowledge as relevant.

Credible. The process should be carried out with professionalism, rigour, fairness, objectivity, impartiality and balance, and be subject to independent checks and verification.

Integrated. The process should address the interrelationships of social, economic and biophysical aspects.

Transparent. The process should have clear, easily understood requirements for EIA content; ensure public access to information; identify the factors that are to be taken into account in decision making; and acknowledge limitations and difficulties.

Systematic. The process should result in full consideration of all relevant information on the affected environment, of proposed alternatives and their impacts, and of the measures necessary to monitor and investigate residual effects.

Following these basic principles should ensure that the stages of EIA are conducted in such a way as to enhance the sustainability of the outcomes whilst accommodating the different values of a diverse set of stakeholders. In addition the World Bank has developed specific guidance on EIA for mining projects (World Bank, 1998). However, there is still a need to ensure that the findings of the EIA are properly integrated into mine management. One approach for ensuring this is through the production and implementation of Environmental Management Plans (EMPs) that can be embedded in Environmental Management Systems where companies operate these. Guidelines for EMPs do exist (for example, Goodwin and Wright, 2008), and the World Bank has also produced a guideline on developing EMPs (World Bank, 1999). EMPs take the mitigation measures and design innovations from an EIA and allocated specific responsibilities and timelines to ensure they are implemented in a timely fashion.

Conclusions

Mining has sustainability implications, and poor mine planning or management will likely mean that these impacts are realised. EIA, as an *ex ante* decision-support tool, can anticipate the implications and either design them out, or mitigate them so that sustainable mining is achieved.

Our discussion thus far has focused on major mining undertakings. Artisanal and small-scale mining (ASM) poses a particular challenge as individual operations may be too small to trigger EIA (not to mention illegal operations which obviously will be unregulated), notwithstanding that the cumulative impact is significant and poses considerable sustainability challenges (Hilson and McQuilken, 2014; Labonne, 2014). Recently Morrison-Saunders *et al.* (2015) posited that EIA preparations for major mining operations could play a constructive role in putting in place appropriate management measures for situations where ASM activity is anticipated to accompany or follow major mining operations in developing nations.

Nevertheless, given the plural nature of interpretations of sustainable development, there remains scope for some stakeholders to be unhappy about the implications of well-planned mining activities. The nature of development means that trade-offs are made between negative and positive implications of any development types. EIA can ensure that the all stakeholder views are embedded in mine planning and management to ensure the most sustainable outcomes, with the least conflict.

Notes

1 www.iaia.org.
2 *Mining Act* 1978 of Western Australia, s26(a).

References

African Union Commission, African Development Bank and United Nations Economic Commission for Africa (2012) *Building a sustainable future for Africa's extractive industry: From vision to action. Action plan for implementing the AMV*. Africa Mining Vision, Addis Ababa, Ethiopia.

Agricola, G. (1556) *De Re Metallica*. In: H. C. Hoover and L. H. Hoover (translators), (1950) New York: Dover Publications, available at: http://archimedes.mpiwg-berlin.mpg.de/docuserver/images/archimedes/agric_remet_002_en/downloads/agric_remet_002_en.text.pdf.

Appiah, D. O. and Osman, B. (2014) 'Environmental impact assessment: Insights from mining communities in Ghana'. *Journal of Environmental Assessment Policy and Management, 16(04)*, 1450031.

Azapagic, A. (2004) 'Developing a framework for sustainable development indicators for the mining and minerals industry'. *Journal of Cleaner Production, 12(6)*, 639–662.

Bice, S. and Moffat, K. (2014) 'Social licence to operate and impact assessment'. *Impact Assessment and Project Appraisal, 32*, 257–262.

Bond, A. and Morrison-Saunders, A. (2011) 'Re-evaluating sustainability assessment: Aligning the vision and the practice'. *Environmental Impact Assessment Review, 31(1)*, 1–7.

Bond, A., Morrison-Saunders, A. and Howitt, R. (2013) *Sustainability assessment: Pluralism, practice and progress*. Taylor and Francis, London.

Bond, A. J., Viegas, C. V., Coelho de Souza Reinisch Coelho, C. and Selig, P. M. (2010) 'Informal knowledge processes: The underpinning for sustainability outcomes in EIA?'. *Journal of Cleaner Production, 18(1)*, 6–13.

Canter, L. W. (1996) *Environmental impact assessment*. McGraw-Hill, New York.

Davies J., Maru Y. and May T. (2012) *Enduring community value from mining: Conceptual framework*, CRC-REP Working Paper CW007. Ninti One, Alice Springs.

DMP and EPA (Department of Mines and Petroleum and Environmental Protection Authority) (2015) *Guidelines for preparing Mine Closure Plans*, available at: http://edit.epa.wa.gov.au/EPADocLib/153549_WEB VERSION – Guidelines for Preparing Mine Closure Plans.pdf.

Downing, T. E., Moles, J., McIntosh, I. and Garcia-Downing Mining, C. (2002) *Indigenous Peoples and Mining Encounters: Strategies and Tactics*, Mining,

Minerals and Sustainable Development (MMSD) No. 57. International Institute for Environment and Development (IIED) and World Business Council for Environment and Development, available at: http://pubs.iied.org/pdfs/G00548.pdf.

Dreyfus, D. and Ingram, H. (1976) 'The National Environmental Policy Act: A view of intent and practice'. *Natural Resources Journal, 16*, 243–262.

Esteves, A. M. (2008) 'Evaluating community investments in the mining sector using multi-criteria decision analysis to integrate SIA with business planning'. *Environmental Impact Assessment Review, 28(4–5)*, 338–348.

Esteves, A. M. and Barclay, M. A. (2011) 'Enhancing the benefits of local content: Integrating social and economic impact assessment into procurement strategies'. *Impact Assessment and Project Appraisal, 29(3)*, 205–215.

Esteves, A. M. and Vanclay, F. (2009) 'Social Development Needs Analysis as a tool for SIA to guide corporate-community investment: Applications in the minerals industry'. *Environmental Impact Assessment Review, 29(2)*, 137–145.

Franks, D. (2015) *Mountain movers: Mining, sustainability and the agents of change*. Routledge, London.

Glasson, J., Therivel, R. and Chadwick, A. (2012) *Introduction to Environmental Impact Assessment*. Routledge, London.

Goodwin, C. and Wright, J. (2008) *Environmental management plans*. Institute of Environmental Management and Assessment, Lincoln.

Hall, N. and Hall, S. (2015) 'Global implications and challenges of evolving mine closure requirements in Western Australia'. In: M. Jarvie-Eggart (ed.), *Responsible mining: Case studies in managing social and environmental risks in the developed world*, Society for Mining, Metallurgy and Exploration, USA, pp. 583–608.

Hanna, K. S. (ed.) (2009) *Environmental impact assessment: Practice and participation*. Oxford University Press, Ontario.

Harvey, B. and Bice, S. (2014) 'Social impact assessment, social development programmes and social licence to operate: Tensions and contradictions in intent and practice in the extractive sector'. *Impact Assessment and Project Appraisal, 32(4)*, 327–335.

Hilson, G. and McQuilken, J. (2014) 'Four decades of support for artisanal and small-scale mining in sub-Saharan Africa: A critical review'. *The Extractive Industries and Society, 1*, 104–118.

Holm, D., Ritchie, L., Snyman, K. and Sunderland, C. (2013) 'Social impact management: A review of current practice in Queensland, Australia'. *Impact Assessment and Project Appraisal, 31(3)*, 214–219.

Horowitz, L. (2006) 'Mining and sustainable development'. *Journal of Cleaner Production, 14 (3–4)*, 307–308.

ICMM (International Council on Mining and Metals) (2005) *Financial assurance for mine closure and reclamation*. London.

ICMM (International Council on Mining and Metals) (2008) *Planning for integrated mine closure: toolkit*, available at www.icmm.com/document/310.

IFC (International Finance Corporation) (2007) *Environmental, health and safety guidelines for mining*, World Bank Group, available at: www.ifc.org/wps/wcm/connect/1f4dc28048855af4879cd76a6515bb18/Final B- BMining.pdf?MOD=AJPERES&id=1323153264157.

Innanen, S. E. R. (2004) 'Environmental impact assessment in Turkey: Capacity building for European Union accession'. *Impact Assessment and Project Appraisal, 22(2)*, 141–151.

International Association for Impact Assessment and Institute of Environmental Assessment (1999) *Principles of environmental impact assessment best practice*, available at http://iaia.org/publicdocuments/special-publications/Principles of IA_web.pdf.

Kessomboom, N., Kessomboom, P., Pengkum, S. and Siriwatanapaiboon, S. (2005) 'Roles of health impact assessment and potash mining project, Thailand'. In Healthy Public Policy and Health Impact Assessment Program, Health Systems Research Institute (ed.), *Towards healthy society: Healthy public policy and health impact assessment in Thailand*. Health Systems Research Institute, Nontaburi, Thailand, pp. 253–276.

Kobus, D. and Lee, N. (1993) 'The role of environmental assessment in the planning and authorisation of extractive industry projects'. *Project Appraisal, 8(3)*, 147–156.

Labonne, B. (2014) 'Who is afraid of artisanal and small-scale mining (ASM)?'. *The Extractive Industries and Society, 1*, 121–123.

Lajoie, G. and Bouchard, M. A. (2006) 'Native involvement in strategic assessment of natural resource development: The example of the Crees living on the Canadian taiga'. *Impact Assessment and Project Appraisal, 24(3)*, 211–220.

Laurence D. (2011) 'Establishing a sustainable mining operation: An overview'. *Journal of Cleaner Production, 19*, 278–284.

Lawrence D. P. (2013) *Impact assessment: Practical solutions to recurrent problems and contemporary challenges*. John Wiley & Sons, New Jersey.

Lockie, S., Franettovich, M., Petkova-Timmer, V., Rolfe, J. and Ivanova, H. (2009) 'Coal mining and the resource community cycle: A longitudinal assessment of the social impacts of the Coppabella coal mine'. *Environmental Impact Assessment Review, 29(5)*, 330–339.

Martinez, C. and Franks, D. M. (2014) 'Does mining company-sponsored community development influence social licence to operate? Evidence from private and state-owned companies in Chile'. *Impact Assessment and Project Appraisal, 32(4)*, 294–303.

MMSD (Mining, Minerals and Sustainable Development) (2002) *Breaking new ground: The report of the mining, minerals and sustainable development project*. Earthscan, London.

Morgan, R. (2012) 'Environmental impact assessment: The state of the art'. *Impact Assessment and Project Appraisal, 30(1)*, 5–14.

Morris, P. and Therivel, R. (eds.) (2009) *Methods of environmental impact assessment*, 3rd edition. Routledge, London.

Morrison-Saunders, A., McHenry, M. P., Rita Sequeira, A., Gorey, P., Mtegha, H. and Doepel, D. (2016) 'Integrating mine closure planning with environmental impact assessment: Challenges and opportunities drawn from African and Australian practice'. *Impact Assessment and Project Appraisal, 34(2)*, 117–128.

Morrison-Saunders, A., McHenry, M. P., Wessels, J. A., Sequeira, A. R., Mtegha, H. and Doepel, D. (2015) 'Planning for artisanal and small-scale mining during EIA: Exploring the potential'. *The Extractive Industries and Society, 2(4)*, 813–819.

Morrison-Saunders, A., Pope, J., Gunn, J., Bond, A. and Retief, F. (2014) 'Strengthening impact assessment: A call for integration and focus'. *Impact Assessment and Project Appraisal, 32(1)*, 2–8.

Mudd, G. M. (2007) 'Sustainable mining – an oxymoron?'. *The Chemical Engineer, 798*, 27–29.

Noble, B. F. and Bronson, J. E. (2005) 'Integrating human health into environmental impact assessment: Case studies of Canada's northern mining resource sector'. *Arctic, 58(4)*, 395–405.

Nwapi, C. (2015) 'Governance considerations relating to social impact assessments for mining development in African communities'. *Journal of Environmental Assessment Policy and Management, 17(02)*, 1550019.

Ogbonna, P. C., Nzegbule, E. C. and Okorie, P. E. (2015) 'Environmental impact assessment of coal mining at Enugu, Nigeria'. *Impact Assessment and Project Appraisal, 33(1)*, 73–79.

O'Riordan, T. (2000) 'The sustainability debate'. In T. O'Riordan (ed.), *Environmental science for environmental management*. Prentice Hall, Harlow, pp. 29–62.

Otto, J. (1997) 'A national mineral policy as a regulatory tool'. *Resources Policy, 23(1/2)*, 1–7.

Parsons, R. and Moffat, K. (2014), 'Integrating impact and relational dimensions of social licence and social impact assessment'. *Impact Assessment and Project Appraisal, 32(4)*, 273–282.

Petts, J., ed (1999a) *Handbook of environmental impact assessment. Volume 1. Environmental impact assessment: Process, methods and potential*. Blackwell Science, Oxford.

Petts, J., ed (1999b) *Handbook of environmental impact assessment. Volume 2. Environmental impact assessment in practice: Impact and limitations*. Blackwell Science, Oxford.

Pritchard, G., Wood, C. and Jones, C. (1995) 'The effect of environmental assessment on extractive industry planning decisions'. *Mineral Planning, 65*, 14–15.

Prno J. and Slocombe, D. S. (2014) 'A systems-based conceptual framework for assessing the determinants of a social license to operate in the mining industry'. *Environmental Management, 53*, 672–689.

Ruckstuhl, K., Thompson-Fawcett, M. and Rae, H. (2014) 'M ori and mining: Indigenous perspectives on reconceptualising and contextualising the social licence to operate'. *Impact Assessment and Project Appraisal, 32(4)*, 304–314.

Sánchez, L. E., Silva-Sánchez, S. S. and Neri, A. C. (2014) *Guide for mine closure planning*. Instituto Brasileiro de Mineração, Lago Sul, Brazil.

Sankoh, O. (1996) 'Making environmental impact assessment convincible to developing countries'. *Journal of Environmental Management, 47*, 185–189.

Sharma, S. (2010) 'The impact of mining on women: Lessons from the coal mining Bowen Basin of Queensland, Australia'. *Impact Assessment and Project Appraisal, 28(3)*, 201–215.

Sheate, W. R. (2009) 'The evolving nature of environmental assessment and management: Linking tools to help deliver sustainability – tools, techniques and approaches for sustainability'. In W. R. Sheate (ed.), *Tools, techniques and approaches for sustainability: Collected writings in environmental assessment policy and management*. World Scientific, Singapore, pp. 1–29.

Sheate, W. R. (2012) 'Purposes, paradigms and pressure groups: Accountability and sustainability in EU environmental assessment, 1985–2010'. *Environmental Impact Assessment Review, 33(1)*, 91–102.

Stacey, J., Naude, A. and Hermanus, M. (2010) 'The socio-economic aspects of mine closure and sustainable development: Literature overview and lessons for the socio-economic aspects of closure – Report 1'. The *Southern African Institute of Mining and Metallurgy, 110*, 379–394.

Suopajärvi, L. (2013) 'Social impact assessment in mining projects in Northern Finland: Comparing practice to theory'. *Environmental Impact Assessment Review*, 42, 25–30.

United Nations (2015) *Sustainable Development Goals: 17 goals to transform our world*, available at www.un.org/sustainabledevelopment.

United Nations Conference on Environment and Development (1992) *Earth Summit '92*. Regency Press, London.

Vanclay, F. (2015) 'Changes in the impact assessment family 2003–2014: Implications for considering achievements, gaps and future directions'. *Journal of Environmental Assessment Policy and Management, 17(1)*, 1550003.

Van Loon, L. (2008) 'Capacity development for environmental impact assessment (EIA): Application and insights in the Republic of Yemen'. MSc thesis submitted in the Faculty of Geosciences, Utrecht University, the Netherlands.

Wathern, P. (1988) *Environmental impact assessment: Theory and practice* Routledge, London.

Wood, C. (2003) *Environmental impact assessment: A comparative review*. Prentice Hall, Edinburgh.

World Bank (1998) *World Bank environmental assessment sourcebook: Update 22 'Environmental assessment of mining projects'*. World Bank, Washington, D.C.

World Bank (1999) *World Bank environmental assessment sourcebook: Update 25 'Environmental Management Plans'*. World Bank, Washington, D.C.

Worrall, R., Neil, D., Brereton, D. and Mulligan, D. (2009) 'Towards a sustainability criteria and indicators framework for legacy mine land'. *Journal of Cleaner Production, 17*, 1426–1434.

Young, J. and Septoff, A. (eds) (undated) *Digging for change: Towards a responsible minerals future, an NGO and community perspective. A Report from Members of the Global Mining Campaign, Mineral Policy Center*, available at: http://bankwatch.org/documents/eir_mineralsfuture.pdf.

Williams, C. C. and Millington, A. C. (2004) 'The diverse and contested meanings of sustainable development'. *The Geographical Journal, 170*, 99–104.

Winkler, M. S., Divall, M. J., Krieger, G. R., Balge, M. Z., Singer, B. H. and Utzinger, J. (2010) 'Assessing health impacts in complex eco-epidemiological settings in the humid tropics: Advancing tools and methods'. *Environmental Impact Assessment Review, 30(1)*, 52–61.

World Commission on Environment and Development (1987) *Our Common Future*. Oxford University Press, Oxford.

5 Using social impact assessment to achieve better outcomes for communities and mining companies

Susan Joyce, Rauno Sairinen and Frank Vanclay

Introduction

Social Impact Assessment (SIA) has traditionally been practiced as a predictive study for the regulatory approval of major mining projects, often under the framework of Environmental Impact Assessment (EIA). Historically, it has been implemented as a one-off, single point-in-time document, primarily a statement of likely negative impacts. In recent years, however, the drivers and focus of SIA, especially in a mining context, have shifted towards greater attention being given to the management of social impacts and to the enhancement of benefits during the whole mining lifecycle – through exploration, feasibility, planning (design and permitting), construction, operations and closure (João *et al.*, 2011; Esteves *et al.*, 2017; Vanclay *et al.*, 2015).

SIA is now being applied to a wide variety of tasks associated with the interactions between a company/project and its local communities. As conflict between communities and mining projects has risen in many regions in the last decade (Hanna *et al.*, 2016a), the mining industry has become increasingly aware that communities do not want to have project impacts thrust on them. In many cases, they want to be active partners in co-development and they want to benefit from private sector projects when these projects proceed. In situations where their concerns have not been adequately addressed, social actors have mobilized against projects, sometimes with sufficient power to block them, at least in the short term (Hanna *et al.*, 2016b).

SIA provides an overarching framework and processes to scope issues, gather and analyze relevant data, determine appropriate mitigation measures, and facilitate participation by various stakeholders. It can also assist in identifying and shaping how a project can contribute to the creation of value for each party (Vanclay *et al.*, 2015). This broader SIA approach is one way to address the fact that project approval has become increasingly complex and is perhaps less predictable than in the past. Approval is not always determined on the basis of the technical merit of the project, or only through the formal permitting process – instead local stakeholders have often taken direct action to halt permits (Hanna *et al.*, 2016b). In addition to government regulatory agencies, many other stakeholders may be involved, either formally or informally, in approving, monitoring or overseeing project approvals and the subsequent social and environmental performance of projects, including local and global NGOs, international financial institutions, international industry associations, the insurance industry, and the project-affected communities themselves (Vanclay *et al.*, 2015).

While national legislation remains important, it is increasingly the international financial institutions – especially the International Finance Corporation (IFC) and other multilateral developments banks, as well as the Equator Principle banks – and the international industry associations that take the lead role in setting standards for industry good practice (IFC, 2012; ICMM, 2012, 2015a, 2015b). Over the last decade or so, the IFC has emerged as the leading agency in codifying international good practice, especially with its shift to Performance Standards (IFC, 2012) which emphasize the development of management plans, systems, and internal capacity to implement these international standards – a shift that has given rise to the concept of 'social performance' (Salazar *et al.*, 2012; Vanclay *et al.*, 2015).

In this chapter, we outline the central role SIA plays in the effective development and implementation of plans to manage social impacts, both mitigating the negative and enhancing the positive, across the full lifecycle of a mine. We pay particular attention to the critical early planning and permitting stages, when the assessment of impacts and the involvement of potentially affected stakeholders have a significant influence on mining projects. However, for SIA to play a more effective role in the development of social management systems, it needs to be integrated into the business decision-making process at a very early stage in order to provide the information critical for planning and adaptive management. It also requires the improved integration of local perspectives into risk assessment and impact management. To lay the basis for this discussion, we provide an initial overview of the practice of social impact assessment, highlight the key role that community engagement and participation play in the identification and management of environmental and social impacts, and discuss SIA's role in managing the social impacts of mining across the mine lifecycle.

What is social impact assessment?

Social Impact Assessment (SIA) arose alongside Environmental Impact Assessment (EIA) in the early 1970s primarily as a regulatory tool, and over time there has been a steady evolution in how SIA has been practiced (Esteves *et al.*, 2012; Vanclay, 2014). Although there is inconsistency in how SIA is undertaken in practice, there is a well-developed international approach endorsed by the International Association for Impact Assessment (Vanclay *et al.*, 2015), including a formal definition and guidance as to the content that should be addressed in each SIA process. The International Principles for Social Impact Assessment (Vanclay, 2003) defined SIA as being "the processes of analyzing, monitoring and managing the intended and unintended social consequences, both positive and negative, of planned interventions (policies, programs, plans, projects) and any social change processes invoked by those interventions." This definition was reconfirmed in the 2015 SIA guidance document published by the International Association for Impact Assessment (Vanclay *et al.*, 2015).

The SIA process is intended to consider the full range of activities associated with the project in question. It attempts to determine the likely social change processes all these activities could invoke, and identify the direct and indirect pathways by which the project activities generate social impacts (Vanclay, 2002). For example, direct pathways include the wages that increase economic wellbeing. Indirect pathways include environmental changes, such as the contamination of water sources, which usually lead to multiple social impacts. SIA is the key tool for social practitioners, inside or outside a mining company, to inform social performance and the management of social issues, and it is applicable to the whole of the project lifecycle (Vanclay *et al.*, 2015; Esteves *et al.*, 2017).

The primary objectives of SIA in mining are to: (1) understand how a proposed mine will change the life of residents, communities and regions; and (2) provide a framework for collaboration with stakeholders and the integration of inputs from affected stakeholders into the planning, design and management of the mine's impacts, both positive and negative, on society. SIA is particularly relevant for mining companies and mining-affected communities because the scale and duration of resource extraction projects usually create a wide range of complex social impacts, many of which are linked to environmental impacts that, in turn, create additional social impacts, which also must be considered (Vanclay *et al.*, 2015). SIA provides an analytical tool for understanding the differing impacts and mitigation measures across the various phases of the mine lifecycle – exploration, design/permitting, construction, operations and closure.

The activities typically undertaken in an SIA process fall under four general headings (Esteves and Vanclay, 2009; Vanclay *et al.*, 2015), which are:

1 understand the issues, including both project/intervention as well as the context, scoping issues and stakeholders, inform and develop participatory processes, and develop an understanding of the social context;
2 predict, analyze and assess the likely impact pathways for social changes and impacts, indirect and cumulative impacts, affected party

responses, the significance of the changes predicted, and project alternatives;

3 develop and implement strategies addressing both negative impact management as well as enhancement of positive impacts (benefits and opportunities), development of the management plans to support effective implementation of these, the agreements and partnerships required to define the actions going forward, a grievance process to provide remedy for complaints, and community support programs to deal with change processes; and
4 design and implement monitoring programs to track predicted incomes, the effectiveness of management strategies and the overall outcomes against desired objectives, supporting ongoing adaptive management and periodic evaluation and review.

These four elements necessarily involve an iterative process, with revision of the predicted impacts and management plans as more information is acquired. They also feed into and receive information back from other studies as the various project components are developed or changed (Vanclay *et al.*, 2015).

Social analysis informed by participation

The nature of social impacts and of social change processes varies with the type and size of a development project, as well as with the characteristics of the community, and broader context in which the project is located (Vanclay, 2002, 2012). In SIA research, a range of theoretical models and concepts are used to assist in investigating the case-specific conditions. The complexity and interconnectedness of social impacts and social change processes require approaches that incorporate the ideas of multiple causality and multiple realities, that is, there can be more than one cause for any particular effect, and there are many understandings about the world and how it works. Social impacts refer not only to deterministic causal relations but also to subjective social meanings and communal values. One of the key characteristics of SIA is that it provides methods for analyzing social effects from the perspectives of the various social groupings (social, age, ethnicity, etc) in the community. SIA seeks to operate within the context of these different perspectives and value sets, because impacts are experienced differently as a result of them.

This analysis is accomplished with the assistance of public participation processes, of which there are many good practice techniques (IFC, 2007, 2014; OECD, 2017). With many justifications being given, there is strong consensus that public participation has an important role in EIA and SIA (Hartley and Wood, 2005; O'Faircheallaigh, 2010). A wide range of benefits from participation have been identified. For example, Glucker *et al.* (2013), drawing on Glicken (1999), identified ten objectives for participation in impact assessment: influencing decisions; enhancing democratic capacity; social learning; empowering and emancipating marginalized individuals and groups; harnessing local information and knowledge; incorporating experiential and value-based knowledge; testing the robustness of information from other sources; generating legitimacy; resolving conflict; and reflection.

The relationship between public participation and SIA should be clearly articulated in the design of the SIA process. Participation should be built into the planning process as a fundamental part of front-end impact assessment followed by participation in collaborative decision-making to design measures to avoid impacts, or to mitigate them where they are unavoidable. Ongoing participatory processes such as community liaison committees and direct engagement with affected people are needed to ensure that the management system has the ability to identify and respond to unanticipated social impacts later in the life of the mine.

Dealing with change and transformation rather than sustaining a previous status quo is an important aspect of SIA (Becker, 1997). This focus for SIA also resonates with Indigenous perspectives on SIA, some which demand that SIA provide a basis for real change. Maintaining the status quo is not acceptable to many Indigenous peoples (O'Faircheallaigh, 2011). The active involvement of social actors and potentially affected people in a process to define and articulate how a project's negative and positive impacts will be managed enhances their resilience and sustainability as a community, and may result in collaborative action and the creation of shared value (Porter and Kramer, 2011; Hidalgo *et al.*, 2014). In this approach, project design and other decisions are taken to meet multiple objectives, including the empowerment of communities.

Structured as an ongoing and embedded process, participation in SIA (including in the subsequent management/monitoring processes) is a cornerstone of respecting human rights (van der Ploeg and Vanclay, 2017a, 2017b). The issues of respect for human rights and having a process that integrates local perceptions into the assessment process may raise questions about the validity of the knowledge and opinion of local communities, and the right of local stakeholders to determine their own destinies independent of outside interference (Kemp and Vanclay, 2013; Vanclay, 2003, 2017), a right underscored for Indigenous people in the right to self-determination (Hanna and Vanclay, 2013). SIA must therefore evaluate, not only the mitigation measures required to reduce impacts to a manageable level, but also whether, for a given project, this mitigation is achievable given the context – the reality is that some projects may not be able to achieve this. While the objective of participatory processes in SIA is to identify how to carry out a project that can create benefit for all parties (Hanna and Vanclay, 2013), the right to self-determination means that "no-go" should be at least a potential outcome of the process.

SIA applies professional expertise to combine a rigorous evidence base with qualitative assessment. It integrates information and participation from all stakeholders to ensure that the understanding of the context is accurate and reflects how local affected people experience the impacts. The result is a more holistic understanding of the local (social) environment, which is necessary to ensure the adequate and effective management of the social issues and likely social changes (Smyth and Vanclay, 2017).

As an ongoing process throughout the mine lifecycle, the outputs from the SIA process should also be ongoing, including regular reporting back to management to integrate new information into management decisions and systems, and to stakeholders and rights-holders. SIA information could be used to inform participatory, multi-actor processes long before the study is actually completed, and should be designed to do so throughout the mine lifecycle through to closure and post-closure. SIA, therefore, is as much a process as it is a product (Vanclay *et al.*, 2015).

SIA and social performance in mining

Mining has a long history of impacting communities and triggering societal change (Veiga *et al.*, 2001; Ballard and Banks, 2003; Esteves *et al.*, 2017). Its impacts can be considerable, affecting not only the natural world, but also fundamental elements of the social environment (Solomon *et al.*, 2008; Petrova and Marinova, 2015). As outlined in the SIA Guidance document (Vanclay *et al.*, 2015), a 'social impact' can be conceived as anything that can be linked to a project that affects or concerns any stakeholder group. The direct social impacts of mining potentially include impacts on people's: employment; socio-economic wellbeing (income and other sources of revenue); traditional livelihoods; sacred sites and cultural heritage; sense of place; housing; social services (access to education, healthcare, etc.); quality of the experienced living environment (e.g., dust, noise, vibrations); land use; access to resources; access to leisure, recreation and tourism opportunities; health and security; community cohesion; levels of social capital; fear and anxiety; the effective functioning of their place of living, society and government; the extent of corruption; as well as many other things (Franks, 2011; Spohr, 2016; Esteves *et al.*, 2017). Environmental impacts may also be social impacts because people depend on the environment for their livelihoods and because people may have a sentimental attachment or spiritual tie to the places where the project is being sited (Vanclay, 2002; Smyth and Vanclay, 2017). Impacts on people's health are also social impacts, but may be addressed in a narrow technical way, without considering the relationships between the environment, health, wellbeing, livelihoods and other social impacts.

Although EIA is well established in many mining countries, SIA tends to be underdeveloped, and where it is undertaken, it is often inadequate and/or undervalued (Suopajärvi, 2013; Hanna *et al.*, 2014; Tiainen and Sairinen, 2014; Tiainen *et al.*, 2015). Too often, social assessments are little more than simple descriptions of an area with no real sense of the local development, history and culture, and no appreciation of the values attached to natural places or of how conditions may differ from one location to another. SIAs can also fail to accommodate local concerns, or fail to enable meaningful participation, so that the regulatory process may create resentment and opposition, with increased risks for mining companies (Hanna *et al.*, 2014).

In an effort to improve social performance, considerable useful guidance has been published in recent years, including the international SIA Guidance document published by the International Association for Impact Assessment (Vanclay *et al.*, 2015) and many guidance documents specifically focused on the extractives sector published by organizations such as: the International Council on Mining and Metals (ICMM); IFC; IPIECA (the global oil and gas industry association for environmental and social issues); the World Bank; and some companies, notably Rio Tinto, and the Socio-Economic Assessment Toolkit of Anglo American. According to these guidance documents, a good understanding of the mining project and how it is likely to affect what is important to local communities and other stakeholders is needed. Being more effective at identifying and managing the complexity of social impacts from mining developments requires an integrative approach, which can be provided by SIA, especially when the key related areas such as health impacts and human rights issues are included (Kemp and Vanclay, 2013; Götzmann *et al.*, 2016).

Management of social impacts over the mine lifecycle

The following sections look at the main stages of the mining lifecycle – exploration, design, planning, permitting, construction, operations and closure – and discuss how SIA can be applied in each stage to ensure identification of principal risks and impacts associated with that phase, in order to guide the management of the social impacts and to enhance social outcomes. Effective management in each phase requires understanding what impacts are typically generated by that phase and how these impacts fit into the overall lifecycle of the mine. It also requires the ability to identify any unusual and/or unexpected impacts when they do occur. To be truly effective, it requires considering the lead-time necessary to enable the uptake of opportunities, and/or to create the conditions to ensure achievement of sustainable development outcomes (Esteves and Vanclay, 2009). Figure 5.1 depicts a typical project cycle and identifies the potential role of SIA at each phase. It should be noted that, in reality, projects seldom progress in a continuous linear way. Rather, for a wide range of internal and/or external reasons most notably fluctuating commodity prices, they typically proceed in a stop-start fashion (Vanclay *et al.*, 2015).

Understanding SIA's role in social management requires consideration of when and how SIA is used. The traditional, formal SIA study is usually carried out only in certain phases of the project cycle. However, the SIA processes of collecting information, evaluating impacts, considering management

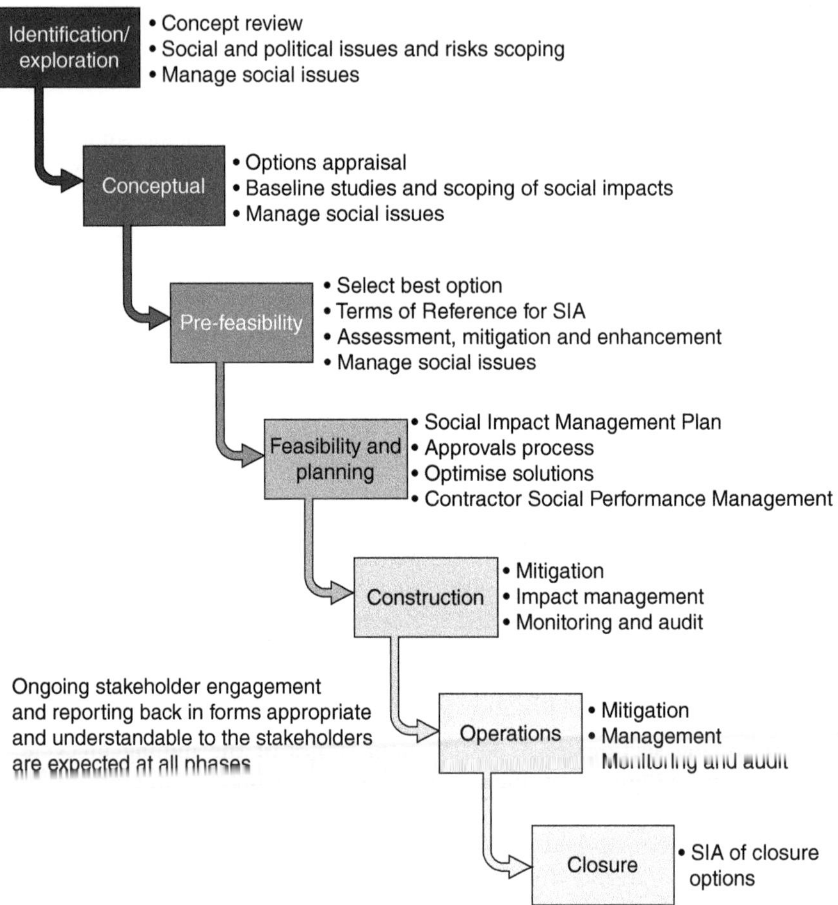

Figure 5.1 SIA can be applied at all phases of the project cycle.
Source: Vanclay *et al.*, 2015.

strategies, and monitoring results should be used in all phases and be an integral part of the company's management systems. The critical points in project development when mining companies (or their consultants) conduct SIA activities are listed here and discussed in detail below:

1 SIA as part of the exploration phase and pre-feasibility studies.
2 SIA and development of social management plans (SMPs) as part of the formal EIA.
3 Ongoing assessment, monitoring and adaptation of SMPs as needed during construction and operations.
4 SIA for mine closure planning.

1 SIA in the early stages of the mining lifecycle

Exploration is the most technically unpredictable stage of the mining lifecycle. It starts with prospecting, sampling and geophysics, advancing to drilling and, if successful, to more intensive drilling. The exploration phase can run from a few drilling seasons to fifteen or more years, and may involve continuous or sporadic activities, or both at different time periods. Compared to the rest of the mining lifecycle, a key feature of exploration is the very high probability of failure, and most exploration projects fail to become mines. For this reason, it is critical to manage any impacts and expectations created during this phase, and to have an exit strategy. This means managing with an eye to social and environmental closure from the beginning. SIA has a very important role in this phase to assess social and economic structures, human rights risks and political dynamics, and to provide the information to manage impacts and expectations in cases where exploration fails to find commercial deposits, as well as when it does.

Typical social issues during exploration that have the ability of the project to generate positive or negative outcomes include:

- the generation of unrealistic expectations about the certainty of mine development and future opportunities;
- creation or amplification of divisions within communities between supporters and opponents (development of conflicts);
- pressure on or weakening of local authority structures;
- reinforcement of local social structures of power and the exclusion of other groups;
- pressure on and changed access to local resources, including increases in land values;
- speculative behavior;
- population influx and local inflation;
- decline in local or traditional activities;
- development of dependency on exploration-related economic flows (distorting local economies, leading to inflation and induced poverty);
- generation of fear, uncertainty and anxiety in relation to the potential changes; and
- potential impacts on human rights associated with these issues.

During the early stages of exploration, SIA can play a critical role in the assessment of the context and early planning to ensure there is respectful engagement with local communities, to assist in learning about the context (through a context analysis and pre-screening), and to ensure there are minimal negative impacts created. Key issues to consider include: the presence of Indigenous people or vulnerable groups; gaps in the legal or regulatory context; the local history of conflict or human rights violations;

problems encountered by current or previous exploration projects; unstable or contested land tenure arrangements; community divisions; and limited access to water or other resources. In order to work effectively, identifying the gaps between national legislation and international standards in terms of expected procedures and the protection and fulfillment of human rights, and collecting broad historical, political and socio-cultural information, are necessary before going to the field. In order to respect the rights of landowners and traditional users, a process of information provision and the gaining of agreement to gain access for exploration activities must take place prior to any significant presence of the company on the ground. If the project is on the land of Indigenous people or other traditional groups, a process to gain their free, prior and informed consent (FPIC) should be obtained (Buxton and Wilson, 2013; Hanna and Vanclay, 2013).

The first social research activity carried out should be a community profile, which provides enough information to guide engagement and to begin mapping the risks or impacts that the communities or stakeholders may face from the mine development. It should develop an initial identification of stakeholders and an assessment of their different needs, interests, values and aspirations. This early work provides the information required to design an appropriate engagement and consultation strategy.

SIA also provides inputs to social investment during exploration, which can help lay the foundation for communities to benefit in the future if a mine is developed. The SIA may show that there is a need to start skills training early, building capacity over a number of years. Preliminary community diagnostics or early baseline studies can:

- identify adult literacy levels and how to structure literacy programs;
- develop transparent employment practices to spread opportunities more widely amongst families;
- identify economic activities or skills of value to a community that match potential future mine employment needs in order to design capacity building programs that will leave positive value even if the project fails; and
- identify economic activities in the communities and their limitations, to better design short- and long-term development support for traditional economic activities to reduce dependency and to support a potential closure strategy.

Once a project looks likely to move into permitting – when the technical information allows for a Pre-Feasibility Study – a full baseline study should be carried out to allow substantive social input into design alternatives aimed at reducing the impacts and knowing which ones are most critical for the affected communities. Typical early decisions include potential siting for key infrastructure; social input can avoid impacts and also identify opportunities for shared value creation from design alternatives.

SIA at this phase includes detailed mapping and analysis of stakeholders beyond the immediate area covered for early engagement, obtaining local inputs and establishing an iterative process to expand and deepen the understanding of social groups, organizations, factions, and distinct positions that affect how specific groups of stakeholders see and relate to the project. Participatory strategies, such as participatory environmental monitoring programs, should be well-developed by the pre-feasibility stage in order to build understanding and confidence of the closest stakeholders that, through SIA work, the project has identified, and is addressing their concerns and priority issues.

Because of the uncertainty associated with exploration, it is important to develop an exit strategy for closure at any point in the project at the same time as preparing local populations and authorities to leverage the opportunities from mining should the mine be developed. Assessment should be done to identify opportunities that are appropriate to the scale of the exploration activity and that enhance the capacity and skills relevant to the community, even if the project does not go ahead, so that a net benefit (or positive legacy) will be left.

Formation of an integrated cross-functional social impact team during exploration, pre-feasibility and feasibility studies helps to improve uptake of social and human rights issues during this stage of the process, as does capacity building with senior financial, project development and engineering design staff. Real opportunity lies in pushing the early planning and therefore the integration of various social management strategies into the mining project's business systems.

2 *SIA as part of the permitting process*

If a project successfully passes early hurdles such as the pre-feasibility study, the company typically moves into project permitting with the formal EIA process, advanced engineering and design as part of the Feasibility Study, and looks to financing for mine development. By the time the project is moving into permitting, feasibility and final design, sufficient information should be on hand to carry out a formal impact assessment process, including evaluating the significance of impacts and development mitigation measures, and management plans for those impacts that could not be avoided.

The requirements for SIA as part of formal regulatory EIA depend on the jurisdiction. In some countries, SIA is understood as a normal part of the EIA process and required in the assessments of projects with significant impacts such as mining. In other countries, the social dimension of the EIA is very limited or totally lacking in the regulatory requirements. It will be included by mining companies that have developed their own standards and procedures for social assessments as part of the company's social performance or by those that use international standards as a reference point.

Companies will also carry out SIAs to international good practice standards if they will be seeking project financing from Equator Principle banks, multilaterals such as the IFC, or the Export Credit Agencies, all of which require that mining projects meet the IFC's Performance Standards.

The SIA for environmental permitting should address mining social impacts during the construction, operations and closure phases. The information gathered and analyzed leading up to and during the permitting process is used to predict and manage the impacts during the subsequent phases of the mine lifecycle. The main outputs of SIA work come at this stage, producing the impact assessment report, as well as mitigation, management and monitoring plans, ideally with participatory processes, and draft closure plans. The SIA and EIA should also address impacts from all associated facilities, necessary related developments and any supply chain requirements. The scope of the final social assessment needs to cross-reference with other impact assessment studies and address potential changes not identified in the social scoping as well as cumulative impacts on society or actors from multiple impacts, project components or projects (Franks *et al.*, 2010).

Changes to the design of the mine, layout of facilities and details of processing can occur during the EIA stage, and SIA should be involved in an iterative process between the technical design, assessment processes, management plans and financial models. This is important to ensure that social issues and priorities are integrated into decision-making, and that documents remain consistent. Any significant design changes may mean that social impacts need to be re-evaluated and management plans revised.

3 SIA to inform social management during construction and operations of mining

Environmental and social management plans are usually developed as an outcome of the preparation of impact statements for project approvals and then periodically updated (Franks, 2012). While environmental management plans are a well-established practice in the mining industry, social management plans (SMPs) are relatively new, but nevertheless are now well established as international good practice and required for compliance with the IFC Performance Standards. The SMP links the SIA to ongoing management practices and allows companies to proactively respond to social and community issues (Franks *et al.*, 2009). For projects adhering to national standards, SMPs are only required in a few countries. However, governments, investors and mining companies are increasingly requiring SMPs, which, depending on the context, may become part of the legal permits to build and operate the mine, or legal covenants in the financing agreements.

An SMP is a management tool for addressing social impacts during the implementation of planned interventions (Franks and Vanclay, 2013). The complexity of social issues, especially during construction, has led to a ballooning number of management plans for social issues including labor and contractor issues, worker accommodation, resettlement, community health and safety, community development and others that have emerged to help meet the requirements of the IFC Performance Standards.

The SMP consolidates the findings of the impact assessments in terms of the implementation of required mitigation measures for negative impacts, or of measures to enhance positive impacts, such as through community development plans, local hiring and procurement plans. As management plans, they should provide estimates of the timing, frequency, duration and cost of management measures; and establish monitoring and reporting procedures (Franks *et al.*, 2009). They address capacity building activities where there are gaps in institutional or community capacity to participate or to play an effective role in the implementation of the plans. Finally, the plans outline the procedures for how social issues will be addressed in site management systems and plans and the development of grievance mechanisms.

The engagement process should inform the planning process on both substantive issues and on how to build participatory processes into the management plans. Plans should encompass multiple mechanisms for involving stakeholders in the oversight, supervision, monitoring and review, and finally reporting on the key impacts they are concerned about during construction of the mine, and should transition from construction through to operations. Once implemented, these participatory mechanisms are the 'real time' transparency of the mining project towards the concerned stakeholders. Establishing a community-based or multi-stakeholder steering group is another mechanism for increased transparency, and can serve for monitoring the implementation of the SMP.

The development of management plans provides an opportunity to enhance benefits by linking the mine's impact mitigation and infrastructure investment with local and regional planning processes and with government planning for services, infrastructure, housing and education. These can include plans for community engagement, community development, procurement and local business development, local and Indigenous employment, housing, community health services, and cultural heritage. Local content, which generally means procurement from and development of the capacity of local suppliers (IPIECA, 2016), is a significant focus here. The negotiation about how the impacts are going to be mitigated or compensated can be documented as a legal contract called an Impacts and Benefits Agreement (IBA) (O'Faircheallaigh, 2010).

IBAs emerged in Canada as a supra-regulatory mechanism for engaging with and addressing the concerns of Indigenous people on whose lands projects are located. Essentially, they are a formal legal agreement (a private contract) of mutual commitments, expectations and processes (Gibson and O'Faircheallaigh, 2010). Although generally perceived as being instruments to defend the interests of Indigenous peoples (Fidler and

Hitch, 2007), IBAs may be negotiated in advance of the EIA/SIA process, limiting the ability of the Indigenous people to protect some things they value, as the assessments are not yet done. This risk may be offset, however, by the added negotiating power the Indigenous people may have before a project is permitted (Gibson and O'Faircheallaigh, 2010, pp. 44–46). In spite of this, for those countries where IBAs are in use (notably Canada and Greenland), the formal EIA and SIA assist in developing these agreements by providing the knowledge base for discussion of potential impacts (Hansen *et al.*, 2016; Tiainen, 2016).

Some variants of community agreements are being implemented in other countries, and the applicability and effectiveness of different models depends on governance, community capacity, local political structures and others (ERM, 2010). Community Development Agreements are being implemented both as regulated and voluntary models depending on the country, and are often designed to address longer-term development objectives as distinct from specific impact mitigation measures (World Bank, 2012). The SIA baseline and ongoing monitoring of socio-economic data can provide the information needed for this broader development planning process.

Moving into the mine construction phase initiates the most challenging stage for social management, with a significant and dramatic ramping-up of activities, influx of multiple companies and non-local workers, transformation of the physical location, and significant movements of people and goods along transport routes – hence the importance of developing the plans, procedures and budgets during the previous stage. Senior management commitment will be necessary in order to ensure social management is integrated into the project management schedule, and respected by other areas as part of the overall strategic management.

The SMP should provide the objectives, indicators and timeframes against which to measure the effectiveness of the designed interventions across the construction and operations phases. Monitoring and follow-up SIAs provide the opportunity to capture and confirm whether the predictions were accurate, and bring any new impacts or risks that have emerged into the management system. These may come from inaccurate predictions made during the IA process, but can also arise from changes to the social environment, including outside shocks such as economic crises external to the sector itself or unanticipated social behavior. Depending on the degree of participation in the SMP process, it should provide for regular feedback to stakeholders and rights-holders on implementation and monitoring results, and a structured process for collaborative efforts to address emerging issues.

4 *SIA to inform mine closure*

Mines close for a variety of reasons, including the exhaustion of the resource, market conditions, environmental disasters and other external influences. The social aspects of mine closure have been well studied (Neil *et al.*, 1992; Sheldon *et al.*, 2002; Kemp *et al.*, 2007; Evans, 2011) and there is some good guidance available (e.g., DITR, 2006; World Bank, 2012; Anglo American, 2013); however, there is still need for research on predicting and managing the social issues of mine closure (Vanclay *et al.*, 2015). Too often, closure is underconsidered in the formal EIA and SIA processes. Kemp *et al.*, (2007) identified that, even in countries where mine closure plans are required or form part of permit conditions, the focus is often only on environmental and physical aspects rather than the social, cultural and economic aspects. A significant challenge for companies and SIA practitioners is how and when to start the process of assessing the impacts of closure, and how to integrate this into the larger framework of community engagement (Evans, 2011). The objective should be to build closure issues into project design and research processes from the start of the project and to update them regularly over the life of the mine (DITR, 2006; World Bank, 2010).

Kemp *et al.* (2007) identified the key social issues typically associated with mine closure. The social impacts will differ depending on whether there is a diversified, thriving economy in the affected area, or whether the local community and economy is highly dependent on the mine being closed. Mine-dependent communities and towns face big social and economic problems when mines are closed and when the main base of regional economy and employment collapses. In these cases, the main challenges concern the possibilities to refocus the local economy and to develop the social resilience of the local communities. Depending on the extent of diversity of the local economy, the closure of a mine can have a significant negative impact on local expenditure due to reduced spending by the mine and its employees. Businesses in town may close, leading to follow-on impacts for their owners and employees. In some cases, new business opportunities such as tourism or environmental rehabilitation may emerge through the closure process. Mine closure and job losses can have flow-on effects in the economy, with declines in real estate values, closure of businesses, outmigration of population, and subsequent impacts to the levels of social support, volunteerism and other civic activities.

Beyond the tangible economic and demographic changes, there can also be a range of social and psychological stresses, and increased fear due to uncertainty. Uncertainty begins, not with the announcement of closure, but rather when assumptions of future closure arise in the community.

Kemp *et al.* (2007) identified the opportunities present when communities have strong leadership, and there is sufficient advance planning for closure. Ongoing engagement through SIA monitoring and participation processes should identify not only the preferred closure options for local residents, but also when these preferred options change. This is particularly likely for mines with a long expected life, or when participation in a mine-based economy leads to significant changes in the expectations and life conditions of the local population, such as might occur in regions with subsistence farmers or Indigenous communities not previously integrated into cash economies. Through regular updating of the closure plans, SIA can identify changing priorities and support the required adaptation of management strategies to reflect them.

SIA, when carried out as part of the evaluation of closure options, will identify the dependencies that may have developed due to mine programs, such as social services or other activities that depend on mine funding or employment. Early identification of these allows the necessary parties the time to develop a transition plan to a more sustainable funding or governance arrangement.

Closures can bring about dramatic changes in many dimensions of local wellbeing and the ability of people and communities to adapt. A key issue for SIA is the identification and assessment of the key community assets that are needed for communities to be resilient to these shocks. The resulting management actions and strategies must be developed and implemented in collaboration with the people, organizations and institutions who will remain after the mine is closed. The participatory process built into (social) impact management throughout the mine life should be designed with closure in mind, to build the capacity and systems needed in local or regional institutions to manage this transition as effectively as possible.

Conclusion

Social impact assessment is the process of using professional expertise to combine a rigorous evidence base with qualitative assessment, with the aim of managing the social issues and impacts of projects in a participatory way, thus providing improved outcomes for communities and companies alike. In the mining sector, this means that SIA has an expanded role of research, engagement, action and monitoring through the full mine lifecycle from early exploration through to closure. SIAs, and EIAs for that matter, are not carried out only for compliance with regulatory requirements, or as a check-box approach to fulfilling international standards or corporate policies – they are done to achieve improved outcomes. This wider application of SIA as a management process has been an important and influential development during last decade with particularly strong uptake in the mining sector.

Mining is a sector in which external standards have created new levels of social performance, and in which leading company policies and national and international sector standards have emerged to guide good practice. Although the IFC Performance Standards are generally taken to represent international good practice, local innovation, and sometimes collaboration with other stakeholders including NGOs, lead to the evolution of good practice for SIA in mining. The IFC Performance Standards consolidated the management systems approach to good practice, allowing the distinctiveness of projects and their particular context to shape specific details of the process, with a focus on management systems and management capacity. The social management plan should map out the impacts, mitigation and enhancement measures, monitoring frameworks, adaptive management processes, and reporting processes to support the planning process in improving outcomes.

To make SIA effective, it is critical to ensure that: the information needed is available; community engagement is effective and inclusive; the local community is involved in the selection of indicators and monitoring processes; and the effectiveness of the company's community work is evaluated against objectives and indicators. SIA provides the frame for the collection and analysis of the information, including the participatory or collaborative work with stakeholders to ensure their inputs – and their voices – are heard throughout the whole process, from the very beginning to after closure. Anticipating the issues, concerns and fears that local stakeholders will have, and developing sound, locally validated responses to these concerns, should start in exploration, so that when a project enters the project permitting stage, the main issues are known and can be actively addressed through the permitting process. Changes within communities and external to them occur immediately in response to the exploration activity, as well as in anticipation of a possible mine. For this reason, SIA and social management need to be initiated early during exploration, and maintained throughout the life of the mine.

References

Anglo American (2012) *SEAT Toolbox: Socio-Economic Assessment Toolbox. Version 3*. Available at: www.angloAmerican.com/~/media/Files/A/Anglo-American-Plc/docs/seat-toolbox-v3.pdf.

Anglo American (2013) *Mine Closure Toolbox*. Available at: www.angloAmerican.com/~/media/Files/A/Anglo-American-PLC-V2/documents/approach-and-policies/environment/toolbox-main-brochure-lr.PDF.

Ballard, C. and Banks, G. (2003) "Resource wars: The anthropology of mining." *Annual Review of Anthropology* 32, 287–313.

Becker, H. (1997). *Social Impact Assessment: Method and Experience in Europe, North America and the Developing World*. London: UCL Press.

Buxton, A. and Wilson, E. (2013) *FPIC and the Extractive Industries: A Guide to Applying the Spirit of Free, Prior and Informed Consent in Industrial Projects*. London: International Institute for Environment and Development. Available at: http://pubs.iied.org/pdfs/16530IIED.pdf.

DITR (Department of Industry, Tourism and Resources) (2006) *Leading Practice Sustainable Development Program for the Mining Industry. Mining Closure and Completion*. Commonwealth of Australia. Available at: www.industry.gov.au/resource/Programs/LPSD/Pages/LPSDhandbooks.aspx#.

ERM (Environmental Resources Management) (2010). *Mining Community Development Agreements: Practical Experiences and Field Studies*. Final report for the

World Bank. Washington, D.C. Available at: http://documents.worldbank.org/curated/en/697211468141279238/pdf/712990v30WP0P10IC00CDA0Report0FINAL.pdf.

Esteves, A.M. and Vanclay, F. (2009) "Social development needs analysis as a tool for SIA to guide corporate-community investment: Applications in the minerals industry." *Environmental Impact Assessment Review 29(2)*, 137–145.

Esteves, A.M., Factor, G., Vanclay, F., Götzmann, N. and Moreiro, S. (2017) "Adapting social impact assessment to address a project's human rights impacts and risks." *Environmental Impact Assessment Review 66*, in press. http://dx.doi.org/10.1016/j.eiar.2017.07.001

Esteves, A.M., Franks, D. and Vanclay, F. (2012) "Social impact assessment: The state of the art." *Impact Assessment and Project Appraisal 30(1)*, 35–44.

Evans, R. (2011) "Closure planning." In: Vanclay, F. and Esteves, A.M. (eds), *New Directions in Social Impact Assessment: Conceptual and Methodological Advances*. Cheltenham, UK: Edward Edgar, pp. 221–232.

Fidler, C. and Hitch, M. (2007) "Impact and benefit agreements: A contentious issue for environmental and Aboriginal justice." *Environments: A Journal of Interdisciplinary Studies 35(2)*, 49–69.

Franks D. (2011) "Management of the social impacts of mining." In Darling, P. (ed.), *SME Mining Engineering Handbook* (3rd edn). Littleton, CO: Society for Mining, Metallurgy, and Exploration, pp. 1817–1825.

Franks, D. (2012) *Social Impact Assessment of Resource Projects*. International Mining for Development Centre Mining for Development: Guide to Australian Practice. Available at: http://im4dc.org/wp-content/uploads/2012/01/UWA_1698_Paper-02_Social-impact-assessment-of-resource-projects1.pdf.

Franks, D. and Vanclay, F. (2013) "Social impact management plans: Innovation in corporate and public policy." *Environmental Impact Assessment Review 43*, 40–48.

Franks, D., Brereton, D., Moran, C.J., Sarker, T. and Cohen, T. (2010) *Cumulative Impacts: A Good Practice Guide for the Australian Coal Mining Industry*. Centre for Social Responsibility in Mining and Centre for Water in the Minerals Industry, Sustainable Minerals Institute, University of Queensland. Australian Coal Association Research Program. Brisbane, Australia. Available at: www.csrm.uq.edu.au/publications/coal-mining-managing-the-cumulative-impacts-of-multiple-mines-on-regional-communities-and-environments-in-australia.

Franks, D., Fidler, C. and Clark, P. (2009) *Leading Practice Strategies for Addressing the Social Impacts of Resource Development*. Brisbane: University of Queensland and Queensland Government. Available at: www.csrm.uq.edu.au/docs/Franks_etal_LeadingPracticeSocialImpacts_2009.pdf.

Gibson, G. and O'Faircheallaigh, C. (2010) *IBA Community Toolkit: Negotiation and Implementation of Impact and Benefit Agreements*. The Walter and Gordon Duncan Foundation, Vancouver, Canada. Available at: http://gordonfoundation.ca/north/iba-community-toolkit.

Glicken, J. (1999) "Effective public involvement in public decisions." *Science Communication 20(3)*, 298–327.

Glucker, A., Driessen, P., Kolhoff, A. and Runhaar, H. (2013) "Public participation in environmental impact assessment: Why, who and how?" *Environmental Impact Assessment Review 43*, 104–111.

Götzmann, N., Vanclay, F. and Seier, F. (2016) "Social and human rights impact assessments: What can they learn from each other?" *Impact Assessment and Project Appraisal 34(1)*, 14–23.

Haley S., Szymoniak, N., Klick, N., Crow, A. and Schwoerer, T. (2011) *Social Indicators for Arctic Mining*. ISER Working Paper 2011.2. Institute of Social and Economic Research, University of Alaska Anchorage. Available at: www.iser.uaa.alaska.edu/Publications/mining-indicators.pdf.

Hanna, P. and Vanclay, F. (2013) "Human rights, Indigenous peoples and the concept of Free, Prior and Informed Consent." *Impact Assessment and Project Appraisal 31(2)*, 146–157.

Hanna, P., Langdon, J. and Vanclay, F. (2016a) "Indigenous rights, performativity and protest." *Land Use Policy 50*, 490–506.

Hanna, P., Vanclay, F., Langdon, E.J. and Arts, J. (2014) "Improving the effectiveness of impact assessment pertaining to Indigenous peoples in the Brazilian environmental licensing procedure." *Environmental Impact Assessment Review 46*, 58–67.

Hanna, P., Vanclay, F., Langdon J. and Arts, J. (2016b) "Conceptualizing social protest and the significance of protest action to large projects." *Extractive Industries and Society 3(1)*, 217–239.

Hansen, A.M., Vanclay, F., Croal, P. and Olsen, A. (2016) "Managing the social impacts of the rapidly expanding extractive industries in Greenland." *Extractive Industries and Society 3(1)*, 25–33.

Hartley, N. and Wood, C. (2005) "Public participation in environmental impact assessment: Implementing the Aarhus Convention." *Environmental Impact Assessment Review 25(4)*, 319–340.

Hidalgo, C., Peterson, K., Smith, D. and Foley, H. (2014) *Extracting with Purpose*. FSG. Available at: http://sharedvalue.org/extracting-purpose.

ICMM (International Council on Mining and Metals) (2012) *Integrating Human Rights Due Diligence into Corporate Risk Management Processes*. London. Available at: www.icmm.com/website/publications/pdfs/3308.pdf.

ICMM (International Council on Mining and Metals) (2015a) *Good Practice Guide: Indigenous Peoples and Mining* (2nd edn). London. Available at: www.icmm.com/website/publications/pdfs/9520.pdf.

ICMM (International Council on Mining and Metals) (2015b) *Understanding Company-Community Relations Toolkit*. London. Available at: www.icmm.com/website/publications/pdfs/9670.pdf.

IFC (International Finance Corporation) (2007) *Stakeholder Engagement: A Good Practice Handbook for Companies Doing Business in Emerging Markets*. Washington, D.C. Available at: www.ifc.org/wps/wcm/connect/topics_ext_content/ifc_external_corporate_site/sustainability-at-ifc/publications/publications_handbook_stakeholderengagement__wci__1319577185063.

IFC (International Finance Corporation) (2012). *Performance Standards and Guidance Notes*. Washington, D.C. Available at: www.ifc.org/performancestandards.

IFC (International Finance Corporation) (2014). *A Strategic Approach to Early Stakeholder Engagement: A Good Practice Handbook for Junior Companies in the Extractive Industries*. Washington, D.C. Available at: www.ifc.org/wps/wcm/connect/topics_ext_content/ifc_external_corporate_site/sustainability-at-ifc/publications/publications_handbook_stakeholderengagement__wci__1319577185063;

also at: https://commdev.org/userfiles/FINAL_IFC_131208_ESSE%20Handbook_web%201013.pdf.

IPIECA (2016). *Local Content: A Guidance Document for the Oil and Gas Industry* (2nd edn). London. Available at: www.ipieca.org/media/1384/local_content_2016.pdf.

João, E., Vanclay, F. and den Broeder, L. (2011) "Emphasising enhancement in all forms of impact assessment." *Impact Assessment and Project Appraisal 29(3)*, 170–180.

Kemp, D. and Vanclay, F. (2013) "Human rights and impact assessment: Clarifying the connections in practice." *Impact Assessment and Project Appraisal 31(2)*, 86–96.

Kemp, D., Clark, P. and Zhang, T. (2007) *Estimating Socio-Economic Impacts of Mine Closure*. Research Paper 8. Centre for Social Responsibility in Mining, University of Queensland. Available at: www.csrm.uq.edu.au/docs/SEIA%20for%20Mine%20Closure_Final%20Draft.pdf.

Neil, C.C., Tykkyläinen, M. and Bradbury, J. (eds) (1992) *Coping with Closure: An International Comparison of Mine Town Experiences*. London: Routledge.

OECD (Organisation for Economic Co-operation and Development) (2017) *OECD Due Diligence Guidance for Meaningful Stakeholder Engagement in the Extractive Sector*. Paris. Available at: www.oecd.org/daf/inv/mne/OECD-Guidance-Extractives-Sector-Stakeholder-Engagement.pdf.

O'Faircheallaigh, C. (2010) "Public participation and environmental impact assessment: Purposes, implications, and lessons for public policy making." *Environmental Impact Assessment Review 30(1)*, 19–27.

O'Faircheallaigh, C. (2011) "Social impact assessment and Indigenous social development." In: Vanclay, F. and Esteves, A.M. (eds), *New Directions in Social Impact Assessment: Conceptual and Methodological Advances*. Cheltenham, UK: Edward Edgar, pp. 138–153.

Petrova, S. and Marinova, D. (2013) "Social impacts of mining: Changes within the local social landscape." *Rural Society 22(2)*, 153–165.

Petrova, S. and Marinova, D. (2015) "Using 'soft' and 'hard' social impact indicators to understand societal change caused by mining: A Western Australia case study." *Impact Assessment and Project Appraisal 33(1)*, 16–27.

Porter, M. and Kramer, M. (2011) "Creating shared value." *Harvard Business Review 89(1–2)*, 62–77.

Sairinen, R. (2011) "Environmental conflict mediation." In: Vanclay, F. and Esteves, A.M. (eds), *New Directions in Social Impact Assessment: Conceptual and Methodological Advances*. Cheltenham, UK: Edward Edgar, pp. 273–287.

Sairinen, R., Rinne, P., Halonen, M., Simonett, O. and Stuhlberger, C. (2012) *Responsible mining: A toolkit for the prevention and mediation of conflicts in the development of the mining sector*. University of Eastern Finland, Gaia Group Oy and Zoï Environment Network. Joensuu. Pp. 1–57. Available at: http://epublications.uef.fi/pub/urn_isbn_978-952-61-0926-8/urn_isbn_978-952-61-0926-8.pdf.

Salazar, J., Husted, B. and Biehl, M. (2012) "Thoughts on the evaluation of Corporate Social Performance through projects." *Journal of Business Ethics 105*, 175–186.

Sheldon, C., Strongman, J. and Weber-Fahr, M. (2002) *It's Not Over When It's Over: Mine Closure around the World*. Washington, D.C.: World Bank and

International Finance Corporation. Available at: http://siteresources.worldbank.org/INTOGMC/Resources/notoverwhenover.pdf.

Smyth, E. and Vanclay, F. (2017) "The Social Framework for Projects: A conceptual but practical model to assist in assessing, planning and managing the social impacts of big projects." *Impact Assessment and Project Appraisal 35(1)*, 65–80.

Solomon, F., Katz, E. and Lovel, R. (2008) "Social dimensions of mining: Research, policy and practice challenges for the minerals industry in Australia." *Resources Policy 33(3)*, 142–149.

Spohr, M. (2016) *Human Rights Risks in Mining: A Baseline Study*. Bonn: German Federal Institute for Geosciences and Natural Resources and Max Planck Foundation for International Peace and the Rule of Law. Available at: www.bmz.de/rue/includes/downloads/BGR_MPFPR__2016__Human_Rights_Risks_in_Mining.pdf.

Suopajärvi, L. (2013) "Social impact assessment in mining projects in Northern Finland: Comparing practice to theory." *Environmental Impact Assessment Review 42*, 25–30.

Tiainen, H. (2016) "Contemplating governance for social sustainability in mining in Greenland." *Resources Policy 49*, 282–289.

Tiainen, H. and Sairinen, R. (2014) "Mining in the Chatkal Valley in Kyrgyzstan: Challenge of social sustainability." *Resources Policy 39*, 80–87.

Tiainen, H., Sairinen, R. and Sidorenko, O. (2015) "Governance of sustainable mining in Arctic countries: Finland, Sweden, Greenland and Russia." *Arctic Yearbook 2015*, 132–157.

van der Ploeg, L. and Vanclay, F. (2017a) "A tool for improving the management of social and human rights risks at project sites: The human rights sphere." *Journal of Cleaner Production 142(Part 4)*, 4072–4084.

van der Ploeg, L. and Vanclay, F. (2017b) "A human rights based approach to project-induced displacement and resettlement." *Impact Assessment and Project Appraisal 35(1)*, 34–52.

Vanclay, F. (2002) "Conceptualising social impacts." *Environmental Impact Assessment Review 22(3)*, 183–211.

Vanclay, F. (2003) "International principles for Social Impact Assessment." *Impact Assessment and Project Appraisal 21(1)*, 5–11.

Vanclay, F. (2012) "The potential application of Social Impact Assessment in integrated coastal zone management." *Ocean and Coastal Management 68*, 149–156.

Vanclay, F. (2014) "Developments in Social Impact Assessment: An introduction to a collection of seminal research papers." In: Vanclay, F. (ed.), *Developments in Social Impact Assessment*, Cheltenham, UK: Edward Elgar, pp. xv–xxxix.

Vanclay, F. (2017) "Project induced displacement and resettlement: From impoverishment risks to an opportunity for development?" *Impact Assessment and Project Appraisal 35(1)*, 3–21.

Vanclay, F., Esteves, A.M., Aucamp, I. and Franks, D. (2015) *Social Impact Assessment: Guidance for assessing and managing the social impacts of projects*. Fargo, ND: International Association for Impact Assessment. Available at: www.iaia.org/uploads/pdf/SIA_Guidance_Document_IAIA.pdf.

Veiga, M., Scoble, M. and McAllister, M. (2001) "Mining with communities." *Natural Resources Forum 25*, 191–202.

World Bank (2010) *Towards Sustainable Decommissioning and Closure of Oil Fields and Mines: A Toolkit to assist Government Agencies* (version 3.0).

Washington, D.C. Available at: http://siteresources.worldbank.org/EXTOGMC/Resources/336929-1258667423902/decommission_toolkit3_full.pdf.

World Bank (2012) *Mining Community Development Agreements Sourcebook*. Washington, D.C. Available at: http://siteresources.worldbank.org/INTOGMC/Resources/mining_community.pdf.

6 Due diligence in the mining sector

An expanding concept

Kendyl Salcito and Mark Wielga

Due diligence: a brief history

"Due diligence" is a term of art with roots in law. Under U.S. law, it assigns liability to a broker managing the sale of a company or stock for failing to disclose problems that could affect the value of stock being sold. Simultaneously, it absolves the broker of responsibility if she can prove she conducted a reasonably careful investigation of the company with the intent to identify such issues (Section 11, Securities Act of 1933, 15 U.S. Code §77k).

It is also a general business term for any prudent investigation of the other side of a transaction. In this sense, "due diligence" includes any risk, not just legal liability. The essential aim of due diligence is to determine if there are any hidden, invisible, but potentially disastrous surprises in what is being purchased, which could decrease a transaction's value. A classic example is legal permitting. If one company wants to purchase a factory that requires a permit for discharging wastewater, due diligence requires that the buyer verify the existence of the permit. But that is not enough. Is the permit valid? When does it have to be renewed? What is the likelihood that the permit will not be renewed? What does the seller say about it? Is the seller's word trustworthy and reliable? Is a legal opinion needed? Does the permit-issuing regulatory agency need to be contacted to provide additional assurances?

This is the nitty-gritty of due diligence. The process takes on a special importance when the business enterprise at issue is in a country which is poor, conflict-prone or weakly governed. In these cases, social due diligence is also a factor: will the community allow the factory wastewater to be discharged, even if there is a legal permit? Political risks need also to be considered. Due diligence, necessarily, becomes much broader and dramatically more complex.

Due diligence for human rights risks

It is natural that this same general concept would be used in the shifting governance paradigms of corporate social responsibilities. When drafting what become the United Nations Guiding Principles on Business and Human Rights (OHCHR and Ruggie, 2011), Prof. John Ruggie tapped into this term so familiar in the business world. In defining the meaning of a corporation's Responsibility to Respect Human Rights, he included this requirement:

> Guiding Principle 15: In order to meet their responsibility to respect human rights, business enterprises should have in place policies and processes appropriate to their size and circumstances, including: [...]
>
> (b) A human rights due diligence process to identify, prevent, mitigate and account for how they address their impacts on human rights.
>
> [...]
>
> Guiding Principle 17: In order to identify, prevent, mitigate and account for how they address their adverse human rights impacts, business enterprises should carry out human rights due diligence. The process should include assessing actual and potential human rights impacts, integrating and acting upon the findings, tracking responses, and communicating how impacts are addressed.

And so "human rights due diligence" was born. As in conventional due diligence, human rights due diligence is concerned with discovering risks. Due diligence may have arisen to consider only financial risk, but it has evolved to consider political, social and other factors that affect a corporate operation. As a human rights tool, its role is not legal but driven by social norms. As Ruggie has since clarified, "It serves to meet a company's social license to operate" (Ruggie and Sherman, 2017).

The moral and financial impetus for human rights due diligence

Social license is a well-established concept that informally parallels legal license to operate (Morrison, 2014) while extending beyond legal requirements (Ruggie, 2017). It requires a project to be viewed as legitimate by the local community in order to move forward, even if necessary legal permissions have already been granted. In the most extreme scenario, when social license is lacking, community members might use civil disobedience to stop the project from being built or to shut it down. Davis and Frank have estimated that the loss of social license can cost a mining project with CAPEX between US$3–5 billion roughly US$20 million per week in delayed production and other direct costs (Davis and Franks, 2014). One company also analyzed its indirect costs and identified a $6 billion value erosion over a two-year period owing to lost social license (Davis and Franks, 2014). In less extreme forms, it can mean the operation is always the subject of costly and constant local hostility and threat. Evaluating social license is an important element of due diligence.

Human rights due diligence, however, is not solely driven by the bottom line. Beyond the financial impetus for human rights due diligence, it has an ethical dimension. The Guiding Principles clearly state that human rights due diligence is focused on risks to human rights or, more specifically, to rightsholders. Furthermore, it extends beyond inquiry. Human rights due diligence is a process that is to include *prevention, mitigation, acting upon the finding and tracking responses*, all of which require actions on the ground, over and above investigation. There is also a duty of communication, as companies must "*account for how they address*" their human rights impacts, and *track responses* to their mitigation measures.

These are not concepts inherent in "due diligence" as that term is used in business, and they are not a part of what business people consider the due diligence process to be. However, they are familiar to mining companies. The extractives are perhaps the only industries well acquainted with the link between duly diligent project preparation and the risks posed to human welfare by an operation's relationships, context and other externalities. This is because extractive companies have incorporated external impacts into their due diligence processes for nearly 40 years, in the form of environmental impact assessment.

Mechanisms for human rights due diligence: impact assessment

The 1970 U.S. Environmental Policy Act required that proponents of any large infrastructure project produce an "Environmental Impact Statement," a detailed, data-driven impact assessment of the operation on each sector of the environment (water, air, fauna, etc.), prepared by scientists with expertise (U.S. Congress, 1969). Environmental Impact Statements are made public, and drafts are open to comments from citizens and experts which are addressed before the project would be given agency approval. The environmental impact evaluation component of the Environmental Policy Act is the most widely copied piece of legislation in the world (Rodgers, 1993) and, slightly renamed, "Environmental Impact Assessments" are now required by most governments, as well as major international lending institutions, such as the World Bank. Many extractive companies commission them for all projects as a matter of corporate policy, regardless of whether they are required by a host government in the country where the project is planned.

The success of environmental impact assessment (EIA) requirements spawned assessments in other substantive areas. Social impact assessment (SIA) now analyzes the social and economic effects of a project. Health impact assessment (HIA) focuses on human health effects. Seeing the overlap, many companies prepare integrated assessments, such as Environmental,

Social and Health Impact Assessments (ESHIAs) and Environmental Safety and Security Impact Assessments (ESSHIAs).

Though analyzing diverse substantive areas, integrated impact assessments have a common method and pattern in the mining sector, identifying impacts and then proposing strategies ("mitigation measures") to reduce negative impacts. Identifying impacts is itself a two-part process, first marking a baseline, and then extrapolating how corporate activities are likely to change that baseline. For an EIA, this means that parameters affecting air, groundwater and surface water quality must be measured before the project is in place. Then predictions are made estimating expected changes in each environmental parameter resulting from the planned project's implementation. This kind of analysis allows intelligent understanding of the effects of the project. If the effects are negative, changes to the project's design or operation may be considered to reduce the negative effects. This is "prevention" if the negative effect is largely eliminated or "mitigation" if is it reduced.

Human rights due diligence is the link joining corporate financial responsibility to shareholders and environmental social and political responsibility to rightsholders. There are notable ties between Ruggie's definition of due diligence and the processes of impact assessment. After hosting a 2006 consultation dedicated exclusively to human rights impact assessment (HRIA), he issued an 11-page update report in 2007 dedicated entirely to the topic (Ruggie, 2007). In it, he explicitly stated that HRIAs should "prioritize the human rights risks that the proposed business activity presents and *make practical recommendations to address those risks*" (italics added). Those recommendations, he advised, "should be incorporated into a management plan that includes provisions for monitoring the baseline indicators and revisiting the issues raised during the HRIA process." Consultation with "affected parties" should be regular. To reinforce the importance of acting on findings, an entire paragraph was dedicated to the necessity of tracking outcomes:

> As valuable as the HRIA process can be, it is not an end in itself. Just as with any risk and impact assessment tool, it is how those involved use the findings and engage with the process that matters – little credit is given simply for going through the exercise.

"Human rights impact assessment," as a term of art, is absent from Ruggie's final guidance documents, but the language used to describe HRIA in 2007 unmistakably parallels his notably expanded definition of "due diligence" in the Guiding Principles in 2011. One reason for the diction change may have been that no HRIA methodology was widely available in 2011. Another was that expectations for corporate social behaviors in general were changing, offering the promise that a variety of impact assessment and social engagement processes would adopt a human rights lens, contributing broadly to human rights due diligence.

Pitfalls in human rights due diligence: far more is required than is generally believed

The Guiding Principles were strategic in incorporating business-friendly terminology to describe corporate human rights responsibilities, but the terminology has also created confusion. Financial due diligence is secret – the first step in financial due diligence is the signing of a confidentiality agreement. Secrecy is necessary to allow the investigating party to see the target's finances, liabilities and personnel problems. Human rights due diligence, on the other hand, is, of necessity, transparent, in order to demonstrate that the "right to participate in public life" (Article 21 of the Universal Declaration of Human Rights (UDHR) and Article 25 of the International Covenant on Civil and Political Rights (ICCPR)) is respected by a corporation (De Schutter *et al.*, 2012). This right guarantees to all citizens the opportunity, without unreasonable restrictions, to take part in the conduct of public affairs directly or through freely chosen representatives and to have equal access to public services. Companies (and their legal teams) have not internalized the fundamental distinction between corporate secrecy and rightsholder entitlements to information.

Furthermore, legal and financial due diligence are desk-based activities, while human rights due diligence is incomplete without the input of affected people. Human rights due diligence should identify "specific impacts on specific people, given a specific context" (UNGP 18, commentary). Companies, which are not staffed, let alone managed, by human rights experts, are generally ill-equipped to identify human rights evaluation processes that are "duly" diligent. Finally, the people who carry out financial due diligence are unqualified to conduct human rights due diligence. The financial analysts and lawyers who oversee traditional due diligence are accustomed to drawing reasoned conclusions from established sets of questions, based on conclusive documentation. Human rights issues are not framed by pre-established research questions, they are often not documented, and they are rarely fully understood quantitatively. Human rights due diligence is fundamentally, substantively and procedurally different from financial due diligence.

A large amount of data is needed for thorough human rights due diligence. These can include such statistics as infant mortality, literacy rates, demographic data, local incomes, incarceration rates, drinking water quality and many others. However, the one common point in all this data is people. People's lives and sentiments are the ultimate object of the study.

Next steps in methodological rigor: blending perceptions and realities in employing the human rights lens

In practice, human rights due diligence considers a suite of human rights clearly spelled out in the Guiding Principles to cover the economic, social, cultural, civil and political dimensions of human life. Political rights (the right to participate in governance decisions, the right to a fair and public trial, the freedom of the press), labor rights (the right to a safe work environment, the right to strike), social rights (freedom of religion, freedom from discrimination), welfare rights (the right to health, the right to education) and basic needs (the right to water, the right to a clean environment) are among these. Clearly, human rights make for a dauntingly wide-ranging scope of analysis.

As people ("rightsholders") are the subject of human rights due diligence, both their objective condition (job income, calories consumed, number of incidents of malaria) *and* perceived condition (fears, anger, hopes) are relevant points of inquiry.

Perceptional studies have a well-established precedent in governance risk evaluation, forming the basis for the World Bank's Governance Indicators (Kaufmaan *et al.*, 2010). In human rights due diligence, perception studies are combined with quantitative data to triangulate findings in an iterative, in-depth process. For example, say a company built a hydroelectric dam to supply power to its mine, creating a stagnant reservoir where malarial mosquitoes could breed. The mine might distribute bed nets to communities, but quantitative data – malaria incidence rates at local clinics prior to and after the construction of the dam – would validate or invalidate the intervention. If rates have risen regardless of the intervention, the impact is not mitigated; then community perceptions must be examined (i.e., qualitative data). When perception studies were carried out in such a situation in Kenya, researchers found that residents believed malaria was only partially caused by mosquitoes, but also by rain, cold weather, certain foods and dirty water. Their belief that bed nets offered insufficient protection caused half of families to forego the inconvenience of nets. Further inquiry revealed that children under five, who are most susceptible to malaria, were not sleeping on the only family bed, which meant they were unprotected by the only family bed net (Alaii *et al.*, 2003). A company operating in such a context would not be duly diligent to supply bed nets to communities; it would only mitigate its impacts by addressing the perceptions to increase bed net usage, or by re-engineering the dam to eliminate stagnant water bodies where mosquitoes breed.

Just as community beliefs can determine the effectiveness of clinically proven interventions, community beliefs also determine the effectiveness of a company's efforts to gain social license. How do community members feel about this company? How do they feel about the company's home country? How will the operation affect their lives? Is there a fear of explosions or poisoned drinking water? Are they afraid of violence from armed guards or police who come to the community to protect the project? How do they see the economic opportunities provided by the project? Answering these questions requires inquiry into human emotions and opinions, regardless of whether those emotions are based on sound science. The question is not whether the people are right, but whether their beliefs are sincere and could drive them to action.

This is an essential role of the human rights lens: it takes a series of concrete, fact-based indicators, and it compares them to the historically, culturally, socially and politically driven perceptions of people, deriving insight from the disconnections. It values the perceived indignities experienced by rightsholders at the same level as the corporate policies meant to prevent indignity, looking to eliminate the gap.

Because these are questions about people's inner feelings, research into them requires direct contact with the people themselves. No-one can speak for them, and they must be able to speak from a position of comfort and openness. Any restriction on their honest and open expression risks leaving resentment buried, posing risks over the long term. Understanding and interpreting perceptions can be difficult. To accomplish it requires direct, unmediated contact between the assessor and the subject, which more closely resembles conversation than any questionnaire format can provide.

The value to understanding these perceptions is, for companies, sometimes quantifiable from a corporate (financial) risk standpoint. Rejection of bed nets increases sickness rates, which increases worker absenteeism. Community beliefs that a mine is troubling mountain spirits can trigger protests that shut down production. The cost of ignoring beliefs can be insurmountably high, destroying community trust irretrievably and eliminating the potential to expand an operation. One of the most high-profile such cases is the $5 billion Conga mine, planned by Newmont Mining in Peru. Two decades of damage to social license at the neighboring Yanacocha mine, coupled with a mounting climate of distrust of mining in the region led Newmont to remove Conga from its reserves in its 2015 SEC filings (Newmont, 2016). Two years prior, Barrick delayed its $8 billion Chilean project, Pasqua Lama, in the face of public protest over perceived environmental risks, although Barrick had secured all relevant environmental permits.

Corporate opposition to the human rights lens

Despite the demonstrable importance of understanding how communities internalize the impacts of companies, and how their perceptions guide their actions, mining companies have resisted human rights due diligence in practice, even as they have embraced it in policy (Salcito *et al.*, 2015). Mine engineers are scientific; they recognize facts as important and mere opinions as irrelevant. Knowing an environmental management system is effective, they are inclined to dismiss communities' environmental fears as biased, ignorant or activist-driven. The human rights lens serves to highlight the fear, contrast it with the reality, and generate an appropriate response. If the fear is river pollution, but the reality is that the river is completely unaffected, the human rights lens focuses on the disjoint between perception and reality. The result may be to recommend an engagement strategy that tackles public fears and draws corporate personnel out to communities to explain environmental management strategies, demystify perceived (or actual) changes in water parameters and build confidence in the monitoring processes.

Companies are not necessarily ready to see the benefit of this time commitment. As such, effective human rights due diligence is controversial. It does not resemble the standard impact assessments produced for companies, and it is not carried out using the standard methodologies employed by environmental and social consultants. Often consultants are trained in survey methods, statistical analysis and sampling procedures, while socially inclusive investigation has been under the purview of anthropologists, cultural epidemiologists and activists. Where there is a willingness to change engagement processes, there is rarely an available trainer to guide new approaches: consulting firms carry out much of their training in-house, and there is a shortage of available human rights trainers. Additionally, there is a business motivation for a contracted consultant to understand the client's needs and be sympathetic to their point of view. Synchronizing assessment findings with the client corporation's understanding is a hallmark of a successful consultant, one who pleases the client sufficiently to be called back for future projects. However gratifying this approach is to the company (and consultant) in the short run, it fails the companies that have commissioned such reports for one clear reason: it leads to false conclusions. False conclusions, in turn, lead to false confidence and actions which can harm the company, and human rights, in the long run.

Human rights due diligence that identifies no risks is unlikely to be duly diligent. Mining projects do not exist in vacuums, and where mines are developed in the vicinity of communities, misunderstandings are common. This is true both in regions with extended history of mining, where historical issues color current perceptions, and in regions with limited or no mining history, where a lack of experience or sophisticated understanding of complex chemical processes generates fear. In both cases, community members will perpetually seek out better, clearer information about environmental and social consequences. That means that a duly diligent human rights investigation will normally produce findings that challenge conventional knowledge on site and push operators to do more to engage with rightsholders. Because human rights conditions are fluid and constantly changing, there will always be more engagement to be done and more potential impacts to evaluate.

Next steps in methodological rigor: filtering out noise

At the same time, a duly diligent evaluation of human rights impacts considers not only which rightsholders are affected, but which ones might be gaming the assessment process. Communities are not monoliths; they are multidimensional and often fragmented by gender, culture, economics, religion, age and other factors. Community members have divergent interests and agendas. Assessors seeking to look past the statistics to understand the stories risk undermining their human rights reporting if they are gamed by community members or activists with an agenda. Each interview subject has a narrative, which must be borne out in fact, triangulated through other sources and types of data, in order to be validated. It is common for minority groups to feel excluded from the benefits of development. Jobseekers at various operations have told the authors that they were denied employment because of their ethnicity. In one case, clear ethno-racial bias in hiring was borne out in employment and wage data. In another, however, the perception was misguided; the reason that the jobseekers were not called back was that the human resources department underwent a personnel change. The new staff expected the jobseekers to call back and enquire about their employment, while jobseekers were patiently waiting for the company to call them. Unconfirmed, claims of ethnic, racial or social bias in hiring are empty allegations. When does a story become a fact, or when does a collection of stories become a trend? There is never the time or resources to check out every story, but there are means to compile and triangulate evidence of *perceived* discrimination, and there are ways to cross-check employment logs to confirm (or invalidate) those perceptions. The process is time consuming but important. If discrimination is real, it needs to be eliminated. If discrimination is purely perceived, the company needs a new communication strategy for its hiring policy.

Carrying out interviews in languages, locations and contexts where power dynamics between assessors and respondents are minimized has been shown to naturally decrease the likelihood that respondents will deliberately misrepresent the truth (Blattman, 2015). Assessors can check their findings for respondents gaming the interviews by noting when individual stories resonate with each other. Consistently repeated story lines increase the credibility of those stories. However, consistently repeated *lines*, issued verbatim from various individuals, increase the likelihood that an agenda is being pursued. Where diction is too similar between respondents to be purely coincidental, assessors must consider whose interests are being promoted. This process is facilitated by qualitative data analysis software (e.g., MAXQDA), which enables researchers to code their interview inputs and note themes.

Sticking to the facts

"Due" diligence requires fact-checking. The challenge of legitimizing findings is inherent in social research and more pronounced when the findings are based on semi-structured, qualitative interviews. Established social science validation methods, conducted by competent, experienced assessors fulfil this role (Salcito *et al.*, 2013). The effort is needed, partly to protect the assessor from being gamed by communities, but also to protect the assessor from being gamed by the corporation's own agents.

Not all human rights analysis is rooted in community misperceptions; company misperceptions are equally important. The human rights lens provides clarity about the impacts of engineering, mine ops and other dimensions of project design and implementation, by retaining a focus on impacted rightsholders. In recent years, the importance of this lens has been made clear repeatedly. Sexual assaults by Barrick security guards in Papua New Guinea was alleged for years before Barrick acknowledged the truth of local complaints. Said then-VP and Deputy General Counsel Jonathan Drimmer, "it was an identity-changing moment. We thought we were a responsible company, but our guards were gang-raping women" (Henderson and Hsieh, 2016). In a more positive incident, the human rights lens was employed at a World Bank funded power plant in Mon State, which helped re-scope the project to be inclusive of downstream agricultural impacts of earthworks on a brownfield site (NomoGaia, 2014). A five-year human rights due diligence process at Paladin Energy's Kayelekera Uranium Mine in Malawi exposed weaknesses in the project's infectious disease management program that resulted in the development of one of the country's premier HIV/AIDS education, testing, counseling and treatment programs (Salcito *et al.*, 2014b).

Conclusion

Despite methodological inconsistencies and corporate resistance, there is cause for optimism. There is a growing body of experts working at the intersection of human rights and business. They are tackling methodological shortcomings while identifying a range of practices that clearly identify iterative questioning, social inclusion and ongoing engagement as central to effective identification and management of human rights risks (Salcito *et al.*, 2013, 2014a). Bold companies are publishing their own human rights due diligence to positive effect. In the mining sector, Nevsun Resources, a Canadian gold mining company, recently published an annual update on its full human rights impact assessment of its Eritrean operations, accompanied by a management plan that includes ongoing engagement with communities (with the assistance of human rights experts). Time will tell whether their human rights due diligence continues to frame their, and the mining industry's, approach to impacted communities.

References

Alaii, J. A., van den Borne, H. W., Kachur, S. P., Shelley, K., Mwenesi, H., Vulule, J. M., Hawley, W. A., Nahlen, B. L. and Phillips-Howard, P. A. 2003. Community reactions to the introduction of permethrin-treated bed nets for malaria control during a randomized controlled trial in western Kenya. *American Journal of Tropical Medicine and Hygiene*, 68, 128–136.

Blattman, C. 2015. Measuring the measurement error: A method to qualitatively validate survey data. *Journal of Development Economics*, forthcoming.

Davis, R. and Franks, D. M. 2014. *Costs of Company–Community Conflict in the Extractive Sector*. Cambridge: CSR Initiative, Harvard Kennedy School.

de Schutter, O., Ramasastry, A., Taylor, M. B. and Thompson, R. C. 2012. *Human Rights Due Diligence: The Role of States*. European Coalition for Corporate Justice, Brussels. Available at: http://corporatejustice.org/hrdd-role-of-states-3-dec-2012.pdf.

Henderson, R. M. and Hsieh, N. 2016. Putting the Guiding Principles into action: Human rights at Barrick Gold (A). *Harvard Business Review*, Case Study 9–315–108.

Kaufmann, D., Kraay, A. and Mastruzzi, M. 2010 *The Worldwide Governance Indicators: Methodology and Analytical Issues*. Washington, D.C.: World Bank. Available at: http://info.worldbank.org/governance/wgi/pdf/wgi.pdf.

Morrison, J. 2014. *The Social License: How to Keep Your Organization Legitimate*. New York: Palgrave Macmillan.

Newmont. 2016. *Form 10-K. Newmont Investor Relations Filings*. Available at: www.newmont.com/investor-relations/financial-reports/sec-filings/sec-filings-details/default.aspx?FilingId=11192434.

Nomogaia. 2014. *Human Rights Risk Assessment: World Bank-Funded Thaton Power Station*. Denver, CO: NomoGaia. Available at: http://nomogaia.org/wp-content/uploads/2014/08/Human-Rights-Risk-Assessment-DRAFT-Thaton-WB.pdf.

OHCHR (Office of the United Nations High Commissioner for Human Rights) and Ruggie, J. G. 2011. *Guiding Principles on Business and Human Rights: Implementing the United Nations "Protect, Respect and Remedy" Framework*. New York: United Nations.

Rodgers, W. H. J. 1993. The seven statutory wonders of U.S. environmental law: Origins and morphology. *Loyola Law Review*, 1009–1022.

Ruggie, J. G. 2007. Report on the Special Representative of the Secretary-General on the issue of human rights and transnational corporations and other business enterprises: Human rights impact assessments – resolving key methodological questions. *Implementation of General Assembly Resolution 60/251 of 15 March 2006 Entitled "Human Rights Council."* Geneva: United Nations General Assembly.

Ruggie, J. G. and Sherman, J. F. 2017. The concept of "due diligence" in the UN Guiding Principles on Business and Human Rights: Reply to Professors Bonnitcha and McCorquodale. *European Journal of International Law*, 28, 14.

Salcito, K., Singer, B. H., Krieger, G. R., Weiss, M. G., Wielga, M. and Utzinger, J. 2014a. Assessing corporate project impacts in changeable contexts: A human rights perspective. *Environmental Impact Assessment Review*, 47, 36–46.

Salcito, K., Singer, B. H., Weiss, M. G., Winkler, M. S., Krieger, G. R., Wielga, M. and Utzinger, J. 2014b. Multinational corporations and infectious disease: Embracing human rights management techniques. *Infectious Diseases of Poverty*, 3, 39.

Salcito, K., Utzinger, J., Weiss, M. G., Münch, A. K., Singer, B. H., Krieger, G. R. and Wielga, M. 2013. Assessing human rights impacts in corporate development projects. *Environmental Impact Assessment Review*, 42, 39–50.

Salcito, K., Wielga, C. and Singer, B. H. 2015. Corporate human rights commitments and the psychology of business acceptance of human rights duties: A multi-industry analysis. *The International Journal of Human Rights*, 19, 673–696.
US Congress. 1969. *National Environmental Protection Act (NEPA)*, §§4321–4347.

7 Financing human rights due diligence in mining projects

Motoko Aizawa, Daniela C. dos Santos and Sara L. Seck

Introduction to human rights due diligence

In 2011, the UN Human Rights Council unanimously endorsed the UN Guiding Principles on Business and Human Rights (UNGPs) (UN, 2011) proposed by the Special Representative of the Secretary-General on human rights and transnational corporations and other business enterprises, Professor John Ruggie. As a direct consequence of the UNGPs, human rights due diligence (HRDD) became a process expected of business enterprises in any sector, anywhere in the world. Professor Ruggie found that the extractives sector was prone to negative human rights impacts (UN, 2015). This meant mine development projects, particularly the large-scale ones, were prime candidates to implement HRDD, through which they would "know" the human rights impacts of their operations and "show" how such impacts are prevented or managed.

HRDD can create two-way benefits for rights holders and mining corporations. Even at an early phase, geological survey and exploration activities can create risk perceptions and negative impacts on a few households or entire villages. Early engagement with potentially affected local communities to disseminate project information and to seek their input can help allay concerns. Identification of stakeholders' perceptions of human rights risks can inform the design of the project and help the project avoid future controversies, delays, shutdowns, and other direct and indirect cost implications (Davis and Franks, 2014). When communities of Indigenous Peoples are involved, early engagement is a prerequisite to obtaining their consent for the proposed project activity. It is in the interest of the mining company to ascertain sooner rather than later that consent may not be forthcoming, in which case it can either terminate the venture altogether or change its scope to ensure consent. HRDD also avoids companies becoming complicit in human rights violations through its activities and relationships in the home or host state or business relationships with certain persons and entities with a record of past or present human rights violations.

In fact, the International Council on Mining and Metals (ICMM) correctly anticipated that human rights impacts from mining operations will have to be tackled by its member companies, and started to provide implementation guidance as early as 2003 (ICMM, 2009). Shortly after the UNGPs came into existence, ICMM published a guide on how to integrate HRDD into corporate risk management processes (ICMM, 2012), and also resolved to obtain the free, prior and informed consent of affected Indigenous Peoples (ICMM, 2013). By the time the UNGPs came into existence, senior mining companies generally had been sufficiently sensitized about the reputational risks and the "above the ground" risks associated with mining projects, including those with social and human rights dimensions.

The business and human rights landscape changed quickly after the UNGPs and it is now populated with many substantive initiatives and meaningful tools that are of direct relevance to the mining sector. Various soft law instruments on business and human rights, and more specifically on HRDD preceded, coincided or followed the UNGPs. Some are instruments of general application, such as the International Standards Organization's ISO 26000 on Social Responsibility (2010) (ISO, 2010); the OECD Guidelines for Multinational Enterprises (2011) (OECD, 2011); the IFC Performance Standards on Environmental and Social Sustainability (2012 version) (IFC, 2012);[1] and the Global Reporting Initiative's G4 Sustainability Reporting Guidelines (2013) (GRI 2013), all of which are aligned with the UNGPs (UN, 2011). Initiatives specific to the extractive sector include the OECD Due Diligence Guidance on Responsible Supply Chains of Minerals from Conflict-Affected and High-Risk Areas (second edition, 2012) (OECD, 2012); and the OECD Due Diligence Guidance for Meaningful Stakeholder Engagement in the Extractive Industries, which specifically addresses the importance of indigenous and local community rights to consultation and consent, as well as the importance of integrating a gender perspective (OECD, 2017). These instruments tend to underscore the importance of due diligence in the context of enterprise or operational risk management and can expose underlying human rights issues in mining.

In addition, some financial institutions that provide project or corporate finance or export credits now require that their corporate clients carry out the process of HRDD. The Equator Principles Financial Institutions updated the Equator Principles in 2013 to align them with the updated IFC Performance Standards and the UNGPs. To ensure the playing field is level, the export credit agencies of the OECD countries recently updated the Common Approaches, also making reference to HRDD (OECD, 2016). If mining companies want to access financial products from the institutions participating in these initiatives, they must abide by the specific requirements.

Alongside these standard setting initiatives, new tools for corporate reporting and benchmarking, namely, the UN Guiding Principles Reporting Framework (UN n.d.(a)) and the Corporate Human Rights Benchmark (CHRB) (Business and Human Rights Resource Centre n.d.), became operational. The former provides a corporate reporting framework consistent with the UNGPs, and the latter benchmarks companies for their specific human rights performance. These two initiatives enable investors to explicitly take into account human rights factors when investing in listed equity. CHRB's initial sectoral focus includes the extractives sector.

The initiatives described above reinforce and complement the UNGPs, by underscoring the importance of making a policy commitment for respecting human rights, and spelling out the generic components of HRDD, from identifying and assessing human rights impacts, preventing and managing adverse impacts, monitoring and communicating performance, to remediating actual impacts. To help with day-to-day implementation, various practical tools are also on offer to help companies walk through a specific methodology of HRDD, often by way of a human rights impact assessment (HRIA) process.[2]

There are now several templates for corporate HRIAs that companies can initiate and carry out in-house or through their consultants, such as the Human Rights Impact Assessment and Management tool, which broadly explain the content and process of HRIAs (UN, 2010), and the Human Rights Compliance Assessment tool by the Danish Institute for Human Rights (DIHR) equipped with numerous indicators (DIHR, n.d.). DIHR more recently published the detailed Human Rights Impact Assessment Guidance and Toolbox (DIHR, n.d.), which provide step-by-step how-to guidance for specialists. These HRIAs can inform planned corporate activities or part or all of existing corporate activities, and be issue-specific or encompass all human rights. Some HRIAs are stand alone, while others are a hybrid where HRIA elements are grafted on to an environmental and social impact assessment (ESIA). At the other end of the spectrum is the community-based HRIA, which can help communities and their designated experts design a ground-up, community-driven process (Oxfam America, n.d.). These could play a valuable role of exposing affected communities' perspectives from the bottom up, and when combined with the usually top-down corporate HRDD processes, could provide powerful rights holder-specific information that corporations might otherwise overlook. Another methodology called Sector-Wide Impact Assessment reviews human rights impacts from a sectoral perspective in a given country. It assesses typical human rights impacts at a project level, as well as the cumulative level, and human rights issues in legal and policy frameworks. (Myanmar Centre for Responsible Business, n.d.)

The need to fully integrate a gender perspective into existing HRIA methodologies is an area of increasing importance for the mining industry. Goal 5 of the recently endorsed 2030 Sustainable Development Goals explicitly identifies the need to "[a]chieve gender equality and empower all women and girls" including through "women's full and effective participation and equal opportunities for leadership" (UN, n.d.(b)). The importance of women's full participation in sustainable mining was earlier recognized in paragraph 46 of the 2002 Johannesburg Plan of Implementation (UN, 2002), an outcome document of the 2002 World Summit on Sustainable Development. The rights of women are also well enshrined in the well-ratified Convention on the Elimination of All Forms of Discrimination Against Women (CEDAW). Yet, a 2014 critical review of the literature on women, mining and development by Katy Jenkins concluded that the situation of women and mining is "unrecognized and untheorized" especially with regard to poor communities of the global south (Jenkins, 2014). Increasingly, gender impact assessment guidance tools are emerging to address this gap (Australian Aid and Oxfam Australia, 2017).

Growing state efforts toward mandatory rules

Multifaceted efforts are ongoing to give a hard legal edge to aspects of the UNGPs, many of them through mandatory disclosure regimes. These include the California Transparency in Supply Chains Act of 2010, the UK Modern Slavery Act of 2015, as well as new EU requirements around non-financial reporting on environmental, social and governance risks (EU Directive 2014/95/EU and its implementing legislation). In France, the new "Devoir de Vigilance" law[3] goes further: It requires large multinationals to set out "vigilance plans" that spell out the steps they will take to identify risks and avoid serious violations of human and labor rights, and damage to the environment, which result from company, subsidiary, supplier and subcontractor activities. This obligation is grounded in an explicit duty of care with respect to human rights. Just across the border from France, Swiss NGOs continue their efforts to persuade Swiss voters to vote in favor of corporate mandatory due diligence in a national referendum (Umlas, n.d.).

In the U.S., the Dodd–Frank Wall Street Reform and Consumer Protection Act of 2010 included specific requirements for mining companies dealing with conflict minerals from the Democratic Republic of Congo (DRC). In 2012, the Securities and Exchange Commission issued the rule under Section 1502 of that Act mandating disclosure of a company's involvement with conflict minerals. Section 1504 required companies to disclose payments made to the U.S. or foreign governments in relation to extraction of minerals as well as oil and natural gas. (However, it should be noted that Section 1504 was repealed in February 2017, and Section 1502 may also suffer a similar fate.) In addition, various federal and state-level legislations and procurement rules now require due diligence or disclosure of information on specific human rights dimensions of corporate or government level activities.[4]

Canada's national CSR Strategy for the Extractive Industry Abroad (Government of Canada 2014), which was updated in 2014, explicitly provides that the government "expects Canadian companies operating abroad to respect human rights and all applicable laws, and to meet or exceed widely-recognized international standards for responsible business conduct." The CSR Strategy promotes the UNGPs as well as other important soft law instruments to the mining industry, several of which are mentioned above.[5] Moreover, it has teeth: Companies that do not embody best practice in CSR and refuse to engage with recommended dispute resolution processes under the Strategy will be denied the benefits of "economic diplomacy" and may lose Canadian export credit financing or support.[6]

HRDD is also implicitly recommended in the *Chinese Guidelines for Social Responsibility in Outbound Mining Investment*, launched in 2014 by the China Chamber of Commerce of Metals, Minerals and Chemicals Importers and Exporters. The Chinese Guidelines include a section on human rights which recommends that companies actively observe the UNGPs throughout the project life-cycle and highlights the importance of seeking free, prior and informed consent of indigenous peoples and other local communities even when operating in states that do not recognize these rights (China Chamber of Commerce, 2014).[7]

Moreover, the importance of respect for human rights and international norms for mining companies as well as governments is noted in the 2013 Mining Policy Framework developed by the Intergovernmental Forum on Mining, Minerals, Metals and Sustainable Development. The Intergovernmental Forum currently has fifty-five member states, and the 2013 Mining Policy Framework endorses several of the international standards noted above.[8]

These developments are taking place at a time when countries are also considering and implementing national action plans on business and human rights. Fourteen countries have launched such an action plan, while just under thirty have some type of development process underway (UN, n.d.(c)). These national action plans create a strong national focus on business and human rights issues and can exert pressure on companies to demonstrate good implementation. Many provisions address corporate behavior when making outbound investments.

In addition, the UN High Commissioner for Human Rights issued guidance to states on how to strengthen aspects of domestic judicial systems to improve accountability and access to remedy for victims of business-related human rights abuses (UN, 2016). This report is expected to stimulate judicial reform to improve legal access to remedies in multiple countries.

These extraordinary efforts to harden the soft law nature of the UNGPs are prompting some commentators to suggest that a mining company's failure to respect human rights may have concrete legal implications (Aftab, 2014). For example, the recent Canadian Hudbay case illustrates the real possibility that a common law court may find a parent company owes a duty of care in negligence directly to foreign plaintiffs, with HRDD under the UNGPs informing the standard of care necessary to avoid liability (*Choc* v. *Hudbay Minerals Inc.*, 2013). The allegations in Hudbay concern human rights violations committed by security forces employed by

Hudbay's Guatemalan subsidiary. A failure of HRDD may also become a relevant trasnational public policy consideration in investor-state arbitration cases arising from resource nationalism where the investor company is seeking compensation from the host state under an investment treaty (Aftab, 2014). While there are examples of investor claims that have been denied admissibility due to bribery, to date there are no examples of a failure of HRDD leading to a similar result, though commentators speculate that this may soon change. Another distinct future possibility is that financial institutions that fail to address human rights concerns associated with mining investments could face liability as well (*Piedra* v. *Copper Mesa Mining Corporation*, 2011). For example, in a novel but unsuccessful case brought in 2011 against the Toronto Stock Exchange (TSX), plaintiffs alleged that the TSX was negligent for listing a mining company and thereby facilitating its access to equity financing, without which the company could not have committed various human rights violating acts against local community members in Ecuador. Specifically, the plaintiffs relied upon letters sent to the TSX ahead of these incidents to warn it of the potential for harm that might arise upon listing.

In this landscape of numerous initiatives prompting HRDD, where the idea of legal responsibility for such due diligence is beginning to take shape, mining companies should not lack drivers to conduct HRDD. In its decision to carry out HRDD, a mining company may be influenced by the level of potential human rights risks, such as community conflicts, that it perceives as a threat to itself, rather than to rights holders. It is also possible that an HRIA is produced because a third party, such as a multilateral development bank (MDB) or another financial institution, requires it. Whether driven by self-preservation or compulsion by others, it would seem obvious that the rewards of HRDD combined with the detriments of not carrying one out would lead mining companies to consistent implementation of HRDD.

Human rights due diligence: state of play

HRDD at the very outset of a mining activity seems like an easy win-win proposition: The process would inform the entire mine development process and help community engagement and impacts prevention and management programs start on a right footing. It is also established from an engineering point of view that the most influential project decisions are made early in the timeline of the investment; that is, the information gained at an early assessment stage can critically modify a project and its success (Mueller, 1986). Yet we do not know whether HRDD/HRIA is as prevalent as the number of initiatives in this area suggests and the business and human rights community wishes it to be. There is a view that a comprehensive HRIA is not necessarily congruent with the company's interest, particularly when human rights risks from a smaller project do not necessitate a comprehensive, open and unbiased HRIA. We do know that there are significant financial and nonfinancial constraints to such due diligence that are inherent in the mining sector, resulting in scant evidence of such due diligence.

According to leading practitioners, HRIAs can have variable price tags and time frames depending on their intended purpose:

- At the low end of the price range, US$30,000 and upward would buy some variant of a rapid assessment, often for internal fact finding and risk management purpose with no or limited stakeholder engagement, but possibly with a strong legal gap analysis. These documents tend to remain confidential.
- A middle-of-the-range HRIA would be a reasonably thorough HRIA with good stakeholder engagement and a good report that can be shared externally. This assumes a context where good level of stakeholder engagement and cooperation with the affected communities is possible. These may cost up to $150,000.
- Certain tailor-made HRIAs for specific damage control purpose, such as in the case of problems or conflict with local communities, are likely to well exceed US$150,000. For example, the Marlin HRIA was conducted in the midst of community conflict in Guatemala, and in response to a shareholder proposal brought forward by a group of socially responsible investors (On Common Ground Consultants, 2010),[9] and its cost is assumed to have far exceeded $150,000.
- According to informal World Bank estimates, a comprehensive ESIA will normally cost around 1–3 percent of total project cost in the case of large infrastructure projects. The cost will increase if the company is responsible for land acquisition, resettlement and compensation.

Although rapid assessments may be complete in a matter of few weeks or months, some HRIAs may last significantly longer, particularly if the process must collect baseline information, such as household surveys in the case of resettlement. This process could encounter further delays if land tenure information is not formalized at a particular location and must be collected and verified manually. Although collection of baseline information typically will serve the company well in the future against negative impacts caused after the baseline data collection by actors other than the company, frequently the benefits are not well understood. Not willing to delay project activities, companies often run the process of baseline information collection alongside other project activities, such as exploration for reserves, which could result in confusion of and conflict with local communities.

Perhaps the more concerning problem is the fact that, with a few exceptions, HRIAs are not typically disclosed. Even the better known HRIAs put out by the extractives sector are not complete. For example, the HRIA for the Tangguh oil and gas project in Indonesia (Human Rights Assessment of the Proposed Tangguh LNG Project, 2002) is said to be the first ever HRIA but only a summary of the document was disclosed and is available today, due to concerns about the host government taking actions against project staff. The assessment for the Marlin mine in Guatemala, due to unsurmountable challenges in engaging local rights holders, was considered a "human rights assessment" rather than a full HRIA by the assessment team (On Common Ground). In contrast, the ongoing HRIA and audit of Nevsun's Bisha Mine in Eritrea holds promise and is worth watching closely (LKL International Consulting, 2015).

This inconsistent and spotty state of practice makes it virtually impossible for affected communities, other stakeholders and observers to monitor whether HRDD is in fact put to use, and its effectiveness. Moreover, while an increasing number of consulting and law firms offer custom process of HRDD, some law firms sell their services based on their ability to confer attorney-client privilege on information divulged by clients. This creates inconsistencies with the UNGPs requirement that companies "know and show" respect for human rights, although the claim is that privilege creates a safe space for companies to learn about potential harms and devise strategies to remedy them. While lawyers can confer attorney-client privilege, they can also make the case to their clients about the benefits of disclosure, even if not complete, so as to better enable the meaningful stakeholder engagement that is essential to earning a social license to operate.

A recent survey also indicates that mining companies tend to withhold any reference to the existence of a specific ongoing or completed HRDD process from their CSR, sustainability or other types of corporate reporting (Shift 2014). Concerns for legal liability and not inflaming an already prickly relationship with nearby affected communities drive mining companies to carry out these processes away from public scrutiny, and avoid any mention of such activities at all to external audiences. In the process, engagement with affected communities is shunned, leaving the very rights holders to bear the burden of project impacts without any knowledge of the company's findings and decisions. It is conceivable that companies are also skipping the process altogether when they can operate below the radar screen of any external scrutiny.

Constraints on human rights due diligence

In this section we explore the specific nature of actors and their activities in the very beginning phases of mine development that create several challenges for the proper implementation of HRDD.

To begin with, the standards and tools designed to help companies implement HRDD do not always squarely apply to early phase mining operations. But the relative scarcity of HRDD by mining companies early in a mine life cycle could be mainly attributable to two prominent traits of the mining sector: (1) the types of mine companies that populate the upstream part of the mine value chain; and (2) the way in which mining projects are financed during the early phases of a mine development process. The combination of these two traits alone likely creates an overwhelming disincentive for HRDD at the outset of mine projects. Below we consider several probable constraints in turn.

1 *Information scarcity and other challenges early on*

ESIAs methodologies and to some extent those of HRIAs depend on clear demarcation of geographic and temporal boundaries of the physical footprint of planned operations. Only once such boundaries are established can specialists project forward potential positive and negative impacts of activities planned within these boundaries over a specified period of time. Mining project boundaries can only be marked with certainty once the locations of reserves are proven and a detailed mine development plan emerges. Until such time, assessment tools operate at less than their full capacity due to scarcity of information at the start of the activities.

Such information scarcity early on in a project life cycle is a common occurrence in all sectors. Assessment specialists get around this challenge usually by carrying out rapid assessments, collecting available information, creating assumptions and scenarios, and deferring work for a later date when information becomes available. But their work is predicated on an awareness that early project activities could still create impacts and that stakeholder communities must be engaged early on.

It is frequently assumed that no significant environmental or social impacts from early activities such as geological survey should be expected. But community impacts or reactions to perceived risks could be significant even at this phase. For example, in the Kalahari Diamonds project in Botswana, BHP Billiton proposed to use a proprietary airborne technology that would help identify diamond reserves in the Kalahari dessert. This technology was meant to enable the company to prioritize licensed areas for later exploration without creating any physical disturbance on the ground through soil sampling and other conventional techniques. In 2003, IFC was approached for a small equity stake in the venture, and worked with BHP Billiton to create an environmental and social management plan that would be largely deferred and triggered once reserves were confirmed (IFC n.d.(a)). However, the presence of hunter-gatherer communities of indigenous people called the San in the license area added a wrinkle to this deferred plan. IFC specialists realized the possibility of inducing anxiety and distress among the San communities in the survey area coming close to circling planes; at the same time, the possibility of over-communication will induce unnecessary anxiety among those communities unlikely to experience overhead flights. Even with the innovative and seemingly innocuous technology, impacts would materialize; at the same time, uncertainty about the geographic boundaries – the flight paths – made the process of communicating the potential impacts to communities constantly on the move challenging. A culturally appropriate community engagement plan had to be put in place for the early survey phase of the project, to be replaced by a more comprehensive management plan for the exploration phase.

The foregoing project took place almost a decade before IFC's requirement for the free, prior and informed consent of the Indigenous Peoples (FPIC) became effective in 2012. Today, potentially affected communities of Indigenous Peoples not only have the right to seek, request and receive information on planned mining projects, but they also have the right to withhold consent to aspects of the proposed project (IFC, 2012: para 7). In projects that may be sited in the vicinity of communities of Indigenous Peoples, the project must anticipate the need for FPIC. Preparation for obtaining such consent could be an extremely time consuming process and engagement with the Indigenous Peoples must start as early as possible. FPIC entails some of the greatest challenges to be encountered by any mining company[10] and the irony is that preparations for FPIC needs to commence exactly at a time when companies are least able to take on such arduous tasks. They can only hope that the host government will have performed some groundwork toward FPIC and engaged with affected communities of Indigenous Peoples before handing out exploration licenses.

2 *Mining sector value chain and financing structure*

Even if some of the technical challenges during an early period of information deficit and lack of organizational preparedness could potentially be overcome, peculiar traits of the mining sector act as even stronger deterrent to HRDD. We begin with an analysis of the particular value chain structure of the mining sector, and the role of junior mining companies, who occupy the upstream space in the chain. A website dedicated to 140 listed Canadian junior mining companies explains the value chain structure as follows:

> Mining companies are defined largely by the way in which they derive their revenues. A senior producer or operator generates its revenues from the production and sale of the commodity it is mining. A junior mining company has no mining operations and is essentially a venture capital company. It must rely almost entirely on the capital markets to finance its exploration activities. There is another category: mid-tier producers. These are generally junior companies that have decided to go into production on properties that they have discovered. There are about 1650 junior mining companies listed in Canada.
>
> (Junior Miners, n.d.)

The definition by Natural Recourses Canada of junior companies, for example, defines them mostly for what they are not: A junior miner is neither a producing company nor the recipient of significant income from production or from some other business venture (Government of Canada, 2017).

As part of the multi-tiered mining industry, prospectors or ex-senior mining company employees with entrepreneurial spirit establish junior companies. It is common that the company will hold one or two assets, and that it will only concentrate on scoping and exploration efforts. Since the vast majority of exploration endeavors do not result in an economic and technically viable project, juniors are cash sinkholes; therefore, the financing of the junior mining sector is mostly undertaken either through the raising of equity or joint ventures with earn-in options (Government of Canada, 2017).

The relatively *sui generis* nature of the junior mining sector and its risk profile has resulted in concentration of juniors home-based in a number of choice financial markets. Canada, for example, dominates the junior public markets with more than 57 percent of junior companies listed in its stock exchanges, accounting for 62 percent of the equity raised globally for mining in 2014 (Mining Association of Canada, 2016). Other important stock exchanges for juniors include the London Stock Exchange (AIM), the Johannesburg Stock Exchange and the Australian Stock Exchange.

The prevailing structure of the mining sector value chain all but assures that the early actors in the chain will not have much to gain from identifying, assessing and managing environmental, social and human rights issues. They will incur only the costs deemed essential for exploration, and it is hardly likely that HRDD will be deemed an essential activity when they will not operate the mines themselves. Even in jurisdictions in which ESIAs are mandatory, this assessment usually takes place at a later phase, typically during the feasibility study, which in turn occurs only after exploration (Harris and Bland, 2015). Environmental permits follow ESIAs, and are likely not required until closer to construction. In the absence of a legislated requirement to consult with local indigenous communities at the exploration stage, as is the case in Ontario (Simons and Collins, 2010; Pardy and Stoehr, 2015), specific risk or reputational concerns, or an MDB taking up an equity stake in an exploration company and calling for HRDD, junior mining companies will have little compelling reason to carry out such diligence for their part in the mining value chain.

As already mentioned, HRIAs come with a range of price tags. Even a very comprehensive HRIAs with proper stakeholder engagement (excluding the process of FPIC in the event that Indigenous Peoples are involved) costing over $150,000 seems financially negligible, particularly in large projects. Even if a comprehensive ESIA that also includes an adequately scoped human rights impact assessment component pushes the cost outlay to tens of millions, or even hundreds of million dollars, this price tag should be seen in the context of the largest projects costing tens of billions of dollars to develop. In mining projects, HRIAs seem hardly extravagant, given the early warning signals that they provide to inform companies of above-the-ground risks.

The stark financial reality, however, is that junior mining companies typically put up very little equity upfront for a mining prospect, and finance various activities incrementally, venture-capital style (Junior Miners n.d.) During geological survey and exploration, there will only be sufficient funds to go around for essential operational activities. Even in subsequent phases, mining companies likely will seek financing for one phase at a time, such as for environmental permits and operational licenses. In this context, a cost outlay of a mere $150,000 for an HRIA could be unwelcome to shareholders.

Funds are not only scarce but they are also of a particular type – equity. The juniors will not and cannot seek project financing loans because they will have no access to operating revenues to service project finance loans. This means, among other things, that the Equator Principles will have no effect since the Principles apply only to project finance and limited corporate finance with known use of proceeds.

Notwithstanding the shoe-string financial model, some expect that if and when a MDB becomes involved later on with project loans or equity, they will help impose the right environmental and social conditions on projects and retrofit the earlier defects. This may in fact be possible, as was the case with the Kalahari Diamonds project with a very early equity participation by IFC. But MDBs cannot always be counted on to right the wrong, particularly if the irreversible wrong occurred early in the process, such as missing the FPIC process altogether.

New multilateral players, such as the Asian Infrastructure Investment Bank (AIIB) and the New Development Bank, now compete for opportunities to fund large transformational projects alongside the World Bank and regional development banks (RDBs). Although AIIB has adopted a set of environmental and social policies, largely modelled after the World Bank safeguard policies, it is not yet clear exactly how they will be applied in operations. Likewise, we do not yet know how the World Bank and the RDBs will react to the new development banks' approach to environmental and social issues – will they soft-pedal application of their own safeguard policies to stay in the project or will they stand their ground and risk being disinvited from the lender group in the next project?

Even if an MDB succeeds in gaining access to a mine project and starts to work to strengthen the mine project's HRIA or ESIA, the mine asset could be grabbed and flipped to another buyer, as seen in the Simandou project in Guinea in 2014 (*The Economist*, 2014), or the Gertler incident in 2012 in the Democratic Republic of Congo (Els 2012). In such a rough and tumble world of mining, it is unavoidable that HRDD will often take a back seat.

New mechanisms to enable human rights due diligence

While the value chain and financial structures of the mining sector present serious impediments to HRDD, we consider the diligence process as an opportunity to create intrinsic value in the mining project, something that a purchaser of the mining prospect should recognize and appreciate (Baumann-Pauly and Posner, 2016). As we debate how junior mining companies should finance HRDD, a tenet of our proposals below is to focus on assisting juniors in obtaining upfront cash, but in ways in which government revenue will not be jeopardized by such incentives or funding mechanisms. We also explore mechanisms associated with the raising of funds both at the home and host country levels, and look at how alternative types of financing may be of assistance to the junior mining sector and beyond.

1 Redefining existing tax benefits

Due to the importance of the mining sector to home and host jurisdictions, many already provide for tax deductions, allowance and credits for expenses incurred during exploration and development, extraction and processing. We do not suggest further tax benefits as a solution for funding HRDD. Instead, the creation and expansion of a class of shares that hold tax benefits to the investor, depending on the type of expenditure, could be implemented. For example, the federal government of Canada already incentivizes the junior mining market in Canada through the use of flow-through shares (FTS) (Jog, 2016). FTS is a tax-based financing incentive that consists of a “flow through” of expenses to investors, who can then claim them in their own personal tax statements (Gravelle, 2012). The junior company issues FTS, and the company agrees to expend a certain amount of costs up to the amount paid by the taxpayer for the share (Jog).

Eligible expenditures under the FTS system are categorized under either “grass-roots” or “pre-production.” Examples of grass-roots expenditure include costs incurred for the purpose of determining the location, extent or quality of a mineral resource, including geological surveys, drilling by rotary or trenching (Gravelle), while pre-production expenses include costs that are incurred to bring the mine into production, such as sinking a mineshaft (PwC, 2012).

In 2016, the Canadian legislature clarified that environmental studies qualify as eligible expenditures (Statutes of Canada, 2016). Furthermore, community consultations, including if undertaken to “obtain a right, licence or privilege,” has also been included in this recent amendment. Therefore, presumably HRDD would qualify as an eligible expenditure (Statutes of Canada, 2016: s.7(1)). It may be beneficial if the FTS system could also be extended to the home-state context and benefit investors making overseas investments, so long as the HRDD component is explicitly covered.

2 IFC's Early Equity Program

IFC's Mining Group has an early equity program, aimed at exploration companies: "Under our unique Early Equity Program, we support mining projects at the pre-feasibility stage by becoming a shareholder and long-term partner" (IFC n.d.(c)). By buying into the project early on, IFC could provide not only the capital needed by exploration companies at the early stage of a mine project, but also due diligence advice on areas that exploration companies frequently overlooked, such as failing to engage appropriate professionals who could identify potentially affected local communities and create a strategy to engage with them. IFC's presence ensured that the exploration companies would take environmental and social issues seriously, and budget the cost of such due diligence appropriately (even though such costs were usually relatively modest). According to IFC, not all shareholders were always interested in such due diligence, and at times it struggled to keep all shareholders focused on such diligence. In some instances, IFC sold its equity where satisfactory action was not being taken.

As a minority shareholder, IFC also faced the risk of being paid out when the exploration companies sold their claims, and losing its influence altogether. Even though this was a fairly common occurrence, there have been exceptions. For example, the Guyana Goldfields project demonstrated that IFC could stay involved in a mine development project over a long term, starting with its early equity program. In this particular project, IFC first purchased its equity in 2006, and completed the financial package in 2014 (Skodeberg, 2014). IFC claims its long-term engagement with the project helped Guyana Goldfields establish an integrated environmental, health, safety and social management system in line with international best practices.

Notwithstanding these benefits, it appears that this instrument is no longer in use at IFC due to the high risks of financing exploration companies. Other MDBs do not seem to offer a similar product. Yet, this is precisely the kind of financial product that multilaterals should carry so they can share the burden of addressing risks at the exploration phase of a mine project, including the risk that these companies might miss an important HRDD step at the outset that could snowball later on to huge problems at the mine development stage.

3 Social impact bonds

A modified version of social impact bonds (SIBs) could be used to fund HRDD/HRIA. SIBs are a relatively novel way of funding social programs with the involvement of the private sector. In some cases, SIB may be a misnomer, as they are not necessarily debt in the traditional sense, and may not be a fixed income instrument.

A typical structure for an SIB is for investors to provide upfront cash to a social impact partner, which is a service provider. The social impact partner is evaluated and paid based on specific key performance indices (KPIs), which means the success of the project is an important component of return on investments. A public entity, usually government, pays the social impact partner, which then returns to investors a rate of return on their investment dependent on achieved KPIs. Many countries, such as Australia, Canada, Mozambique, South Africa, the United Kingdom and the United States, have funded SIBs (Nicholas, 2013).

In the case of financing the junior mining sector for the purpose of conducting HRDD/HRIAs, the use of SIBs could be twofold. First, a straight-up slightly modified SIB could be used to fund HRDD/HRIA costs. Instead of a government entity paying the bill of the social impact partner, major mining companies, institutional investors or impact investors would bear the upfront costs. Second, once the modified SIB is created, it could be securitized with returns based on HRDD/HRIA KPIs. This securitized HRDD/HRIA could then be sold and/or transferred to another investor if the original investor either does not want to continue with the project or for any other reason.

Both alternatives above bundle the HRDD/HRIA interest and commoditizes it. One of the benefits of commoditizing the HRDD/HRIA Bond is the standardization of the quality of HRDD/HRIAs endeavors. This quality measure would be recognized by other players in the markets and, therefore, could ultimately increase the valuation of the junior, and thus improve its chance for a possible sale to a major.

A bundled HRDD/HRIA Bond could also be sold to civil society and/or impact investors, and they could be restructured as convertible bonds. In exercising the convertible bonds, the HRDD/HRIA Bond could become non-voting preference shares if the project goes forward. Note that a non-voting requirement may be important so as not to create a chilling effect on sales to third parties.

The host country, in order to incentivize local service providers and social impact partners, could also encourage such HRDD/HRIA Bonds by: (a) assisting in establishing local guidelines and norms for such bundles, with specific quality control standards; and (b) require local content, thus fostering local participation and opening local markets for such investments.

Listing HRDD/HRIA Bonds on social stock exchanges (SSE) could be a novel way of marketing and raising funds. Brazil, Canada, Kenya, Singapore, South Africa and the United Kingdom, to name a few, have opened SSEs. Each has different platform conceptions, ranging from an online matchmaking platform to a quasi-full-fledged stock exchange. In its many forms, SSEs' main function is to list social businesses, so that investors can finance, either through equity or debt, social businesses by mission, geographic location and so on (Chhichhia, 2015).

An issue with regards to SSEs is whether the social purpose of the business needs to be either its primary social purpose, or just one of its core purposes. The Brazilian model, for example, requires neither; it lists socio-environmental projects for investors (Chhichhia, 2015; BVSA, n.d.). This may be a hurdle that is insurmountable for traditional mining companies. However, it may be a distinct possibility for mining companies with an ownership structure that reflects the growth in social enterprises, B-corporations, and benefit corporate structures with local indigenous communities holding an ownership interest, for example. But, considering that HRDD/HRIA's core and main purpose is the preservation of human rights, then it an interesting proposition to bundle these services in such a way that could deliver access to social investors and other types of impact financing to critical portions of mining projects. The assumption here is that mining, as an industry and a business proposition, will not end in the near future. As such, increased participation of civil society and impact financiers is an important way to raise ethical and human rights considerations.

4 *Equity crowd funding*

Equity crowd funding may be an option whether at the home country or the host country. Equity crowd funding, also known as crowd-sourced equity funding, allows unlisted companies to seek equity investment from members of the public (Gullifer and Payne, 2015). Generally, a website is the crowdfunding platform, and investors can invest small amounts of money.

In the mining sector, Red Cloud Klondike Strike Inc. in Canada (www.klondikestrike.com) was reportedly the world's first mining crowdfund launched in 2016 (Christensen, 2016). The Red Cloud platform used by the company, allows for the raising of financing in a range from CND $500,000 to 10 million. While investors can invest as little as $2,500 per investor, the maximum amount the investor can invest will depend on the type of investor and specificities of securities regulation (Red Cloud).

Australian legislators have recently approved crowdfunding legislation, and Mineral Intelligence, a mining crowdfund platform, is in the market, allowing investments of even US$500. The question then is whether other jurisdictions will follow suit.

The possibility of crowdfunding could be an important way for the local population to become involved in the mining project. By investing in HRDD/HRIAs and providing the junior with upfront cash, returns for such investment could be a share of the project should it go ahead. Of course, the problem is that local communities, especially in developing countries, will not have access to funds. Nevertheless, the host government or non-governmental organizations could potentially provide financial support.

Conclusions

The mining sector is presently suffering one of the worst slumps in recent memory. Financing opportunities are hard to come by, and in these cost-cutting times initiatives that are non-core may simply be scrapped. At the same time, considering the number of very public cases of human rights breaches, such as the Barrick Porgera mine in Papua New Guinea and Goldcorp's Marlin Mine in Guatemala, surely HRDD cannot entirely escape the attention of junior companies. In the previous section, we reviewed how such costs could be borne by junior mining companies faced with specific financing and other constraints, and suggested some existing mechanisms in which shareholders, investors and taxpayers could take the financial responsibility for HRDD.

We conclude this chapter by drawing several observations and inferences from our proposition on financial mechanisms. The first is that it is the role of the market to reward junior mining companies that spend its limited capital well to maximize the value of the prospect, and that the market should be given explicit encouragement to understand the enhanced financial value that can be created through HRDD. Anecdotal evidence indicates that there is no practice of investors in and buyers of mining prospects paying price premia for well-designed and executed HRDD.[11] We are also not aware of any senior mining companies willing to explicitly signal readiness to reward juniors with price premia for HRDD. However, the market could and should become sensitized to the fact that appropriate HRDD carried out at the outset of mine development will enhance the financial value of the mine project by the multiples of the original cost of the due diligence. The value enhancement should come from the avoided cost of future conflict, project delays and shutdowns (IFC, n.d.(b)),[12] as well as avoidance of litigation risk. To ensure that the market understands the financial value that HRDD can create, juniors could be much more explicit about the existence of such due diligence by pushing out their due diligence information in their prospectuses and disclosure documents. We also expect a pull factor from securities regulators and stock exchanges: While no securities regulator currently requires listed extractive companies to perform HRDD, we should see a growing trend in favor of disclosure rules for human rights-related issues, including community consultation and transparency of payments (OSC, 2013; SEC, 2016).

The second observation is that the examples of financing mechanisms potentially point to a new model of HRDD, where the "ownership" of the process no longer resides exclusively with the mining company. As shareholders, investors, taxpayers and, potentially, buyers begin to play a significant role in financing HRDD of the junior mining company, they will have a greater say on the scope of such due diligence. Many financing entities will push for the HRDD process to involve affected communities and stakeholders, which will require disclosure of salient information much earlier in a mine development process. Junior mining companies obtain financing through equity, and often through private placement or a non-public offering of securities, which means it is only after an initial public offering that the activities of a large chunk of the junior mining sector ever becomes public and therefore open to public scrutiny. The new model could change the dynamics altogether. Effectively, the new transparent HRIA process and products will be pushed out of companies and into the public domain.

If enough HRDD can be financed and implemented this way, we will create a movement whereby HRDD and HRIAs can be bought and managed, and even passed on, like a commodity, entirely in the public domain. With adequate financing, the asset can remain with the mine project throughout its full life-cycle but managed outside the company in a parallel process. This has the added benefit that additional HRDD, as and when necessary as new human rights issues inevitably arise, can be carried out and implemented. It will be available to address the ultimate challenge of mine closure and managing the long-term social and human rights impacts on the communities, which will outlast short-term reclamation and environmental projects typical at mine closure. In this way, HRDD will serve the needs of affected communities from cradle to grave of mine development projects, and not only at the outset of projects.

Our final observation is that home and host states alike must create a regulatory environment in which the financial mechanisms discussed, or something similar, can thrive. The obligation to protect human rights lies squarely with nation states. Host and home states should therefore engage with the mining community and provide incentives for miners to undertake preventative measures and financing mechanisms to help such measures. Such actions will not only benefit the host state and the community, but also the junior company's return on investment when the asset is sold. Above all, developed home states, where financing opportunities flow more readily and where profits return to, ought to foster an environment that encourage prevention and mitigation of negative human rights impacts.

Notes

1 IFC's Performance Standard 7 on Indigenous Peoples introduced for the first time a requirement for the free, prior and informed consent of the affected communities of Indigenous Peoples.
2 Although the UNGPs suggest a human rights due diligence process (Principle 7(b)) and refers to assessments of human rights impacts in a generic way, the term "HRIA" is not used.
3 Law No. 2017–399 (Loi n° 2017–399 du 27 mars 2017 relative au devoir de vigilance des sociétés mères et des entreprises donneuses d'ordre).
4 See Executive Order 13627 – Strengthening Protections Against Trafficking In Persons In Federal Contracts (www.hsdl.org/?abstract&did=723091); and the rule amending the Federal Acquisition Regulation (FAR) in order to implement the Executive Order (www.federalregister.gov/documents/2015/01/29/2015–01524/

federal-acquisition-regulation-ending-trafficking-in-persons). Also, California Transparency in Supply Chains Act of 2010.

5 The Canadian CSR Strategy refers to the following soft law instruments specifically: the OECD Guidelines for Multinational Enterprises; the Voluntary Principles on Security and Human Rights; IFC Performance Standards; the OECD Due Diligence Guidance on Responsible Supply Chains of Minerals from Conflict-Affected and High-Risk Areas; and the Global Reporting Initiative.

6 These dispute resolution mechanisms include the National Contact Point for the OECD MNE Guidelines, as well as the Office of the Extractive Sector CSR Counsellor.

7 Section 2.4, especially 2.4.4 and 2.4.5.

8 These include the IFC Performance Standards, the Voluntary Principles on Security and Human Rights, as well as the OECD Guidelines for Multinational Enterprises. While the Mining Policy Framework does refer to the UN Declaration on Human Rights and the UN Declaration on the Rights of Indigenous Peoples, it does not explicitly refer to the UNGPs.

9 The shareholder groups included Ethical Funds, SHARE, the Public Service Alliance of Canada Staff Pension Fund, and two Swedish National Pension Funds.

10 According to IFC Performance Standard 7, such engagement should be based on stakeholder analysis, engagement planning, disclosure of information, consultation and culturally appropriate participation, and the project proponent needs to provide sufficient time for decision making.

11 On the other hand, anecdotal evidence also indicates that price is discounted for poor human rights management, as with any other liability. In acquisitions (and attempted acquisitions) in difficult jurisdictions with complicated human rights issues, such as in Guinea, Liberia, Mozambique, Democratic Republic of Congo and South Africa, discounts were demanded for assets with many complications including human rights complications. The result ironically meant certain Chinese companies stepping in to complete the deal because they would not necessarily discount for human rights liabilities of the mines.

12 IFC's Financial Valuation Tool (IFC n.d.) helps companies assess the downside financial risk of not doing anything to manage future environmental, social and human rights risks. It calculates the current cost of future noncompliance or failure to act to manage these nonfinancial risks. The tool is sponsored by Newmont Mining and Rio Tinto among others.

References

Aftab, Y. (n.d.) *The Role of Legal Counsel in Human Rights Strategy*, www.enodorights.com/assets/pdf/human-rights-due-diligence.pdf.

Aftab, Y. (2014) "The Intersection of Law and Corporate Social Responsibility: Human Rights Strategy and Litigation Readiness for Extractive-Sector Companies," in *Proceedings of 60th Annual Rocky Mountain Mineral Law Institute*, 19-1–19-31.

Asia Infrastructure Investment Bank (n.d.) *Environmental and Social Framework 2016*, www.aiib.org/en/policies-strategies/operational-policies/environmental-social-framework.html.

Australian Aid and Oxfam Australia (2017) *A Guide to Gender Impact Assessment for the Extractive Industries*, www.oxfam.org.au/wp-content/uploads/2017/04/2017-PA-001-Gender-impact-assessments-in-mining-report_FA_WEB.pdf.

Baumann-Pauly, D. and Posner, M. (2016) "Making the Business Case for Human Rights: An Assessment," in *Business and Human Rights: From Principles to*

Practice, ed. Dorothee Baumann-Pauly and Justine Nolan, Routledge, New York.

Business and Human Rights Resource Centre (2016) *Corporate Human Rights Benchmark, Pilot Methodology 2016*, https://business-humanrights.org/sites/default/files/CHRB_report_06_singles.pdf.

BVSA (Bolsa de Valores Socioambientais) (n.d.) www.bvsa.org.br/bvsa.

CEDAW (Convention on the Elimination of All Forms of Discrimination against Women) (18 December 1979) GA res 34/180, 34 UN GAOR Supp (No 46) at 193, UN Doc A/34/46; 1249 UNTS 13; 19 ILM 33 (1980), www.un.org/womenwatch/daw/cedaw.

Center for Global Development (2013) *Investing in Social Outcomes: Development Impact Bonds – The Report of the Development Impact Bond Working Group*, www.cgdev.org/sites/default/files/investing-in-social-outcomes-development-impact-bonds.pdf.

Chhichhia, B. (2015) "The Rise of Social Stock Exchanges: A New Innovative Platform is Helping More Investors Support Social Enterprises," *Stanford Social Innovation Review*, https://ssir.org/articles/entry/the_rise_of_social_stock_exchanges.

China Chamber of Commerce of Metals Minerals and Chemical Importers and Exporters (2014) *Guidelines for Social Responsibility in Outbound Mining Investment*, www.emm-network.org/wp-content/uploads/2015/03/Guidelines_for_Social_Responsibility_in_Outbound_Mining_Investments.pdf.

Choc v. *Hudbay Minerals Inc.* (2013) ONSC 1414, www.chocversushudbay.com/wp-content/uploads/2010/10/Judgment-permitting-lawsuits-to-proceed-to-trial-in-Canada.pdf.

Christensen, N. (2016) "Crowdfunding Comes to Mining Sector," *Forbes*, www.forbes.com/sites/kitconews/2016/03/23/crowdfunding-comes-to-mining-sector/#4f7090447e37.

Davis, R. and Franks, D.M. (2014) "Costs of Company-Community Conflict in the Extractive Sector," *Harvard Kennedy School*, www.hks.harvard.edu/m-rcbg/CSRI/research/Costs%20of%20Conflict_Davis%20%20Franks.pdf.

Depres, B. (2016) "Crowdfunding: Will the UK be Next to Join this Trend?" *Canadian Mining Journal*, www.canadianminingjournal.com/features/crowdfunding-will-the-uk-be-next-to-join-this-trend.

DIHR (Danish Institute for Human Rights) (n.d.) *Human Rights Compliance Assessment*, https://hrca2.humanrightsbusiness.org.

DIHR (Danish Institute for Human Rights) (n.d.) *Human Crowdfunding Comes to Mining Sector*, www.humanrights.dk/business/human-rights-impact-assessment-guidance-toolbox-material.

Els, F. (2012) "Meet the Israeli Middleman Said to Have "Stripped And Flipped" First Quantum's DRC Mine," *Mining.com*, www.mining.com/meet-the-israeli-middleman-said-to-have-stripped-and-flipped-first-quantums-drc-mine-76979.

Equator Principles (2013) *Equator Principles III*, www.equator-principles.com/index.php/ep3.

Government of Canada (2014) "Doing Business the Canadian Way: A Strategy to Advance Corporate Social Responsibility in Canada's Extractive Sector Abroad," Global Affairs Canada, www.international.gc.ca/trade-agreements-accords-commerciaux/topics-domaines/other-autre/csr-strat-rse.aspx?lang=eng.

Government of Canada (2017) *Mineral Exploration*, Natural Resources Canada, www.nrcan.gc.ca/mining-materials/statistics/8854.

Gowling (2016) *Crowdfunding in the Mining Sector*, https://gowlingwlg.com/en/canada/insights-resources/crowdfunding-in-the-mining-sector.

Gravelle, J. (2012) "Examining Flow-Through Shares in the Mining Sectors," *Canadian Mining Journal* 133(5): 34.

GRI (2013) *G4 Sustainability Reporting Guidelines*, www.globalreporting.org/information/g4/Pages/default.aspx.

Gullifer, L. and Payne, J. (2015) *Corporate Finance Law: Principles and Policy*, 2nd edn., Hart Publishing, Oxford, UK.

Harris, E. and Bland, L. (2015) "The Effectiveness of ESIA in Meeting Project Financing Requirements: A Mining Sector Perspective," paper presented at International Association for Impact Assessment conference, Florence, Italy, April 20–23.

Holland, E. (n.d.) *French Duty of Vigilance Law Takes Trend toward Mandated Corporate Disclosure Regimes to New Level*, Freshfields Bruckhaus Deringer, http://humanrights.freshfields.com/post/102e4aq/french-duty-of-vigilance-law-takes-trend-toward-mandated-corporate-disclosure-reg.

Human Rights Assessment of the Proposed Tangguh LNG Project (2002), www.ideaspaz.org/tools/download/47408.

ICMM (International Council on Mining and Metals) (2009) *Human Rights in the Mining and Metals Industry: Overview, Management Approach and Issues*, www.icmm.com/en-gb/publications/mining-and-communities/human-rights-in-the-mining-and-metals-industry--overview-management-approach-and-issues.

ICMM (International Council on Mining and Metals) (2012) *Integrating Human Rights Due Diligence into Corporate Risk Management Processes*, www.icmm.com/en-gb/publications/mining-and-communities/integrating-human-rights-due-diligence-into-corporate-risk-management-processes.

ICMM (International Council on Mining and Metals) (2013) *Indigenous Peoples and Mining Position Statement*, www.icmm.com/en-gb/publications/indigenous-peoples-and-mining-position-statement.

Iddon, C., Hettihewa, S. and Wright, C.S. (2013) "Junior Mining Sector Capital-Raising: The Effect of Information Asymmetry and Uncertainty Issues," *Journal of Applied Business and Economics* 15(3): 56–67.

IFC (International Finance Corporation) (n.d.(a)) *IFC Project Information Portal*, http://ifcext.ifc.org/ifcext/spiwebsite1.nsf/ProjectDisplay/ERS20426.

IFC (International Finance Corporation) (n.d.(b)) *Financial Valuation Tool for Sustainability Investments*, www.fvtool.com.

IFC (International Finance Corporation) (n.d.(c)) *Oil, Gas and Mining*, www.ifc.org/wps/wcm/connect/industry_ext_content/ifc_external_corporate_site/industries/oil,+gas+and+mining/mining/miningcontent.

IFC (International Finance Corporation) (2012) *IFC Performance Standards on Environmental and Social Sustainability*, Performance Standard 7, www.ifc.org/wps/wcm/connect/c8f524004a73daeca09afdf998895a12/IFC_Performance_Standards.pdf?MOD=AJPERES.

Intergovernmental Forum on Mining, Minerals Metals and Sustainable Development (2013) *Mining Policy Framework*, http://globaldialogue.info/MPFOct2013.pdf.

ISO (International Standards Organization) (2010) *ISO 26000 Social Responsibility*, www.iso.org/iso/home/standards/iso26000.htm.

Jenkins, K. (2014) "Women, Mining and Development: An Emerging Research Agenda," *The Extractive Industries and Society* 1: 329–339.

Jog, V. (2016) "Rates of Return on Flow-Through Shares: Investors and Governments Beware," *School of Public Policy SPP Research Papers* 9(4), University of Calgary, www.policyschool.ca/wp-content/uploads/2016/03/flow-through-shares-jog.pdf.

Junior Miners (n.d.) List of Junior Miners, www.juniorminers.com/companies.html#axzz4Dqj7WfyY.

LKL International Consulting (2015) *Human Rights Impact Assessment of the Bisha Mine in Eritrea: 2015 Audit*, www.nevsun.com/responsibility/human-rights/Bisha-HRIA-Audit-2015.pdf.

Mineral Intelligence (n.d.) *Connecting the Mining Investment Community*, https://mineralintelligence.com/about.

Mining Association of Canada (2016) *Mining Facts*, http://mining.ca/resources/mining-facts.

Mueller, F.W. (1986) *Integrated Costs and Schedule Control for Construction Projects*, Van Nostrand Reinhold, New York.

Myanmar Centre for Responsible Business (n.d.) *Sector-Wide Impact Assessments*, www.myanmar-responsiblebusiness.org/news/swia.

Nicholas, P. (2013) *Social Investment and Mining: Creating a Win–Win with Development Impact Bonds*, Mines and Money London 2013 Conference, London, December 1–5.

OECD (Organisation for Economic Co-operation and Development) (2011) *Guidelines for Multinational Enterprises*, www.oecd.org/corporate/mne/48004323.pdf.

OECD (Organisation for Economic Co-operation and Development) (2012) *Due Diligence Guidelines on Responsible Supply Chains of Minerals from Conflict-Affected and High-Risk Areas*, 2nd edn., www.oecd.org/corporate/mne/GuidanceEdition2.pdf.

OECD (Organisation for Economic Co-operation and Development) (2016) *OECD Recommendations (Common Approaches)*, www.oecd.org/tad/xcred/oecd-recommendations.htm.

OECD (Organisation for Economic Co-operation and Development) (2017) *Due Diligence Guidance for Meaningful Stakeholder Engagement in the Extractive Sector*, https://mneguidelines.oecd.org/stakeholder-engagement-extractive-industries.htm.

On Common Ground Consultants (2010) *Human Rights Assessment of Goldcorp's Marlin Mine*, http://csr.goldcorp.com/2011/docs/2010_human_full_en.pdf .

OSC (Ontario Securities Commission) (2013) Staff Notice 43–705, "Report on Staff's Review of Technical Reports of Ontario Mining Issuers" pp. 7, 9–10, www.osc.gov.on.ca/documents/en/Securities-Category1/sn_20130627_43-705_rpt-tech-rpt-mining-issuers.pdf.

Oxfam America (n.d.) *Community Voice in Human Rights Impact Assessments*, www.oxfamamerica.org/static/media/files/COHBRA_formatted_07-15_Final.pdf.

Pardy, B. and Stoehr, A. (2015) "The Failed Reform of Ontario's Mining Laws," *Journal of Environmental Law and Practice* 23, 1.

Piedra v. *Copper Mesa Mining Corporation* (2011) ONCA 191, www.ramirezversuscoppermesa.com.

PwC (2012) *Flow Through Shares for the Mining Executive*, www.pwc.com/ca/en/mining/publications/pwc-flow-through-shares-2012-05-en.pdf.

Roy, M.J., McHugh, N. and Sinclair, S. (2017) "Social Impact Bonds: Evidence-Based

Policy or Ideology?" in Greve, B. (ed.), *Handbook of Social Policy Evaluation*, Edward Elgar Pub, Northampton, MA.

SEC (Securities Exchange Commission) (2016) Press Release 2016–132, June 27, 2016, "SEC Adopts Rules for Resource Extraction Issuers under the Dodd–Frank Act," www.sec.gov/news/pressrelease/2016-132.html.

Shift (2014) "Evidence of Corporate Disclosure Relevant to the UN Guiding Principles on Business and Human Rights," http://shiftproject.org/sites/default/files/Evidence%20of%20Corporate%20Disclosure%20Relevant%20to%20the%20UN%20Guiding%20Principles%20on%20Business%20and%20Human%20Rights.pdf.

Simons, P. and Collins, L. (2010) "Participatory Rights in the Ontario Mining Sector: An International Human Rights Perspective," *McGill International Journal of Sustainable Development Law and Policy* 6(2), www.mcgill.ca/mjsdl/files/mjsdl/6_2_4_simons_and_collins_0.pdf.

Skodeberg, J. (2014) "IFC Closes Landmark Financing for Guyana Goldfields", IFC, http://ifcext.ifc.org/IFCExt/pressroom/IFCPressRoom.nsf/0/E247C1B6B7B6DC0285257D480060E98C?OpenDocument.

Statutes of Canada (2016) First Session, Forty-Second Parliament 64–65 Elizabeth II, (2015–2016), http://laws-lois.justice.gc.ca/PDF/2016_7.pdf.

The Economist (2014) "Crying Foul Guinea: Africa's Largest Iron-Ore Mining Project has been Bedeviled by Dust-Ups and Delays," www.economist.com/news/business/21635522-africas-largest-iron-ore-mining-project-has-been-bedevilled-dust-ups-and-delays-crying-foul.

Umlas, E. (n.d.) *Human Rights Due Diligence: Swiss Civil Society Pushes the Envelope*, Business and Human Rights Resource Centre, https://business-humanrights.org/en/human-rights-due-diligence-swiss-civil-society-pushes-the-envelope.

UN (n.d.(a)) *Guiding Principles Reporting Framework*, www.ungpreporting.org.

UN (n.d.(b)) Sustainable Development Goals (UN SDG), https://sustainabledevelopment.un.org/?menu=1300.

UN (n.d.(c)) *National Action Plans*, Human Rights Office of the High Commissioner, www.ohchr.org/EN/Issues/Business/Pages/NationalActionPlans.aspx.

UN (2002) *Johannesburg Plan of Implementation of Report of the World Summit on Sustainable Development*, UN Doc. A/CONF.199/20.

UN (2010) *Guide to Human Rights Impact Assessment and Management*, Global Compact, www.unglobalcompact.org/library/25.

UN (2011) *UN Guiding Principles on Business and Human Rights*, Human Rights Office of the High Commissioner, www.ohchr.org/Documents/Publications/GuidingPrinciplesBusinessHR_EN.pdf.

UN (2015), *Report of the United Nations High Commissioner on Human Rights on the Sector Consultation Entitled "Human rights and the extractive industry"*, E/CN.4/2006/92, https://documents-dds-ny.un.org/doc/UNDOC/GEN/G05/167/21/PDF/G0516721.pdf?OpenElement.

UN (2016) *Improving Accountability and Access to Remedy for Victims of Business-Related Human Rights Abuse*, Human Rights Council, www.ohchr.org/Documents/Issucs/Business/DomesticLawRemedies/A_HRC_32_19_AEV.pdf.

UN General Assembly (2015) *Transforming our world: the 2030 Agenda for Sustainable Development*, UNGAOR, 70th Sess, A/RES/70/1, [hereinafter 2030 Agenda for Sustainable Development], www.un.org/ga/search/view_doc.asp?symbol=A/RES/70/1&Lang=E.

Wielga, M. (2016) "Human Rights Impact Assessment," in *Teaching Business and Human Rights Handbook*, http://tbhrforum.org/teaching-notes/human-rights-impact-assessment.

Whittens and McKeough Lawyers and Consultants (2017) *Briefing Note "Crowd Sourced Funding Legislation Passed by Australian Parliament,"* http://whittens.com.au/briefing-note-crowd-sourced-funding-legislation-passed-by-australian-parliament.

Part III

Contemporary sustainability challenges

8 Mining, development and Indigenous peoples

Ciaran O'Faircheallaigh

Introduction

For many Indigenous people, there is an inherent contradiction between mining and sustainability. For them, the values, technologies and impacts associated with large-scale extractive industries are incommensurate with maintenance of their identity and survival as Indigenous people, with their own 'sustainability'. In terms of values, the mining industry is ultimately driven by the search for profit. Indigenous values, while certainly requiring robust systems of economic production, regard the maintenance of the ancestral land and sea country which supports these systems, and the cultural, social and spiritual practices essential for their maintenance, as having priority over financial gain. Technologies of mineral production that can reshape landscapes, change river flows and generate pollution that harms people and lands far from sites of extraction are regarded as the antithesis of 'sustainability'. In the words of Yvonne Margarula, who led the Mirrar people's fight against a second uranium mine on their traditional country in Australia's Northern Territory:

> We do not feel that our people or our country have been protected since mining came here. Government has forced us to accept mining in the past and we are concerned that you will force mining development upon us again. Previous mining agreements have not protected us or given our communities strength to survive development. A new mine will make our future worthless and destroy more of our country. We oppose any further mining development in our country.
>
> (Cited in Laszlo, 1997)

To make matters worse, decision making processes associated with large-scale mineral development have marginalised Indigenous peoples, undermining their capacity to control what occurs on their ancestral lands, with negative consequences that go well beyond the immediate impact of mining (Evans *et al.*, 2002; O'Faircheallaigh, 2016, 42–46; Sawyer and Gomez, 2012).

In sum, many Indigenous people reject the fundamental proposition that there are circumstances in which mining can contribute to sustainable development. It would be misleading to start writing on the subject of 'mining and sustainable development' in an Indigenous context without first acknowledging this point.

There are also Indigenous peoples who believe that mining can contribute to sustainable development of Indigenous peoples and communities, *if* it is conducted in a way that allows them to share substantially in its economic benefits and to control its social, environmental and cultural impacts (Bergmann, 2010; Gibson Macdonald, Zoe and Satterfield, 2014). The issue of Indigenous control is paramount. In my experience, and this is reinforced by the literature, very few Indigenous people trust corporations or state regulators to protect Indigenous interests. As I have noted elsewhere, in discussing the impact of colonisation in Australia and Canada, 'Aboriginal suspicion of the State, its motives and its actions is deeply entrenched' (O'Faircheallaigh, 2016, 40; see also Coates, 2004, 100–101, who makes the same point in relation to Indigenous peoples globally). This distrust of corporations and the state is, for example, fundamental to the sustained international campaign by Indigenous groups to achieve recognition of the principle of Indigenous Free Prior and Informed Consent (IFPIC), which requires that Indigenous peoples should be able to control whether development occurs on their lands and, if it does, what form it should take (O'Faircheallaigh, 2012).

This chapter is written from the second perspective, that mining can in principle contribute to Indigenous development, but only if it is conducted in a way that gives Indigenous peoples the power to control its impact, and by so doing allows them to share in its benefits and minimise its costs. Given the importance of control, the chapter begins with a discussion of decision making in the extractive industries, and the Indigenous role (or lack of it) in making decisions about development on their ancestral lands. I then examine two specific issues that are central to the interaction between extractive industries, Indigenous peoples and sustainability. In relation to ecological sustainability, the chapter will illustrate the way in which Indigenous participation in environmental management of large resource projects serves to minimise their negative ecological impacts. This in turn contributes to the sustainability of Indigenous societies and to the mining industry's net contribution to sustainable development. In terms of economic sustainability, the focus is on the use of mineral revenues accruing to Indigenous peoples to promote economic and social development that can be sustained after mining ends.

In addressing the conditions necessary to drive innovation and reform that can help increase mining's contribution to sustainable development, I argue that these lie in arenas broader than the management of individual mining projects. What are required are system-wide approaches designed to enhance the ability of Indigenous peoples to engage with states and the mining industry on a basis of equality. In particular, progress in mobilising the ability of Indigenous people to help mining contribute to sustainable development requires state authorities to recognise and support the capacity of Indigenous peoples to shape the basis on which they interact with extractive industries.

Sustainability and Indigenous control

Historically, Indigenous people have had little control over mineral development on their lands. While the situation varied to some extent across the globe, until the 1970s virtually all Indigenous peoples, from the Amazon rainforest to the Australian desert, from the Canadian or Soviet Arctic to the Pacific islands, faced a similar situation. State authorities disposed of mineral resources on Indigenous lands, and corporations decided whether and how to develop them, with no reference to Indigenous peoples or their interests.

This situation resulted from the denial to most Indigenous people of civil and political rights and state failure to recognise their interests in land, both of which reflected dominant racist ideologies; their lack of numerical influence in most jurisdictions; and their remote location and lack of access to financial and technical resources. The degree of violence employed in dealing with them varied across countries and over time, but the end result for nearly all Indigenous peoples affected by mining was similar (Blaser *et al.*, 2004; Coates, 2004; Wilson, 1998). They were dispossessed of their lands without compensation when these were required for mining, a reality which prevailed in Australia at least until the 1960s, and continues to prevail in parts of Asia, Africa and South America today (Bebbington and Bury, 2013; Sawyer and Gomez, 2012). They failed to share substantially in the wealth extracted from their ancestral lands, and indeed Indigenous populations in mineral-rich regions continue to be severely disadvantaged relative to their non-Indigenous neighbours (Langton and Mazel, 2008). Their cultural heritage, including sites and areas of great spiritual significance, were destroyed with impunity, and they endured social impacts created by large inflows of outsiders who generally had scant regard for their culture or values and often exploited them ruthlessly (Dixon and Dillon, 1990). Richie Howitt's summary of the experience of Aboriginal people in Western Australia's Eastern Goldfields region – 'All they get is dust' – could apply to Indigenous peoples globally (Howitt, 1990).

Matters began to change, slowly and very unevenly, from the 1970s. In an initiative that was slow to be replicated elsewhere, in 1976 the Australian government passed land rights legislation[1] that conferred on traditional owners of Aboriginal freehold land in the Northern Territory the right to reject or approve applications for exploration (and so ultimately for mining) licences. At about the same time, those Indian tribes in the United States which had been able to maintain ownership over mineral-rich lands and were recognised in law as 'dependent sovereign nations', such as the Navajo, threw off the bureaucratic control formerly exercised by the Bureau of Indian Affairs. They started to take their own decisions about development on their reserves and to deal directly with developers wishing to exploit energy and mineral resources (Jorgensen *et al.*, 1978). Of critical importance in the context of this discussion, as soon as Indigenous people were able to exercise a measure of control, immediate and rapid change occurred in the share of benefits accruing to Indigenous landowners. In the Northern Territory, for example, within just two years of the passage of land rights legislation, Aboriginal traditional owners who had previously received no economic benefits from mining on their land negotiated royalty payments at levels comparable to those traditionally applied by state or national governments in mineral-rich jurisdictions.[2] Equally significant, traditional owners also negotiated substantial cultural heritage and environmental protections in addition to those available under state regulations (O'Faircheallaigh, 2002). Perhaps most important of all, in numerous cases where they believed that mining would, on balance, not contribute to sustainable development, traditional owners refused to allow it to proceed (O'Faircheallaigh, 1988).

Elsewhere, including in large parts of Australia and the United States, the legal rights of Indigenous people changed little. They did increasingly use other means, including media campaigns, direct action and building alliances with sympathetic non-Indigenous groups, to oppose mining projects they believed would threaten their livelihoods and their cultures. Groups in disparate countries including Brazil, the Soviet Union, Canada, Papua New Guinea and Indonesia fought hard to control development, but in many cases their efforts ended in failure and, in developing countries, often in violent repression (Anguelovski, 2008; Ballard, 2001).

From the 1980s onwards, the efforts of individual Indigenous peoples were supplemented by a growing international Indigenous movement that sought recognition and protection of Indigenous rights in fora such as the United Nations, the International Labour Organisation (ILO) and the Inter-American Court of Human Rights. These efforts bore fruit with the adoption by the ILO of International Labour Office Convention 169 on the Rights of Indigenous Peoples. The Convention states that 'the rights of ownership and possession of the peoples concerned over the lands which they traditionally occupy shall be recognised' (Article 14), and that 'the rights of indigenous peoples to the natural resources pertaining to their lands shall be specifically safeguarded' (Article 15). The right to IFPIC is cited in relation to any proposed activities that require relocation of indigenous peoples, which should take place 'only with their free and informed consent' (Article 16.2). While only a small number of countries have adopted ILO 169 and while serious issues remain about its implementation, its adoption was an indication that change, however slow, was occurring in the relationship between Indigenous peoples, the State and extractive industries.

Over the last 30 years this change has continued. More Indigenous groups have been able to establish an ability to negotiate regarding the terms on which development may occur on their lands, though it is still the case today that very few have the ability to reject development if they consider its impact will render their societies unsustainable. For instance, many groups in Australia, as a result of Federal recognition of inherent Indigenous rights in land through the *Native Title Act 1993*, and in Canada, through provisions of comprehensive land claim settlements, have a right to negotiate 'impact and benefit' agreements that provide for sharing of project benefits and additional impact mitigation measures. Even in countries where such legal rights do not exist, the political mobilisation of Indigenous peoples, in some cases combined with the adoption by extractive industries of 'corporate social responsibility' policies, are resulting in the negotiation of company–Indigenous agreements (Bebbington and Bury, 2013; O'Faircheallaigh and Ali, 2008; RESOLVE, 2015).

However a 'right to negotiate' provides only an opportunity to pursue a degree of Indigenous control, it does not guarantee it. Mining companies, while often prepared to allocate at least some economic benefit to Indigenous groups, are generally very reluctant to enter agreements that give Indigenous people substantial control over the design or operation of mining projects. The result is that in only a small minority of cases where Indigenous groups are able to mobilise substantial organisational, political and reputational resources to place pressure on corporations are they able to achieve such control. For example the author's study of 45 Australian agreements found that in only a quarter were the Indigenous participants able to negotiate provisions that allowed them a substantial role in managing project environmental impacts or added significantly to the inadequate protection of Indigenous cultural heritage offered by state legislation (O'Faircheallaigh, 2016, 83–96; see also O'Neill, 2015).

In recent years the international movement for recognition of Indigenous rights has gathered momentum, culminating in the adoption by the United Nations General Assembly of the UN Declaration on the Rights of Indigenous Peoples in 2007. Indigenous control of development, through application of the principle of free prior informed consent (FPIC), constitutes a central element of the Declaration, as for example in Article 32:

1 Indigenous peoples have the right to determine and develop priorities and strategies for the development or use of their lands or territories and other resources.
2 States shall consult and cooperate in good faith with the indigenous peoples concerned through their own representative institutions in order to obtain their free and informed consent prior to the approval of any project affecting their lands or territories and other resources, particularly in connection with the development, utilization or exploitation of mineral, water or other resources.

The Declaration is not legally binding on state authorities, and states that have adopted it continue in many cases to reject its principles. For example, in Australia governments regularly use compulsory acquisition powers to acquire Indigenous land and force through projects without achieving the consent, and often against the active opposition, of Indigenous peoples (O'Faircheallaigh, 2015, 54–55). In some developing countries, states continue to use repression and violence to that same end (Bebbington and Bury, 2013; Sawyer and Gomez, 2012). Neither is the Declaration binding on the extractive industries, and many companies still regard achievement of Indigenous consent as an aspiration rather than as a necessary precondition for investing in projects on Indigenous land (Papillon and Rodon, 2017), though there are important exceptions in this regard (see, for example, Shell, 2017, 49). The principle of FPIC and the UN Declaration do constitute an important legal and moral platform from which Indigenous people can assert their demands for control over development. However, the reality is that only where they can apply economic and political pressure on domestic decision makers can they achieve acceptance of these demands (O'Faircheallaigh, 2012).

Despite some progress in recent decades, Ken Coates' general summary of the situation regarding Indigenous control over land applies equally well to the specific case of mineral development: 'even late-twentieth and early-twenty-first century efforts to establish a tiny measure of indigenous responsibility have made few inroads' (2004, 139). This constitutes a huge problem in terms of ensuring that mining contributes to sustainable development. It means that Indigenous people cannot stop projects that are inherently incapable of making such a contribution, and can only rarely insist on changes to project design and operation that might enhance the contribution of projects to sustainable development. I return to this point in discussing the conditions necessary to drive innovation and reform.

Indigenous peoples and the environmental impacts of mining

Managing the environmental impacts of mining represents an issue of critical importance both to the mining industry and Indigenous peoples. The cost to industry of failure to effectively manage environmental impacts is illustrated by other contributions to this volume. For Indigenous people the cost of failure is even greater in that it can destroy their livelihoods and social and cultural survival (Kirsch, 2014). Given this context there are, in principle, strong incentives for industry and Indigenous peoples to cooperate to minimise mining's negative effects on the environment. Indigenous peoples are often in a unique position to assist mining companies in minimising negative environmental impacts and in rehabilitating mine sites to acceptable environmental standards.

One critical resource they possess is time depth in relation to information on the existing environment ('base line data'). Typically, mining companies only start collecting base line data which they use in assessing likely project impacts, in establishing acceptable impacts, and in designing environmental monitoring and management systems, some 2–3 years before project construction is planned to commence. The difficulty is that environmental conditions can be highly variable over time, and a few years' data may not provide a sufficient basis on which to develop an understanding of environmental dynamics. Indigenous landowners draw not only on decades of experience in observing environmental conditions, an understanding of which is vital to their subsistence activities, but also on generations of experience handed down to them. Thus their participation is essential in achieving a full and accurate understanding of existing environmental dynamics, which in turn is the foundation for effective environmental protection (Nadasdy, 2003; Usher, 2000).

A second area involves the intimate and ongoing contact that many indigenous people have with their ancestral lands and waters.[3] This can place them in an excellent position to assess what environmental impacts are likely to be most significant, and what measures are likely to be effective in avoiding or mitigating them. It also allows them to quickly detect ecological changes that may signal problems with a mine's environmental management system, helping to avoid potential damage. On one occasion the author, while travelling across country with traditional owners of a major mine in north Australia, encountered a small area of lush vegetation in a place that elders said would normally be dry at that time of year. They alerted mine management to what they believed was a leak of water from the mine's open pit into sub-surface drainage channels. The mine's environmental section initially rejected this possibility, stating that its extensive water monitoring system had not picked up any sign of water moving out of the open pit. After a subsequent visit to the area revealed a further increase in vegetation, the traditional owners insisted that the mine undertake additional investigations. These revealed that water was indeed leaving the open pit, and the company was able to take remedial action.

A range of more specific indigenous knowledge can also greatly assist effective environmental management. This can include understanding of animal and bird behaviour essential in devising effective wildlife monitoring and management regimes; and knowledge of the soil and drainage conditions required for specific plants to thrive, critical for successful rehabilitation of areas disturbed by mining and associated activities (O'Faircheallaigh, 2010a).

Despite the obvious contribution Indigenous people could make in addressing a matter of enormous economic and political significance to the mining industry, in general mining companies fail to take advantage of Indigenous environmental knowledge. Indeed an extensive analysis of negotiated agreements in Australia indicates that the opposite is the case. Few companies using the opportunity agreements provide to secure Indigenous participation, and some sought to use agreements to reduce Indigenous input below that allowed by environmental legislation (O'Faircheallaigh and Corbett, 2005). These findings are consistent with the author's own experience in agreement negotiations and with Canadian research (Cragg and Greenbaum, 2002: 321–322). Even where companies are prepared to accept provisions strongly favourable to Aboriginal landowners in areas such as financial compensation, cultural heritage protection, and employment and training, they tend to strongly resist sharing control over environmental management.

Reflecting this situation, in those few cases where Indigenous peoples do manage to influence project design and operations, this usually results from protracted negotiations that require Indigenous negotiators to overcome resistance from companies, and in some cases from state authorities. Two examples illustrate this point, and at the same time highlight the potential contribution of Indigenous people to ecological sustainability.

The first involves the Voisey's Bay nickel project in Labrador, Canada. Over a number of years the project's then owner, Inco Ltd, and the Province of Newfoundland and Labrador refused to accept proposals by the area's Indigenous owners, the Innu and Inuit, to reduce the scale of the project, to minimise its impact on marine ecosystems, and to enhance the effectiveness of ongoing environmental monitoring. Decreasing the scale of the project was seen as especially important by the Innu and Inuit. It would reduce the project's environmental footprint, for example by allowing shipping schedules to be organised to minimise impact on sea ice. It would also extend project life, allowing the Innu and Inuit more time to develop the skills and organisational capacity required to take advantage of development opportunities generated by the project. Reducing project scale would thus contribute simultaneously to ecological, economic and social sustainability. Only after the Innu and Inuit demonstrated their capacity to stop the project entirely through litigation and direct action did Inco and Newfoundland accept their environmental proposals. After Voisey's Bay achieved commercial production in 2006, complete with enhanced environmental protection and at less than half the size initially planned by Inco, it operated very profitably. This is especially significant given Inco's earlier assertions that the project would not be economically viable at the smaller scale demanded by the Innu and Inuit (O'Faircheallaigh, 2016, 174–198).

The second example involves a Liquefied Natural Gas (LNG) project planned for a site north of Broome, in the Kimberley region of Western Australia (WA), by the WA State Government and a consortium of energy companies led by Woodside Energy Ltd (WEL). Here also the Aboriginal traditional owners and their regional organisation, the Kimberley Land Council, had to apply substantial financial, organisational and political resources in an extended negotiation before WA and WEL would accept a substantial Aboriginal role in environmental planning, monitoring and management. Measures ultimately included in project agreements with Aboriginal traditional owners included a requirement for WEL to build a water desalination plant if withdrawal of water from aquafers threatens significant environmental damage; and that the State must employ a compliance officer specifically for the LNG Precinct throughout its life, which could exceed 50 years, to monitor and ensure compliance with environmental conditions.

This last provision is highly significant given that state governments and other regulatory authorities have historically been ineffective in ensuring that environmental conditions continue to be monitored and enforced throughout project life (Morrison-Saunders and Arts, 2005). In recent years their deficiency in this regard has worsened as governments have cut numbers of environmental inspectors and other regulatory staff in response to budgetary pressures and political demands for 'smaller government' and less 'green tape'. For example, in 2012–2013 a newly elected conservative government in Queensland, one of Australia's largest mining states, eliminated 1,400 jobs across government departments dealing with environmental regulation, including those of 30 inspectors whose role was to check on resource development projects with environmental conditions attached. Similar trends are evident across the globe (Campbell, 2009; Goodland, 2012; Novaes and de Franca Souza, 2013; Steinzor, Glicksman and Havemann, 2014). In the case of Kimberley LNG, only Indigenous intervention ensured that monitoring of environmental of environmental compliance would be guaranteed throughout project life, with benefits not just for traditional owners but for the community as a whole.

At exactly the same time (2010–2011) as Kimberley Aboriginal Traditional Owners were negotiating these terms, similar LNG projects were being developed at Gladstone, in Central Queensland, by consortia that included some of the same energy companies involved in the Kimberley and under legislative provisions identical to those that applied in Western Australia. It is telling that in Gladstone, where Aboriginal landowners lacked the financial and political resources and the media profile enjoyed by their counterparts in the Kimberley, project agreements with traditional owners make no reference at all to environmental planning or management. This did not result from any lack of interest or environmental expertise on the part of the Gladstone traditional owners. They simply did not have the bargaining power to *insist* that industry allow them to have a role in improving the ecological sustainability of the projects involved, and so industry did not respond to their wish to play such a role (O'Faircheallaigh, 2013; O'Neill, 2015).

The reluctance of industry to afford Indigenous peoples a substantial role in environmental planning and management reflects a number of factors. One involves a general reluctance by project operators to have any external entity constrain their freedom of action in relation to aspects of project design and operations that can have a major impact on profitability and corporate reputation. Another may arise from the fact that Indigenous communities, or segments of those communities, may oppose mining projects, especially when they are initially proposed and before it is clear what their impacts might be. Companies may then suspect the motives of Indigenous leaders who insist on having a major say in environmental planning and management, fearing that they may use access to information they obtain through their participation to oppose a project on environmental grounds. But given the history of Indigenous–mining relations over many centuries, the mining industry cannot expect that Indigenous peoples will immediately welcome proposed mines with open arms. This does not mean that, if companies approach Indigenous communities with a willingness to engage and offer them a degree of control over what happens on their ancestral lands, they will not be prepared to contribute their knowledge and experience to enhance the ecological sustainability of mining projects. After all, Indigenous groups have a fundamental interest in achieving such an outcome. Finally, some company personnel may display racist or paternalist attitudes, assuming that Indigenous people have little of worth to contribute and that all wisdom resides with their own, conventional 'scientific' environmental expertise.

Industry leaders must take a role in changing attitudes towards the potential contribution of Indigenous people in reducing the environmental impacts associated with mining. Failure to do so will significantly reduce mining's net contribution to sustainable development, and at the same time leave the industry more exposed to environmental risks and their economic and reputational consequences.

Mineral revenues and Indigenous development

The issue of mining revenues and Indigenous development is contentious. Some analysts argue that it constitutes the critical mechanism through which extractive industries can contribute to the sustainable economic and social development of Indigenous peoples. Others, echoing the 'resource curse' literature, claim that mineral revenues foster dependency, cause social conflict and encourage waste and corruption. Elsewhere I have documented cases where Indigenous royalties are used to establish long-term investments funds that can generate an income after mining ends; to supplement inadequate education and health services; and to foster cultural activity and transmission of cultural knowledge (O'Faircheallaigh, 2002, 2010b; see also Gibson Macdonald *et al.*, 2014). Yet there are also many cases where Indigenous revenues have been misappropriated, used to fund substance abuse, or spent on short-term consumption of consumer goods, in the process undermining cultural practices and social structures and relationships (O'Faircheallaigh, 2002; Wild, 2016). Thus mineral revenues have the potential to destroy, as well as to promote, sustainable development.

How mineral revenues are used is obviously a critical consideration, but another and prior point must be made in relation to mineral revenues and Indigenous development. While mines on Indigenous lands in some regions of Australia, Canada and the United States generate significant payments to Indigenous landowners, in other parts of those countries and more generally across the globe, Indigenous people are usually excluded from sharing in mineral revenues. For instance, while certain communities in North Australia are entitled to royalty payments which rise with project revenues and receive millions of dollars annually, in the coal mining regions of central Queensland and New South Wales or in the gold producing regions of Western Australia, Aboriginal traditional owners typically receive fixed cash that represent only a tiny percentage of the value of minerals extracted from their land. For example, one coal agreement in New South Wales provides for a single payment of $50,000 from a project whose turnover exceeds $1 billion. Internationally, very few Indigenous groups gain a significant share of project revenues. Company allocations in most cases consist of grants for projects that are typically selected by community relations departments with a view to generating positive publicity and deflecting opposition to the company, in part by maximising local political leverage. What an Indigenous community believes is most important for its long-term sustainable development is a secondary consideration (Ballard, 2001; Cleary, 2014; Kapelus, 2002; Welker, 2014).

An obvious but important implication of this situation is that if mineral revenues are to contribute to sustainable Indigenous development, the mining industry needs to direct a much larger share of wealth generated by mining to the Indigenous owners of land from which it is extracted, and to do so more evenly across regions and projects. The minority of mines that are required to allocate substantial revenue streams to Indigenous peoples continue to operate profitably, indicating that there is no conflict between this requirement and the economic viability of the industry.

Even if this change can be achieved, revenues must be applied productively if they are to contribute to economic development, and equitably if they are to support social and cultural sustainability. Both research on mining revenues and Indigenous peoples, and the wider 'resource curse' literature, indicate that the quality and integrity of the Indigenous institutions that receive mineral revenues will be critical if these goals are to be achieved. However, existing writing on the subject is much less clear about how such institutions can be developed where they do not already exist (O'Faircheallaigh, 2011, 22). This is a particularly pressing issue for Indigenous peoples because their existing institutions have usually been developed for purposes quite different to those involved in effectively managing mineral revenues. Substantial additional research is required in the area of institutional development at the interface between mining and Indigenous peoples, but the following points can be made.

First, it is not possible to create effective institutional arrangements for managing mineral revenues which operate in isolation from their wider social and political context. Rather, the quality of governance in relation to revenues will mirror the overall quality of governance in an Indigenous society. Yet the typical response of mining companies which make payments to Indigenous groups is to create separate, non-Indigenous institutional structures, such as charitable trusts or foundations, to manage these payments (see, for example, Strelein and Tran, 2007, 5). The substantial resources needed to create legal forms and to build personal and institutional capacity are then focused on these structures. Mining companies wish to create separate and 'dedicated' institutions in the expectation that these will ensure that revenues are used in ways that are 'productive' according to the company's set of values; help to protect its 'social licence to operate'; and do not reflect badly on its reputation. Broadly, this means that revenues should be used for 'community purposes', such as service provision and infrastructure, and to generate activity valued by the mining industry, for example formal employment and establishment of business enterprises (Kapelus, 2002, 289; O'Faircheallaigh, 2016, 120, 140, 142). However, institutions created to reflect corporate rather than Indigenous values are inevitably fragile. In particular, their non-Indigenous legal forms and processes lack transparency to the community members for whose benefit they supposedly operate, and as a result they are vulnerable to exploitation by politically astute Indigenous individuals and groups pursuing their own agendas.

A recent illustration of this problem is the Groote Eylandt Aboriginal Trust, which received millions of dollars annually in royalties from BHP Billiton's manganese mine in Australia's Northern Territory. The Trust was established as a 'charitable' entity whose objectives are to 'use royalty payments and donations for the education benefit, welfare comfort and general advancement in life of the aboriginal people from time to time resident on Groote Eylandt'. However, in a period of rapidly growing revenues due to rising mineral prices towards the end of the last decade, the Trust's office holders were able to siphon off millions of dollars of revenues for their personal use (Wild 2016). This occurred against a background where community members were not in a position, for instance, to monitor and understand the financial reports of the Trust's auditors who were raising warnings about patterns of expenditure a number of years before the problem became obvious to the community.

The mining industry's hopes of controlling Indigenous revenues by using familiar, non-Indigenous institutional forms are likely to prove illusory. It would be much better advised to help build the capacity of existing institutions whose operations are well understood by Indigenous people so that these institutions can take on the additional role of allocating and managing mineral revenues. Building capacity in this way takes time. One of the clear lessons from experience to date is that the prospects for successfully managing Indigenous revenues from mining are best when institution building begins well before substantial revenues actually arrive. If work on developing institutions is only commencing at the time when payments begin to occur, political forces intent on immediately appropriating revenues are mobilised, causing internal competition and conflict. This atmosphere is far from conducive to the information provision, deliberation and negotiation that a community will need to identify broadly accepted norms and processes on which to base effective long-term management of mining revenues. Preparations need to start well before a project becomes operational. This may be difficult to achieve, for mining companies and Indigenous communities. Both tend to be preoccupied with decisions about whether or not a project will be approved, with negotiation terms of a project agreement and with managing the immediate effects of project construction. In addition, companies may be fearful of raising expectations regarding the size of revenue streams if they make an early start on building institutional capacity to manage them. But these challenges must be met, because the evidence is unequivocal that leaving institution building until a point where revenue streams have already commenced is a recipe for failure (O'Faircheallaigh, 2002, 2010b).

A final point involves the wider participation of Indigenous people in state and corporate decision making processes regarding development on Indigenous lands. As noted earlier, until very recently, and still today in many places, Indigenous people are excluded from decision making on design, approval and operation of mining projects. Yet in common with all social groups, Indigenous people learn how to take informed and effective decisions by engaging in decision making. To the extent that Indigenous peoples have the opportunity to exercise decision making in relation to other aspects of mineral development, they will enhance their capacity to make the 'right' decisions, in terms of their own values and priorities, in allocating and managing mining revenues.

Innovation and reform

The discussion so far highlights the fact that many of the world's Indigenous peoples have little opportunity to engage with the mining industry in ways that would enhance its contribution to sustainable development, including Indigenous development. For reasons explained in detail above, Indigenous control is central to any effort to change this situation. Against a background of prolonged marginalisation, dispossession and exclusion from decision making, Indigenous peoples are generally unwilling to commit to engagement with states and corporations designed to promote sustainable development unless there is a real measure of Indigenous over what happens on Indigenous lands. Another major issue is that governments and corporations have shown little inclination to willingly acknowledge the potential contribution of Indigenous people in enhancing sustainability.

Given this reality, innovation and reform that can help increase mining's contribution to sustainable development must involve systemic and fundamental change that allows Indigenous peoples to negotiate with companies and the state from a position of equality. Change at the level of corporate policy towards individual projects will not be sufficient. Such policy change is subject to reversal as a result of shifting corporate priorities, reflecting for example, declining commodity prices or changes in project ownership. In addition, state action is required to change key decision making processes that currently exclude Indigenous peoples, including those that allocate Indigenous land for mineral exploitation; decide whether or not projects should proceed; and determine project environmental conditions. More broadly, the political marginalisation and state repression applied to Indigenous people in many parts of the globe must cease.

From this perspective, a genuine commitment by government to the principles which underlie the UN Declaration and which would afford Indigenous peoples substantial control over development is essential. Such a commitment will not be easy to achieve. Across the globe governments are primarily concerned to facilitate smooth establishment of mining projects, and tend to see any attempt by Indigenous people to assert their right to control development as incompatible with this goal. State authorities must recognise that current models of governance in extractive industries are inadequate to the task of ensuring that mining is conducted in a way that gains the confidence of Indigenous people, and is consistent with principles of sustainable development. A basic change in the attitudes of political and corporate leaders towards Indigenous peoples is an essential first step, from condemning them as an 'obstacle to development', to seeing them as an asset in the pursuit of sustainable development. At a more practical level, states and corporations must support the capacity of Indigenous people to participate effectively in planning and managing mining projects on their traditional lands, in particular by helping to build Indigenous institutions that are autonomous and driven by Indigenous priorities. Only through such institutions can the potential of Indigenous people to help mining contribute to sustainable development be realised.

Conclusion

The weight of historical evidence is firmly on the side of those Indigenous people who take the view that mining is incompatible with their sustainable development and indeed with the survival of their Indigenous identity. For centuries the states and corporations that control mineral development did nothing to protect Indigenous interests, let alone to ensure that mining would contribute to Indigenous development. Little wonder that Indigenous peoples so often oppose development they are not in a position to control.

Where they do achieve a degree of control over mining, Indigenous peoples play a significant role in ensuring that the industry operates in a way that minimises its ecological impact and so increases its net contribution to sustainable development. Their role in this regard is rarely acknowledged by corporate and state decision makers and, partly as a result, Indigenous peoples continue to be excluded from decisions regarding development on their land across most of the globe. For the mining industry, this exclusion constitutes a wasted opportunity, and one it can ill afford.

Greater Indigenous control also brings with it an immediate increase in the share of revenues from mining that accrue to Indigenous peoples. This revenue does have the potential to contribute to their sustainable development, but only where they are able to build robust Indigenous institutions to allocate and use it. Industry and government can do much more to support Indigenous people in building such institutions, in part by resisting the temptation to try and impose non-Indigenous legal and institutional forms that offer them the illusion of control, but in reality are more likely to result in dissipation of valuable mineral revenues.

This returns us to the starting point for the chapter. Indigenous control of mining is the key to making it compatible with Indigenous sustainable development. Until corporations and states accept this reality, mining will in many cases act to undermine sustainable development, not promote it.

Notes

1 The *Aboriginal Land Rights (Northern Territory) Act 1976.*

2 Early agreements in the Northern Territory provided for royalties of between 3.5 and 4.5 of the value of minerals produced, at least on a par with rates charged in most mineral-rich countries, states or provinces at that time.

3 This discussion draws on O'Faircheallaigh, 2010a.

References

Anguelovski, I. (2008) 'Environmental Justice Concerns with Transnational Mining Operations: Exploring the Limitations of Post-Crisis Community Dialogues in Peru'. In O'Faircheallaigh, C. and Ali, S. (eds), *Earth Matters: Indigenous Peoples, Extractive Industries and Corporate Social Responsibility.* Greenleaf Publishing, Sheffield, 198–221.

Ballard, C. (2001) *Human Rights and the Mining Sector in Indonesia: A Baseline Study Prepared for the Mining Minerals and Sustainable Development Project of the International Institute for Environment.* Australian National University, Canberra.

Bebbington, A. and Bury, J. (eds) (2013) *Subterranean Struggles: New Dynamics of Mining, Oil and Gas in Latin America.* University of Texas Press, Austin.

Bergmann, W. (2010) 'Greens should not Force Poverty on Traditional Owners', *The Australian*, 5 April. Available at www.theaustralian.com.au/news/opinion/greens-should-not-force-poverty-on-traditional-owners/story-e6frg6zo-1225849632605.

Blaser, M., Feit, H.A. and McRae, G. (2004) *In the Way of Development: Indigenous Peoples, Life Projects and Globalization.* Zed Books, London.

Campbell, B. (ed.) (2009) *Mining in Africa: Regulation and development*. Pluto Press, London.

Cleary, P. (2014) 'Native Title Contestation in Western Australia's Pilbara Region'. *International Journal for Crime, Justice and Social Democracy* 3, 3, 133–148.

Coates, K. (2004) *A Global History of Indigenous Peoples: Struggle and Survival*. Palgrave Macmillan. London.

Cragg, W. and Greenbaum, A. (2002) 'Reasoning about Responsibilities: Mining Company Managers on What Stakeholders are Owed'. *Journal of Business Ethics* 39, 319–335.

Dixon, R. and Dillon, M. (eds) (1990) *Aborigines and Diamond Mining: The Politics of Resource Development in the East Kimberley*. University of Western Australia Press, Nedlands.

Evans, G., Goodman, J. and Lansbury, N. (eds) (2002) *Moving Mountains: Communities Confront Mining and Globalisation*. Zed Books, London.

Gibson MacDonald, G., Zoe, J.B. and Satterfield, T. (2014) 'Reciprocity in the Canadian Dene Diamond Mining Economy'. In Gilberthorpe, E. and Hilson, G. (eds), *Natural Resource Extraction and Indigenous Livelihoods: Development Challenges in an Era of Globalization*. Ashgate, Aldershot, 57–74.

Goodland, R. (2012) *Responsible Mining: The Key to Profitable Resource Development*. Institute for Environmental Diplomacy and Security, University of Vermont, Burlington.

Howitt, R. (1990) *'All They Get is the Dust': Aborigines, Mining and Regional Restructuring in Western Australia's Eastern Goldfields*. Economic and Regional Restructuring Unit Working Paper No 1, University of Sydney, Sydney.

Jorgensen, J.G., Clemmer, R.O., Little, R.L., Owens, N.J. and Robbins, L.A. (1978) *Native Americans and Energy Development*. Anthropology Resource Centre, Cambridge, Mass.

Kapelus, P. (2002) 'Mining, Corporate Social Responsibility and the "Community": The Case of Rio Tinto, Richards Bay Minerals and the Mbonambi'. *Journal of Business Ethics* 39, 275–296.

Kirsch, K. (2014) *Mining Capitalism: The Relationship between Corporations and Their Critics*. University of California Press, Oakland.

Langton, M. and Mazel, O. (2008) 'Poverty in the Midst of Plenty: Aboriginal People, the "Resource Curse" and Australia's Mining Boom'. *Journal of Energy and Natural Resources Law* 36, 1, 31–65.

Laszlo, S. (1997) 'Traditional Owners say 'No' to Jabiluka Uranium'. Available at www.greenleft.org.au/node/14464.

Morrison-Saunders, A. and Arts, J. (2005) *Assessing Impact: Handbook of EIA and SEA Follow-Up*. Earthscan, London.

Nadasdy, P. (2003) *Hunters and Bureaucrats: Power, Knowledge and Aboriginal–State Relations in the Southwest Yukon*. UBC Press, Vancouver

Novaes, R.L.M. and de Franca Souza, R. (2013) 'Legalizing Environmental Exploitation in Brazil: The Retreat of Public Policies for Biodiversity Protection'. *Tropical Conservation Science* 6, 4, 477–483.

Nwapi, C. (2011) 'Legal and Policy Responses to Environmental Offences in Relation to Alberta Oil Sands'. *Resources* 115, 1–9.

O'Faircheallaigh, C. (1988) 'Land Rights and Mineral Exploration: The Northern Territory Experience'. *Australian Quarterly* 60, 1, 70–84.

O'Faircheallaigh, C. (2002) *A New Model of Policy Evaluation: Mining and Indigenous People.* Ashgate Press, Aldershot.

O'Faircheallaigh, C. (2010a) 'CSR, the Mining Industry and Indigenous Peoples in Australia and Canada: From Cost and Risk Minimisation to Value Creation and Sustainable Development'. In Louche, C., Idowu, S.O. and Filho, W.L. (eds), *Innovative CSR: From Risk Management to Value Creation.* Greenleaf Publishing, Sheffield, 398–418.

O'Faircheallaigh, C. (2010b) 'Aboriginal Investment Funds in Australia'. In Yichong, X. and Bahgat, G. (eds), *The Political Economy of Sovereign Wealth Funds.* Palgrave Macmillan, London, 157–176.

O'Faircheallaigh, C. (2011) *Use and Management of Revenues from Indigenous–Mining Company Agreements: Theoretical Perspectives.* ATNS Working Paper No 1. Available at www.atns.net.au/atns/references/attachments/ATNSWP1_2011_OFaircheallaigh.pdf.

O'Faircheallaigh, C. (2012) 'International Recognition of Indigenous Rights, Indigenous Control of Development and Domestic Political Mobilization'. *Australian Journal of Political Science* 47, 4, 531–46.

O'Faircheallaigh, C. (2013) 'Extractive Industries and Indigenous Peoples: A Changing Dynamic?'. *Journal of Rural Studies* 30, 20–30.

O'Faircheallaigh, C. (2015) 'ESD and Community Participation: The Strategic Assessment of the Proposed Kimberley LNG Precinct, 2007–2013'. *Australasian Journal of Environmental Management* 22, 1, 46–61.

O'Faircheallaigh, C. (2016) *Negotiations in the Indigenous World: Aboriginal Peoples and Extractive Industry in Australia and Canada.* Routledge, New York.

O'Faircheallaigh, C. and Ali, S. (eds) (2008) *Earth Matters: Indigenous Peoples, Extractive Industries and Corporate Social Responsibility.* Greenleaf Publishing, Sheffield.

O'Faircheallaigh, C. and Corbett, T. (2005) 'Indigenous Participation in Environmental Management of Mining Projects: The Role of Negotiated Agreements'. *Environmental Politics* 14, 5, 629–647.

O'Neill, L. (2015) 'The Role of State Governments in Native Title Negotiations: A Tale of Two Agreements'. *Australian Indigenous Law Review* 18, 2, 29–42.

Papillon, M. and Rodon, T. (2017) 'Proponent-Indigenous Agreements and the Implementation of the Right of Free, Prior Informed Consent in Canada'. *Environmental Impact Assessment Review* 62, 216–224.

RESOLVE (2015) *From Rights to Results: An Examination of Agreements between International Mining and Petroleum Companies and Indigenous Communities in Latin America.* Available at http://solutions-network.org/site-fpic/files/2015/09/From-Rights-to-Results-Sept-2015-FINAL-ENG.pdf.

Sawyer, S. and Gomez, E.T. (eds) (2012) *The Politics of Resources Extraction: Indigenous Peoples, Multinational Corporations and the State.* Palgrave Macmillan, London.

Shell (2017) *Shell Sustainability Report 2016.* Available at https://reports.shell.com/sustainability-report/2016.

Steinzor, R., Glicksman, R.L. and Havemann, A. (2014) 'EPA's Retreat from Enforcement will Harm Chesapeake Bay'. Available at http://progressivereform.org/articles/EPA_StrategicPlan_IssueAlert_1402.pdf.

Strelein, L. and Tran, T. (2007) *Taxation, Trusts and the Distribution of Benefits under Native Title Agreements*. Australian Institute for Aboriginal and Torres Strait Islander Studies, Canberra.

Usher, P.J. (2000) 'Traditional Ecological Knowledge in Environmental Assessment and Management'. *Arctic* 53, 2, 183–193.

Welker, M. (2014) *Enacting the Corporation: An American Mining Firm in Post-Authoritarian Indonesia*. University of California Press, Berkeley.

Wilson, J. (1998) *The Earth Shall Weep: A History of Native America*. Picador, London.

Wild, K. (2016) 'Rosalie Lalara, Ex-Public Officer of Australia's Richest Land Trust, Pleads Guilty to $475k Theft'. ABC News, 29 March. Available at www.abc.net.au/news/2016-03-29/rosalie-lalara-ex-land-trust-official-pleads-guilty-475k-theft/7282378.

9 Transit worker accommodation in remote Australian mining communities

Push and pull factors

Fiona Haslam McKenzie and Guy Singleton

Introduction

Mining booms in Australian history have had enduring social and economic legacies since gold was discovered in 1851. Since then, successive boom and bust periods have been responsible for strong population growth with concomitant expansion of towns and subsequent population and community contraction. In the past, the most affected towns were those near to the mine sites. The most recent resources boom (2001–2014) had different impacts. While there was significant economic and population growth, particularly in Western Australia and Queensland, the epicentres of mining activity during the boom, most of the growth occurred in the capital cities, Perth and Brisbane, hundreds of kilometres from the mine sites. The local towns close to mining activity experienced some growth, but compared to that of Perth and Brisbane, it was modest. Instead of living locally, a significant proportion of mine workers regularly commute on mining company-chartered flights from their home or *source* communities to the *host* community, where they live in company sponsored accommodation, transit worker accommodation (TWA) for compressed blocks of work periods. While there, the company provides full board and, in most cases, leisure activities, support services and transport to and from the mine site. Large transit worker accommodation facilities, especially those close to established towns in mining areas have attracted criticism, with many local community leaders, politicians and business owners claiming they prevent the towns from expanding and developing as sustainable and viable urban centres.

Long-distance commuting (LDC) practices such as fly-in/fly-out (FIFO) and drive-in/drive-out are not new, nor is labour mobility in Australia (Haslam McKenzie, 2016a), but the scale of labour mobility and the escalation of the practice during the most recent resources boom attracted considerable community, media and policy-maker attention (Bowler, 2003; House of Representatives Standing Committee on Regional Australia, 2013; Probyn, 2013).

This chapter will discuss the reasons for the proliferation of a non-residential mine workforce and the future of TWA in the face of community and political antagonism in Western Australia. For a variety of reasons which will be considered in the next section, what most excites angst in regional community leadership, local government and business organisations is where and how transient and LDC workers are accommodated and the perceived lack of investment in *host* communities by mining companies and their employees (Miller *et al.*, 2012; Rolfe and Kinnear, 2013). The next section will present the key concerns and the complex economic and social consequences transit worker accommodation present for *host* communities. The changes in policy and workplace conditions that provide the context for a transformation in the way mine work is conducted will then be outlined, followed by an overview of the social conditions and expectations of the modern Australian workforce. The corporate perspective on labour force management priorities and accommodation conditions, particularly in remote locations, will then be presented. The implications of the options for both the mining industry and the local communities will be discussed, particularly in light of the transition from the labour-intensive construction phase of the mining boom to a more steady-state operational phase. The chapter will conclude with a summary of the multiple reasons for LDC and why it is a practice which is not likely to abate, but rather, continue in increasingly straitened economic conditions. Developing strategies to enhance shared benefits is therefore a community, government and corporate priority.

The drivers for long distance commuting and transit worker accommodation

Long-distance commuting has been a feature of the Australian mining industry for several decades. The reasons for this are various, including geography, neoliberal economic policies, changing social expectations and the imposition of sophisticated technologies. Long-distance commuting was of little concern to community leaders and politicians until the most recent iron-ore boom which lasted for more than a decade, with iron-ore prices reaching unprecedented levels for prolonged periods. At the same time that global iron-ore prices were reaching unprecedented levels, other commodities, for example, gold, were experiencing a downturn. Underscoring the interrelated nature of the resources industries and the boom and bust cycles, all industry sectors were impacted by high demand for skilled and experienced labour and especially the demand for mining services. Mining companies responded rapidly to international market demand, principally from China, expanding their labour force as quickly as possible, and due to accommodation shortages, TWAs were a convenient and efficient option.

Most large resource deposits are located in remote areas of Western Australia (see Figure 9.1). The largest and highest value iron-ore projects are concentrated in the Pilbara region, in the northwest, with smaller and

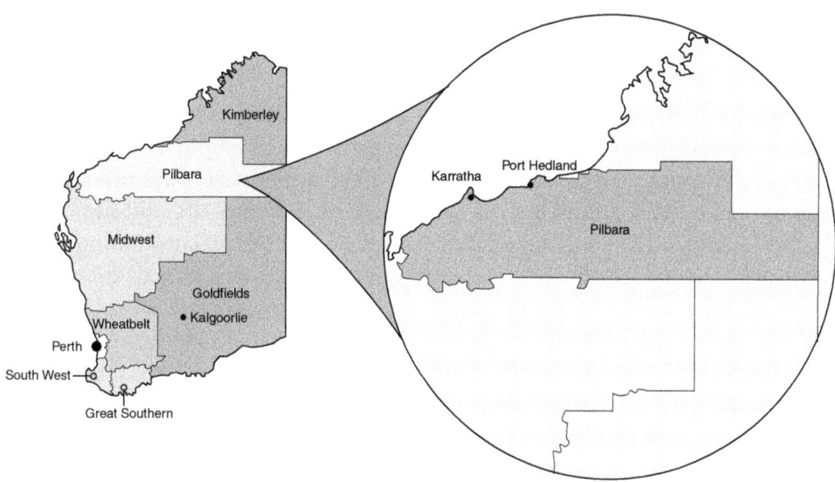

Figure 9.1 Western Australian resource locations.

Source: Bureau of Resources and Energy Economics, 2012.

marginal deposits in the Mid West region. Gold and other resources are concentrated in the eastern regions north of Kalgoorlie-Boulder. The two major towns of the Pilbara region, Karratha and Port Hedland, located 1,500 and 1,750 kilometres respectively from Perth, were under extreme growth pressures from 2002. In 2001, their populations were 15,800 and 13,000. Between 2001 and 2013 the number of people employed in mining more than tripled (Australian Bureau of Statistics, 2013) and the towns were not able to cope with the demand for accommodation and other services.

Between 2001 and 2006 the population of the Shire of Roebourne (Karratha) increased by 17 per cent and Port Hedland at a similar rate (Australian Bureau of Statistics, 2012), putting the towns under considerable pressure. Services such as education, health, policing, childcare, retail and small businesses all came under pressure from increased demand but also because accommodation became extremely expensive. Mining communities exhibit housing tenure characteristics different from the Australian average, with significantly lower levels of housing ownership, consistent with the more transient and temporary nature of the population in mining towns (Haslam McKenzie *et al.*, 2009). In the case of the Pilbara towns, there had been no forward planning for increased housing or accommodation and there were highly complex legal and administrative processes including title and mining leases which constrained or delayed land release.

For more than three decades, Australia has followed a neoliberal policy agenda; government has withdrawn from sectors where market forces are judged to work effectively and efficiently. Government therefore had few policy levers with which to address the particular issues of a boom town economy (Cheshire, 2010). On the contrary, there were taxation and policy agenda that pushed the private market away from providing housing and services in remote communities and which made TWA a more attractive option for mining companies and their employees. Perhaps the most catalytic was the introduction of the Fringe Benefits Tax in 1986 which imposed a tax on employers for non-cash benefits provided to employees. Company-supplied housing attracted this tax. The alternative, accommodating employees in TWA and flying the workforce to the mine site, did not attract the tax. Instead, the costs associated with a long-distance commuting workforce are deemed an employer cost and are therefore a tax deduction. In addition, there are tax advantages for the commuting worker, who can claim a living away from home allowance and remote work allowances.

Industrial relations laws and agreements shifted from strongly unionised and standardised working arrangements in the 1980s to arrangements giving the employer and employee considerably more flexibility. Compressed work arrangements with 12 hour shifts and block rosters are an accepted work practice enabling companies to operate at maximum capacity 24/7 and providing employees with the opportunity to have blocks of leisure time in their home community. TWA enabled employers to maximise their accommodation investment, as shown in Figures 9.2 and 9.3, and minimise their capital costs.

Figures 9.2 High density TWA in Gap Ridge Karratha.

Source: Google Earth, 19 August 2016.

Figure 9.3 High density TWA at Port Haven Port Hedland airport.
Source: Google Earth, 19 August 2016.

Long-distance commuting and *host* communities

For most Australian mining towns, even the more established regional centres such as Kalgoorlie-Boulder, Broken Hill and Mount Isa, the boom and bust cycle is a feature of their history. The mining towns of the Western Australian North West are relatively young, (established in the 1960s), and have struggled to be robust communities. Community leaders and business owners in the Pilbara were keen to grow their towns on the back of the most recent super-boom and looked to mining companies and government to encourage a less transient workforce and entice people to live, invest and spend locally for all but the most remote mine sites. They complained of 'the fly-over effect' whereby remote management, outsourcing of services and the use of non-resident workers and contractors mean that there is limited local economic or social input or throughput and therefore limited impetus for business growth. Even where companies have a local procurement policy, smaller towns typically do not have sufficient capacity or levels of diversification to supply large-scale mining operations, except for minor supply goods.

Community leaders also protest at the unrecorded cost of long-distance commuting work arrangements, particularly on public infrastructure and utilities. Part of this problem is that agencies such as the Australian Bureau of Statistics do not adequately record labour force mobility. The five-yearly census does not specifically ask about labour force mobility. As noted by Haslam McKenzie (2016a, p. 17)

> accurate data is important for State governments and local government authorities which depend upon Commonwealth grants and payments for a range of service delivery commitments including health, education, disability services and affordable housing. Payments are made based on Commonwealth estimates of growth factors, including population. In places where there is a high rate of workforce mobility there are invariably complaints of demand exceeding supply of services or inadequate infrastructure investment.

A high-density TWA facility can be operational within six months and have an immediate impact on water, electricity and other infrastructure which can compromise the capacity for local government and similar agencies to service other planned developments.

Local government has some influence and jurisdiction over TWA when the facility is located in a town area, but exploration camps and TWA on mining leases do not need planning approval from local government when approved through State-level agreements. Some State Agreements, many of which were negotiated decades ago, exempted mining companies from paying local government rates. Some Agreements were settled in the 1960s when there were few reliable transport links in remote parts of Western Australia and mining companies built their own facilities including entire towns. For established, 'open' towns, State and Federal government had a much bigger role in resourcing communities and regional towns. ('Normalisation' (the transformation of 'closed' company-owned towns to 'open', publicly accessible towns with local government and services provided by the state) for most company-owned mining towns in Western Australia began in the early 1980s.) The four local government authorities in the Pilbara consider themselves at a significant disadvantage not being able to charge some of their largest land holders rates, one of the few avenues by which the local government sector can raise revenue.

Nonetheless, most companies operating in Western Australia take their social licence to operate seriously and regularly liaise with the local authorities and sponsor local activities and partner in a variety of community-building arrangements. As noted by Cheshire (2010, p. 12), depictions of mining companies as greedy and self-serving is unfortunate as 'the dynamics of corporations involved in governance are at least as complex and challenging as those of governments and communities'.

Community leaders complain that transient workers do not have a sense of place of community and do not invest themselves or any of their assets in mining communities. When presented with these claims in research interview sessions, many workers agree, although they also claim they do not actively cause negative impacts in the communities where they work, which is contrary to the claims made by Carrington *et al.* (2012). Community leaders also complain of 'churn' but many (Storey and Shrimpton, 1991; Rolfe, 2013) would argue that contractors and resource workers are part of a peripatetic industry.

Work and lifestyle choices

Public policy context and aligning housing and infrastructure supply with production demands are just a few of the factors contributing to the increasing reliance of mining companies and contracting firms on TWA and long-distance commuting employment practices. Perhaps a stronger driver is work and lifestyle choices of the twenty-first century employee and their families. Population patterns throughout Australia have followed a trend of people moving away from rural and remote areas to live in the capital cities with all the concomitant services, facilities and opportunities. During the mining boom, demand for labour and mine services usually exceeded local supply and consequently labour was sourced from outside the local areas, usually the capital cities.

Mobile labour attracts a premium salary and conditions to compensate for the time spent away from home and social networks. For many employees this gave them the opportunity to invest and set themselves and their families up with assets, which they would not otherwise be able to afford. The extent of benefits for local development in the *host* community are relatively limited but the long-distance commuting workforce is effectively transferring the economic and social benefits of employment away from host communities to those where the workforce resides with considerable multiplier effect, particularly for those who live in other rural, regional and remote communities (McKenzie *et al.*, 2014).

While the mining employee is willing to work in remote locations, their family's needs and wants are not easily accommodated. Families are often reluctant to relocate themselves to remote and rural communities where jobs for partners, and education, health, recreation and other social services are not comparable to those where they are currently located, or to move away from where family and social networks are established. For those workers (for example, construction workers and contractors) with peripatetic work patterns, long-distance commuting means that their family base, services and infrastructure are constant while they are often changing jobs and job locations.

Sophisticated technological advances mean that mine lifecycles are increasingly shorter and previously 'hard to get' resources are accessible.

Long-distance commuting arrangements provide employers and employees considerable flexibility and the workforce is less tied to particular jobs, locations and even resources, potentially enhancing career opportunities. This is particularly the case for contractors whose work patterns are variable, generally shorter and for specific tasks.

Most mine workers work compressed block shifts with a mix of day and night rosters of 12 hour, sometimes longer, shifts. There is little time to do anything but work and recuperate in readiness for the following shift. The long-distance commuting workforce who reside in company-provided TWA do not have to prepare meals, clean their accommodation or, for some, drive between the minesite and the TWA, giving them longer time to rest between shifts.

Industry perspective

At the heart of this discussion lies a cyclic tug of war between the resource proponent's objective of reaching and maintaining a state of project profitability, and policy makers within local and state government and other key stakeholders, keenly looking for ways to avoid Western Australia's resource-rich regional zones from continued exposure to potential issues associated with the resource curse and Dutch disease. It is clear there are sound arguments for both cases; the socio-economic benefit from more diverse and resilient economies in regional areas is in both the state and national interest. However, some consideration should be given to the fundamental drivers within industry which influence its preference for working arrangements that include the use of LDC and TWA. A more informed understanding of the industry perspective may shift perceptions for the greater net good of regional communities through all stages of market cycles.

It should be noted that the often portrayed pan-resource sector is in reality a facile take on what is a highly diverse and multi-tiered sector – not only with regard to company scale and market capitalisation, but also in relevant areas of life of operations, commodity price volatility, and location of the resource to be mined. All these factors play into a company's ability to finance a project, mobilise goods and services to develop a project, and to service it with the required labour force.

For example, the longevity of a resource project can, in a simplistic sense, influence its capital allocation and operating structure; assuming similar positive market conditions, a 30-year iron-ore strip mine is likely to be more attractive to project financers than an underground gold mine with a projected three year life. Both projects may well return a profit, but there is greater uncertainty and risk with the shorter-life gold mine. The gold price is exposed to greater levels of market shock, while iron-ore values have been historically more stable. The profit margins, or economics, of each project respectively vary considerably.

This plays into how the project's infrastructure and labour supply is both required and administered. The long life iron-ore mine may have greater access to finance and be physically larger than the gold mine. The infrastructure required for the iron-ore mine will be significantly greater, and in turn, the initial construction-phase of the mine will be larger and run for a longer period of time. The company will need to employ a greater number of fixed-term workers to construct the project. Once completed, employee numbers will be reduced to only meet operational needs.

If this scenario is layered over the Pilbara in Western Australia, the recent boom and bust transition is perhaps usefully depicted as the transition from a construction to an operational state. In its construction state, that happened to coincide with other Pilbara-based commodities' price strength, and local labour markets were quickly exhausted. Companies needed to look further afield to meet their needs. Given the temporary nature of this stage of the project, both companies and workers are often reluctant to overcommit to permanently relocating and investing in their place of employment, knowing that at some point, the need to hire this workforce would cease.

Much of the mining activity that fed the 'mining boom' rhetoric was catalysed by sustained bull-pricing in iron-ore, gas and oil pricing (caused by rapid market expansion in nearby southeast Asian markets). This led to an influx of capital investment into Western Australia's Pilbara region as a range of domestic and international companies rushed to increase production levels and get their products to market. The exhaustion of local labour markets was intensified by this market condition.

As discussed earlier in this chapter, companies relied on TWA to accommodate this temporary workforce. The change in workforce needs has left some of these facilities underutilised, or simply redundant. Critics of transient workforce arrangements argue that now the workforce has reduced to a level likely to be maintained for the duration of the actual mining component of the project, it would be preferable for the companies to switch completely from transient to residential workforce arrangements, as both companies and employees are afforded some medium-term assurance of tenure and project life.

There is clearly some merit to this approach – that industry could do more to facilitate a residential labour transition. However, both industry and the labour markets would need to be aligned to make this work. With the rapidly increasing technological applications across the resource sector, a significant number of highly skilled employees would need to be willing to relocate themselves and their families to their place of employment. The difference with this workforce over that needed for the construction phase is that they likely hold much higher levels of sector mobility, meaning they can and will move to other industries if the conditions of employment do not suit them or their families. Few companies are willing to risk compromising their skilled and experienced labour force.

If we go back to consider the gold mine throughout this period, its journey through the last ten years may have been slightly different. Its construction stage would have been much smaller and the period shorter. The workforce would have been accommodated in the same accommodation facility intended for the future operational staff. As with much of the gold sector, its proximity to regional towns or settlements is unfeasibly distant in order to be relied upon. Employees are required to work at least 12-hour shifts, and it is deemed unsafe to travel medium to long distances either side of a shift.

The planned three-year life of the underground mine, while it may roll over many times to become a much longer operational period than originally planned, does not allow for capital allocation beyond each three-year period. Investment in permanent residential workforce accommodation within distant regional centres is again unfeasible.

Acknowledging the hypothetical characterisations between the gold and iron-ore mine are both simplistic and at the extreme of sectoral diversity. However, they have been included in this chapter to highlight that the case for or against residential and long-distance commuting workforces within the resource sector needs to consider the varying drivers and operational realities experienced between those organisations, employees and regions that make up this reality.

Discussion

In a neoliberal policy environment it is likely that long-distance commuting will continue to be a feature of the Australian workplace. Long-distance commuting arrangements offer mining companies workforce flexibility and the opportunity to quickly react to market and other forces. However, the future of TWA is not as assured. Community leaders, local politicians and small business owners have been vocal in their condemnation of LDC and its perceived suppression of growth in the towns that support mining activities due to company-owned TWA. While they agree that a long-distance commuting workforce is appropriate for remote locations where there is not a town or services nearby, but where there are large TWA complexes such as those in Figures 9.2 and 9.3, both of which are located near regional centres (Karratha and Port Hedland), they are urging companies to close the facilities, especially when there is surplus accommodation vacant in the towns. As the mining boom slows and the frenetic development and construction phase transitions to a steady operational state, there have been demands on resource companies to use local housing and accommodation facilities and services. They are particularly keen on urging companies to use local labour for cleaning, gardening and security services and hence maintain the population locally.

In 2015 BHP Billiton negotiated with the Western Australian government to extend the lease of a 1,200-bed TWA in Newman, a small town (servicing the iron-ore industry) of approximately 7,000 people in the inland of the Pilbara region, for a further 20 years. It caused considerable local and political anger in some quarters because the company had established the facility in the 2004 as a temporary TWA with the intention of demobilising it in mid-2007. The facility, aesthetically, looked temporary, and the company admitted that less than half of the facility would be maintained. However, the real issue was that the occupants of a TWA do not need to use town facilities or patronise local businesses. The local member of parliament, Mr Brendon Grylls, was particularly vocal, claiming it no longer made economic sense for companies facing decade-low commodity prices to continue to maintain large fly-in/fly-out workforces when most people could afford to live in a mining town (Burrell, 2016). Mining companies do not divulge the cost per employee of maintaining a TWA but Mr Grylls claims it is about $70,000–90,000 per employee per year in addition to the regular transport costs of flying workers to the *host* community. After considerable media and lobbying, the company agreed to close the TWA and accommodate the employees in unoccupied company-owned houses in the town.

At a similar time, the Western Australian Chamber of Minerals and Energy undertook a workforce survey which indicated that only one in four FIFO workers would stay in the job if it changed to a local role, despite the job market being considerably tighter than it was two years prior. The resources industry is also at pains to emphasise that not all its employees are FIFO workers and that approximately half live locally. Research has clearly shown that the LDC lifestyle does not suit everyone and the tenure of LDC employees is mixed (Haslam McKenzie and Hoath, 2014; Whalen and Schmidt, 2016).

Mining companies and employees are mindful of the mercurial and often unpredictable nature of the resources industries. As noted by Markey *et al*., (2015), the corporate sector places great importance on productivity, the reduction of production costs and the rationalisation of unproductive operations, and companies react quickly to mitigate unnecessary costs. Petrova and Marinova (2013) and Franks *et al*., (2013) explain the interrelated nature of the social and economic impacts of mining, which are often mutually dependent, cumulative and synergistic. The communities, especially in the Pilbara, are mono-economies and their fortunes are closely tied to that of the local commodities. As global prices have contracted, so too has the workforce and many employees are unwilling to move permanently to these towns when their job tenure is not guaranteed and employment prospects for their partner and families is precarious.

Government and community leaders maintain that the cost of maintaining a TWA, particularly during a downturn, is more expensive than a residential workforce. Companies, on the other hand, argue there are additional fixed costs and other costs, which they either do not understand or have not factored into their assessments. The Fringe Benefits Tax (FBT), for example, introduced in 1986, imposes a tax on the employer for any non-salary benefits provided to employees. Company-paid housing attracts the tax whereas TWA and costs associated with long-distance commuting are an operational expense and therefore exempt from FBT. Many of the resources companies have sold off their residential property portfolios, claiming they are not in the business of real estate. From a social perspective, company-owned facilities keep a large workforce influx contained, thus limiting impacts on local housing and employment markets (Haslam McKenzie, 2016b), and also addressing some of the anti-social behaviour issues reported by Carrington and Pereira (2011).

In 2016, the Pilbara communities are struggling with the post-boom realities of accommodation glut, depopulation and businesses closing. In the event that politicians and local community leaders were successful in lobbying mining companies to limit LDC and encourage a higher proportion of local employment, there would be a strong demand for big ticket services such as schools, health providers, policing and justice during the boom period, but underutilised facilities in the post-boom period. The TWA arrangements therefore have the potential to protect the local community and government from the excesses of the highs and lows of the market. Realistically, then, in a neoliberal policy environment with tight public budgetary controls and severe fiscal equalisation tax redistributions away from resource-rich state, it is unlikely that government will push too hard to limit TWA and the LDC workforce.

Not all companies are committed to long-distance commuting, however. A large ammonia production facility is being built in Karratha and the company has particularly targeted workers with families in their recruitment drive, claiming a local, residential workforce will enhance workforce continuity. Importantly, however, the company has not made housing part of the recruitment package; housing arrangements are the responsibility of the employee – a very different scenario to the boom times.

Conclusion

This chapter has focused on the reasons why long-distance commuting arrangements have proliferated throughout all industry sectors, but particularly in the resources industries over the last two decades. It contributes to the small but growing literature, which informs a more nuanced perspective on the socio-economic impacts of labour mobility, the use of TWA and the drivers which have resulted in their widespread use across a variety of industry sectors, but particularly the resources sector. It acknowledges the complex economic and social consequences of the arrangements on the *host* communities and on employees who regularly commute long distances away from home for work.

There is considerable literature on the negative impacts of long-distance commuting, particularly FIFO. Long-distance commuting does not suit everyone and, for many, the high remuneration and other incentives associated with the workforce practice is not enough to compensate for not being amongst family and the local community. Many do not like the living arrangements in TWA, and they do not usually last long in jobs that require LDC. However, for many, LDC is their preferred work arrangement. For companies, there are many advantages associated with labour mobility. The shortcomings of TWA have received considerable public exposure, but to date there has been limited assessment of the benefits, and why companies choose TWA over residential housing.

Companies work hard to minimise costs. It is therefore a concern that community leaders and politicians are applying considerable pressure to close TWA when the alternatives do not appear to have been properly thought through. Few mining operations in proximity to towns are wholly accommodated in TWA. Mining operations do and will require different mixes of residential and non-residential living arrangements for a variety of reasons. The risks of 'fly-over and 'hollow economy' effects need to be addressed and companies should work with local communities to ensure local businesses derive benefits. Communities must therefore work to identify their points of leverage to ensure they benefit from LDC rather than bearing the costs.

The need for longer-term and more strategic benefits for local communities should be addressed more systematically by industry and government. While 'partnering' is an often used axiom in resources industry public relations, there is a need for greater collaboration across the resources sector, incorporating a better understanding of potential shared benefits for communities and mining projects' business. Companies need to develop strategies to ensure local and regional businesses are given the opportunity to derive benefits from LDC worker arrangements and the mining industry. Similarly, communities and politicians must also have an appreciation of company priorities and be mindful of what they wish for, since many are not necessarily reaping the results they hoped.

References

Australian Bureau of Statistics. 2012. *Census of Population and Housing*. Canberra.

Australian Bureau of Statistics. 2013. *Australian Social Trends: Towns of the mining boom*. Canberra.

Bowler, J. 2003. Fly-in, fly-out issues. *Western Australian Parliament*. Perth: Hansard, 14 August.

Burrell, A. 2016. Wind up FIFO camps in Pilbara, Nationals tell miners. *The Australian*, 25 January.

Carrington, K. and Pereira, M. 2011. Assessing the social impacts of the resources boom on rural communities. *Rural Society* 21, 2–20.

Carrington, K., Hogg, R., Mcintosh, A. and Scott, J. 2012. Crime talk, FIFO workers and cultural conflict on the mining boom frontier. *Australian Humanities Review* 53, 1–14.

Cheshire, L. 2010. A corporate responsibility? The constitution of fly-in, fly-out mining companies as governance partners in remote, mine affected localities. *Journal of Rural Studies* 26, 12–20.

Franks, D., Brereton, D. and Moran, C. 2013. The cumulative dimensions of impact in resource regions. *Resources Policy* 38, 640–647.

Haslam McKenzie, F. 2016a. Long distance commuting in Australia. In: Haslam McKenzie, F. (ed.), *Labour Force Mobility in the Australian Resources Industry: Socio-economic and Regional Impacts.* Singapore: Springer.

Haslam McKenzie, F. 2016b. The socio-economic impacts of long distance commuting on people and communities. In: Haslam McKenzie, F. (ed.), *Labour Force Mobility in the Australian Resources Industry: Socio-economic and Regional Impacts.* Singapore: Springer.

Haslam McKenzie, F. and Hoath, A. 2014. The socio-economic impact of mine industry commuting labour force on source communities. *Resources Policy* 42, 45–52.

Haslam McKenzie, F., Rowley, S., Phillips, R., Birdsall-Jones, C. and Brereton, D. 2009. *Housing Market Dynamics in Resource Boom Towns.* Perth: Australian Housing and Urban Research Institute (www.ahuri.edu.au/publications/p80370).

House of Representatives Standing Committee on Regional Australia. 2013. *Cancer of the bush or salvation of our cities.* Canberra: Parliament of the Commonwealth of Australia.

Markey, S., Ryser, L. and Halseth, G. 2015. 'We're in this all together': Community impacts of long-distance labour commuting. *Rural Society* 24, 131–153.

McKenzie, F., Haslam McKenzie, F. and Hoath, A. 2014. Fly-in/fly-out, flexibility and the future: Does becoming a regional FIFO source community present opportunity or burden? *Geographical Research* 52(4), 430–441.

Miller, E., Van Megen, K. and Buys, L. 2012. Diversification for sustainable development in rural and regional Australia: How local community leaders conceptualise the impacts and opportunities from agriculture, tourism and mining. *Rural Society* 22, 2–16.

Petrova, S. and Marinova, D. 2013. Social impacts of mining: Changes within the local social landscape. *Rural Society* 22, 153–165.

Probyn, A. 2013. Windsor tax war on FIFO. *The West Australian*, 11 February, p. 4.

Rolfe, J. 2013. Predicting the economic and demographic impacts of long distance commuting in the resources sector: A Surat basin case study. *Resources Policy* 38, 723–732.

Rolfe, J. and Kinnear, A. 2013. Populating regional Australia: What are the impacts of non-resident labour force practices on demographic growth in resource regions? *Rural Society* 22, 125–137.

Storey, K. and Shrimpton, M. 1991. 'Fly-in' mining: Pluses and minuses of long distance commuting. *Mining Review* 15, 27–35.

Whalen, H. and Schmidt, G. 2016. The women who remain behind: Challenges in the LDC lifestyle. *Rural Society* 25, 1–14.

Part IV

Corporate sustainability approaches

10 Sustainability reporting in the mining industry

Current status and future research directions

Sumit K. Lodhia

Introduction

This chapter focuses on sustainability reporting practices in the mining industry, based on a review of the existing literature in this area. An overview of sustainability reporting is provided at the outset before emphasis shifts to the literature on sustainability reporting in the mining industry. The chapter concludes with future directions into research in areas that have not been adequately covered in prior literature.

Initially, the chapter focuses on the accounting process which is the primary tool to measure business performance. It is highlighted that sustainability accounting and reporting is an extension of accounting with a focus on the management and reporting of social and environmental issues. Sustainability reporting is the concern of this chapter, with the rest of the section discussing disclosure media, benefits and criticisms of sustainability reporting, and the prominent theories and methods used in prior literature on sustainability reporting. The emphasis then shifts to sustainability reporting in the mining industry.

The literature on sustainability reporting in the mining industry is analysed on the basis of the key findings before the contexts, theories and methods discussed in these studies are highlighted. The initial literature with a primary focus on reporting across the entire minerals industry has been succeeded by studies that address specific contexts and issues, employing newer theories and focusing on a range of media for disclosure.

The chapter concludes with directions for future research into sustainability reporting in the mining industry. Emphasis is on environmental issues such as climate change and water management, broader social issues, integrated reporting, assurance of sustainability reporting and social media communication.

Sustainability reporting

The increasing focus on social and environmental issues in contemporary times has been accompanied by an increasing emphasis on the role of corporations in addressing such issues (Lodhia, 2007). This is especially the case for industries that are socially and/or environmentally sensitive.

Accounting has been at the forefront of measurement of business performance, providing an understanding of an organisation's profitability, financial position and cash flow. Internal mechanisms such as management accounting provide the tools to manage an organisation through a focus on planning, control and decision making. Monetary and non-monetary measures are used to provide information to enable these tasks to be accomplished. The other component of accounting is financial accounting, which provides information to those external to an organisation in order to enable the users of this accounting information to assess the organisation's performance over an accounting period (which is usually one year). The annual report is the outcome of the financial accounting process, providing an understanding of financial performance in a particular year. Accounting standards, corporate law and stock exchange listing requirements provide mandatory requirements for disclosure of information through these reports. Further, an assurance/auditing process is undertaken to ensure that the financial information is an accurate reflection of what has transpired in an organisation over the accounting period.

The increasing emphasis on social and environmental issues has led to a need for a much broader focus on organisational performance (Burritt and Schaltegger, 2010). Merely focusing on financial information at the expense of an organisation's social and environmental impacts is no longer the norm (Bebbington *et al.*, 2014). The users of accounting information are now complemented by other stakeholders who would have an interest in the financial, social and environmental aspects of business performance. Consequently, there is a need to extend the measures for organisational performance with social and environmental information to complement financial information.

Sustainability accounting and reporting has emerged as a response to the increasing importance of social and environmental issues and the rise of a range of different stakeholders (Lodhia, 2013). Drawing upon the accounting tools of management accounting and financial accounting, sustainability accounting and reporting focuses on two major components. Sustainability management addresses the internal management of social and environmental issues within an organisation while sustainability reporting requires the disclosure of social and environmental information to a broad range of external stakeholders.

The focus of this chapter is on sustainability reporting because there is a depth of evidence on this phenomenon compared to the internal aspects of sustainability accounting and reporting. This is because reporting practices can be ascertained through publicly available reports and information on corporate websites. An assessment of management practices requires engagement with managers, and often accessibility to such personnel may be limited. Assessing sustainability reporting in the mining industry provides focus to this study and ensures that there is sufficient evidence available to draw generalisations on the current status of practices in the mining industry.

Sustainability reporting provides accountability of an organisation's social and environmental performance to its stakeholders (Lodhia, 2013). Disclosure of such information is not merely limited to financial information, both monetary and non-monetary (physical)[1] information is of importance in conjunction with narrative information on sustainability performance (Schaltegger *et al.*, 2006). The initial disclosure of social and environmental issues was in annual reports, given that is the primary document organisations use to communicate their financial performance (Lodhia, 2004b). More recently, the increasing importance of social and environmental issues has led to separate standalone reports which address these issues specifically (Lodhia, 2004b). These reports have varying titles such as environmental reports, social and environmental reports, community reports, health and safety reports, as well as sustainability reports. Corporate websites (Lodhia, 2010) and social media (Lodhia and Stone, 2017) can be used to disclose social and environmental information on a more timely basis than periodic disclosure media such as annual reports and sustainability reports. The personnel involved in sustainability reporting include communications and public relations staff, in conjunction with sustainability/environmental staff and, to a limited extent, accountants.

Sustainability reporting provides many benefits to organisations. It enhances the reputation and image of an organisation (Melo and Garrido-Morgado, 2012), assists in gaining stakeholder confidence (Kaur and Lodhia, 2014, 2016, forthcoming), could lead to operational and management improvements (Gray *et al.*, 2014), improves the management of risks (Bebbington *et al.*, 2008), assists to benchmark and differentiate organisational performance (Gray *et al.*, 2014), assists in meeting voluntary and mandatory reporting requirements (Gray *et al.*, 2014) and could improve financial performance (Dhaliwal *et al.*, 2014).

The sustainability reporting process has also been subject to criticisms. Foremost is its voluntary status (Bebbington *et al.*, 2014). Unlike financial reporting through annual reports, sustainability reporting is not subject to the corporate law in a number of countries. Similarly, there are no stock exchange listing requirements for sustainability information (unlike those that exist for financial information) and there are no specific mandatory accounting standards that address social and environmental matters. However, there is legislation dealing with specific environmental and social matters, even though these do not require disclosure in reports. A number of voluntary guidelines also exist for sustainability reporting. Prominent among these are the Global Reporting Initiative (GRI) which provides indicators for measuring social and environmental performance. The GRI also has sector specific guidelines (including one for the mining industry) and technical protocols for measurement of social and environmental issues.

Another criticism directed at sustainability reporting is the use of the term 'sustainability' itself. Milne and Gray (2013) argue that such reporting does not address sustainability which has a long-term orientation and an emphasis on future generations. A mere emphasis on social and environmental matters, the authors further argue, does not address critical issues such as the ecological footprint and social justice.

A number of theories have been used to highlight why organisations engage in sustainability reporting. The most common theory used in prior literature is Legitimacy Theory (Dowling and Pfeffer, 1975; Lindblom, 1993) which suggests that organisations have a 'social contract with society' and will disclose their social and environmental performance to stakeholders in order to legitimise their existence to them. Legitimacy can be maintained, gained or repaired (Suchman, 1995). An organisation can seek to maintain its existing level of expectations from stakeholders or it could seek to be proactive and gain legitimacy. On the other hand, it could be reactive and respond to specific events or incidents to repair its legitimacy. Lindblom (1993) also highlights that there are a number of strategies that organisations use to manage their legitimacy. These include conforming to society's expectations, altering society's perceptions, altering society's expectations and manipulating society's perceptions. Legitimacy theory provides useful explanations for corporate reporting behaviour, especially in industries that are socially and environmentally sensitive.

Closely related to legitimacy theory is stakeholder theory (Freeman, 1984), which suggests that in order to manage a diverse range of stakeholders, an organisation needs to disclose social and environmental information. Ullmann (1985) has developed a framework for social and environmental reporting based on stakeholder theory. Ullmann's framework highlights that stakeholder power, strategic posture and economic performance influence social and environmental reporting practices. Mitchell *et al.* (1997) suggest that stakeholders are managed based on their salience with the attributes of power, legitimacy and urgency determining who the salient stakeholders are. These developments indicate that stakeholder theory has the potential to provide an in-depth understanding of stakeholder relationships and their influence on the resultant sustainability reporting process.

More recent developments in the theorisation for sustainability reporting include the use of new institutional theory (Di Maggio and Powell, 1983) and Reputation Risk Management (Bebbington *et al.*, 2008). New institutional theory suggests that external pressures lead to specific organisational practices. Coercive (rules and regulation), mimetic (replicating successful practices of others) and normative (professionalisation and development of networks) pressures lead to homogenisation of organisational practices, a process referred to as isomorphism (Di Maggio and Powell, 1983). These pressures could drive the homogenisation of sustainability reporting practices in specific industries. Reputation Risk Management, on the other hand, is an attempt to expand legitimacy theory explanations by linking reputation elements and management strategies to sustainability reporting (Bebbington *et al.*, 2008).

Content analysis is the most commonly used research method in sustainability reporting. The content, incidence and depth of disclosures in reports are analysed to comprehend the sustainability reporting practice. Other methods include engaging with organisational staff to comprehend their perceptions, motivations and approaches to disclosing social and environmental information. Interviews have often been used for these purposes, even though surveys could also be used to garner organisational views.

The mining industry is an environmentally and socially sensitive industry (Moran *et al.*, 2014). Its impacts are highly visible and incidents such as Ok Tedi in Papua New Guinea and Samarco in Brazil have the potential to tarnish the image of this industry. Mining companies all over the world are increasingly under pressure to be accountable to stakeholders over their social and environmental impacts (Deloitte, 2013). Consequently, their social and environmental performance is as important as their financial performance (Lodhia and Hess, 2014) with the term 'social licence to operate' often being used by mining corporations to describe their relationship with society. This term closely resembles the social contract terminology used in legitimacy theory. Sustainability reporting is a mechanism that can used by mining corporations to highlight their accountability for their social and environmental impacts and thereby maintain their social licence to operate.

Sustainability reporting in the mining industry

As highlighted by Lodhia and Hess (2014), the focus on management and reporting aspects differentiates sustainability accounting and reporting literature from other similar research domains such as corporate social responsibility and even business ethics. Accordingly, the focus on the analysis of prior literature on sustainability reporting in the mining industry is specifically on studies that explore the reporting of social and environmental issues.

Emphasis in this section is on the significant studies on sustainability reporting in the mining industry, rather than a discussion of every possible study on sustainability reporting. This process did involve judgement on the part of the author but ensured that the chosen approach focused on publications in journals that publish sustainability accounting and reporting research extensively. These include not just accounting journals but also several multidisciplinary journals. A common example is the *Journal of Cleaner Production* (*JCP*), which has published a significant number of papers on sustainability accounting and reporting as highlighted by Lodhia and Hess (2014). The article by Lodhia and Hess enabled an assessment of relevant literature in this journal on sustainability accounting and reporting from 2004 to 2013, while the 2014 introductory article of *JCP* (Moran *et al.*, 2014) mentioned the sustainability accounting and reporting articles in the special issue. In addition to a focus on journals, the significance of articles was also evaluated by their citations, enabling an assessment of literature that made an impact on understanding of sustainability reporting in the mining industry.

The early literature on the mining industry explored environmental reporting, and utilised content analysis, and stakeholder and legitimacy theoretical frameworks. Given the rise in prominence of environmental issues in the 1990s, these issues were more extensively explored in the earlier literature. These studies were primarily focused on all the companies in the industry, with the notable exception being literature on the OK Tedi incident and the BHP mining company.

Christopher *et al.* (1998) utilised Ullmann's (1985) stakeholder framework to Australian mining companies' environmental reporting practices. They only found support for the stakeholder power dimension. More specifically, only large companies and those with membership of the industry association had a range of stakeholder influences and tended to have a higher level of environmental disclosure.

Jantadej and Kent (1999) studied the disclosure of the Australian mining company, BHP, before and after the widely publicised OK Tedi incident in Papua New Guinea. Consistent with legitimacy theory, the authors found an increase in disclosure of environmental information during the period of the study. The OK Tedi incident was also explored by Deegan *et al.* (2000) in relation to major social and environmental incidents in Australia. This study confirmed the legitimacy theory explanation related to this incident.

Deegan *et al.* (2002) explored the social and environmental disclosures of BHP from 1983 to 1997 and found that this reporting was consistent with legitimacy theory explanations. In this process, the authors also disputed a 100-year study into BHP by Guthrie and Parker (1989) which found a limited explanatory potential through the use of legitimacy theory. The use of the media attention variable as symbolic of community concern led to the difference in results.

Peck and Sinding (2003) studied the environmental reporting practice of 30 global mining companies through the content analysis of their environmental reports. A major finding was that Australian companies were leading best practice in environmental reporting compared with companies in Canada and the US. The reports of these companies were found to be data rich and were regarded as being influenced by high expectations of environmental performance by citizens of their country. Various voluntary initiatives, such as the MCA code of environmental management and the Greenhouse Challenge Program, were suggested to have a positive impact on the disclosure levels of Australian companies.

Yongvanich and Guthrie (2005) developed an extended performance reporting framework which focused on intellectual capital and non-economic information, such as social and environmental disclosures, and applied this to the Australian mining companies listed on the Australian Stock Exchange (Top 100) at that point in time. Stakeholder theory was used to highlight that companies would manage their stakeholders through disclosure of issues important to them. The authors found that these companies tended to focus more on intellectual capital disclosures rather than social and environmental disclosures.

Jenkins and Yakovleva (2006) explored social and environmental disclosure in the annual report and social and environmental reports (1999–2003) of the ten largest global mining companies. The authors suggest that whilst such disclosure has increased and has become more sophisticated, reporting companies can be classified according to a 'leaders to laggards' continuum. 'Mature reporters', 'adolescents' and 'infants' were used to categorise the variation in these companies' social and environmental reporting (Jenkins and Yakovleva, 2006, 279). It was also found that the media for communicating social and environmental issues was evolving and that there was an increasing take-up of reporting on the internet. This study highlighted that strong leadership and cooperation from the leading companies was needed to support the laggards of the industry.

Deegan and Bloomquist (2006) explored the influence a World Wide Fund for Nature (WWF) initiative had on environmental reporting in the mining industry. WWF undertook the 'Ore or Overburden' survey of environmental reports of Australian mining companies in response to the industry association's development of a code of environmental management. Interviews with the concerned parties highlighted that this development influenced revisions to the code and the subsequent reporting behaviour of companies in the Australian minerals industry. This finding was consistent with the basic premises of legitimacy theory.

More recent literature has become more sophisticated and critical, and explored a broader range of issues than simply the reporting practices of companies in the mining industry. These have addressed specific contexts in detail and looked at broader issues such as assurances processes, climate change, the use of the global reporting initiative for sustainability reporting and the use of the World Wide Web (web) as an alternative to traditional disclosure media.

Perez and Sanchez (2009) explored the social and environmental reporting practices of four mining companies from 2001 to 2006. These companies were BHP Billiton (Australia), Anglo American (UK), Lafarge (France) and Cemex (Mexico). Through a content analysis of their reports, the authors highlighted that social and environmental reporting has evolved in relation to report comprehensiveness and depth. Social and environmental disclosures were improving and the commitment to address these issues was also addressed. However, third-party verification and details of measurement methodologies were areas that needed significant improvement.

Fonseca (2010) explored the assurance of mining companies' sustainability reports in light of the International Council of Mining and Metals (ICMM) new assurance procedure. The author found that the assurance statements suffered from the problems identified in literature, such as a limited scope and diversity of verification opinions, caused by mining companies having control over the assurance process. It was highlighted that the ICMM assurance procedure may provide consistency and breadth in assurance but could not guarantee trust in the reported information.

Hogan and Lodhia (2011) utilised the Reputation Risk Management (RRM) perspective to examine the sustainability disclosures of BHP Billiton before and after a reputation-damaging event of proposed regulation in the form of carbon pricing. They analysed BHP's annual reports, sustainability reports and various other disclosures made via the web. The authors found extensive support for the RRM perspective, with disclosure around carbon-related issues increasing since a carbon pricing mechanism was first proposed.

Pellegrino and Lodhia (2012) explored the disclosure practices of two leading mining companies, BHP Billiton and Rio Tinto, as well as two key industry bodies, the Minerals Council of Australia (MCA) and the Australian Coal Association (ACA), in response to the legitimising threat of climate change and impending carbon pricing requirements. Through a content analysis of reports and website information and the use of Lindblom's legitimacy strategies, the author's found that both the companies and the industry associations used voluntary disclosure on sustainability issues to execute a number of legitimacy strategies. The companies focused on their own performance while the industry bodies addressed broader policy issues in order to ensure the continuation of their 'social licence to operate'.

Murguía and Bohling (2013) questioned the effectiveness of sustainability reporting in mining through a case study on the Bajo de La Alumbrera mine, Argentina. Through the use of stakeholder theory and a content analysis of disclosures based on the GRI, the authors found high compliance with this initiative but a low quality of disclosure being reported. This was especially the case for environmental disclosures and for other contentious issues. The authors state that this places doubts on the credibility of these disclosures and implied that stakeholders were managed rather than being engaged. Sustainability reporting was perceived as having an adverse role and exasperating conflicts with stakeholders in this context.

An important contribution to the literature on sustainability reporting in the mining industry is the work of Lodhia (2005, 2006a, 2006b, 2012, 2014) on the use of the web for sustainability reporting. Lodhia (2005) applied legitimacy theory to environmental reporting through the web by focusing on the various motives for legitimacy as highlighted by Suchman (1995). Through a study of the online disclosure practices of all the companies associated with the Minerals Council of Australia, the author found that these companies used the web primarily to maintain their legitimacy and were reluctant to gain or repair legitimacy through online disclosure. In the same research context, Lodhia (2006a) explored the use of the communication potential of the web through the use of the media richness framework developed in earlier work (Lodhia, 2004). It was found that companies in the Australian mining industry were not fully utilising the communication potential of the web but there were some companies whose practices were significantly more developed than others in the industry. Lodhia (2006b) sought the views of environmental and communication managers in three mining companies on the use of the web for environmental reporting. The author found that both technical and socio-political factors impacted the use of the web for such reporting, suggesting that these had implications for theoretical perspectives used to explore web-based reporting on social and environmental issues.

Lodhia (2012) explored the communication of social and environmental issues on websites of three Australian mining companies through a longitudinal analysis of their websites, and interviews with sustainability and communication managers from these companies. The media richness framework was used to assess the use of the communication potential of the web. His findings suggested that companies are still learning about web-based social and environmental communication and that there was varying usage of different web capabilities across the three companies. Managers were willing to utilise the organisational and mass communication capabilities of the web more than its timeliness and presentation features. Limited consideration was given to the interactive potential of the web.

Using the same research context as in Lodhia (2012), Lodhia (2014) explored the factors that influenced the use of the web for sustainability communication. The study initially identified economic, internal organisational and external stakeholder influences, which were confirmed in the interviews with sustainability and communication managers of the three Australian mining companies. The interviews also revealed that the web was a 'double-edged sword' for sustainability communication, coupled with organisation restructuring having a negative effect on the use of the web for sustainability communication.

The *Journal of Cleaner Production* published a special issue (Lodhia *et al.*, 2013) in 2014 with a number of papers on sustainability reporting.[2] Studies focused on newer contexts such as South Africa and China, used other theoretical perspectives such as new institutional theory and Dryzek's 'discursive democracy', and critiqued the usefulness of the GRI for mining companies.

De Villiers *et al.* (2014a) analysed the social and environmental disclosures of listed South African mining companies, and compared the larger companies' practices to the smaller companies. They found that the common premise in prior literature that larger companies disclose more than smaller companies only applied to social disclosures. Using new institutional theory, the authors suggest that findings in relation to environmental disclosures were due to normative isomorphism. The professionalisation aspect of normative isomorphism suggested that environmental disclosures among mining companies had reached maturity and were at a stage where smaller companies disclosed very similarly to the larger companies.

Dong *et al.* (2014) focused on the stakeholder salience of the Chinese mining industries' sustainability reporting and found that the central government and international consumers were found to be salient stakeholders. Surprisingly, industry associations, local communities and employees were not found to have salience. An urgent need for diversity in the salience of stakeholders for the Chinese mining industry was highlighted by the authors so that sustainability reporting practices were reflective of a range of critical stakeholders.

Fonseca *et al.* (2014) explored the appropriateness of GRI guidelines for providing mining companies' sustainability performance information. Through semi-structured interviews with 41 mining practitioners, it was found that the GRI guidelines for mining companies do not address a number of principles of sustainability assessment and reporting and that specific changes were required in mining frameworks in order to provide meaningful and accurate information about sustainability progress. The authors conclude that meaningful and reliable standardised disclosures of the contribution to sustainability are unlikely to emerge in future.

Leong *et al.* (2014) focused on the water-related disclosures of mining companies in the Australian state of New South Wales. The authors focused on effectiveness of mandatory environmental reporting requirements when compared to voluntary initiatives. Using Dryzek's discursive democracy theoretical framework, the authors highlighted that when compared to the voluntary requirements, the mandatory system was well designed with publicly available information and community consultation, but there was scope for improvement.

The overview of the literature presented here suggests that the Australian minerals industry has been the primary research context for a number of studies. This could be due to the various initiatives in this industry, such as the codes for environmental management and sustainable development, which require disclosure of social and environmental information (Lodhia, 2007). Even though global studies have been undertaken, there is a need for studies of specific contexts other than Australia. As discussed previously, recent literature has addressed newer contexts and further studies are needed in this regard. Studies into the practices in developing countries, for example, are essential, especially since the requirements for mining in these countries are not as stringent as those in the developed part of the world. Multinationals operating in such contexts therefore have an accountability over their operations and it would be of interest whether sustainability report disclosures provide such accountability.

Legitimacy theory and to some extent stakeholder theory have been extensively utilised in studies on sustainability reporting in the mining industry. This is consistent with prior literature on sustainability reporting. However, further developments in theorisation have been observed in the analysis here with Reputation Risk Management (RRM), new institutional theory, media richness framework and Dryzek's discursive democracy theoretical framework being used. Indeed, there is a need for further developments in theoretical perspectives for sustainability reporting in the mining industry. For instance, the RRM perspective suggested by Bebbington *et al.* (2008) could provide a refined and in-depth understanding of corporate attempts to manage reputation during a crisis. Social and environmental incidents such as OK Tedi and Samarco provide an ideal opportunity to explore how organisations use sustainability reporting to manage their reputational risk during such events. New institutional theory also provides extensive potential for theorising sustainability reporting practices, with concepts such as institutional logics (Thornton and Ocasio 2008) and institutional entrepreneurship (Battilana *et al.*, 2009) providing the tools to examine the processes through which disclosure decisions are made.

The research methods used for the studies discussed here have primarily been content analysis and interviews. These have provided useful insights into current practices in sustainability reporting in the mining industry. There is potential for enhancing the methods used to undertake such research with observation, ethnography and action research methods providing additional approaches for exploring mining industry practices. These methods would enable researchers to engage with mining practitioners, providing insights into sustainability reporting 'in action' and enabling research with practical relevance. Such research is consistent with Adams and Larrinaga-Gonzalez's (2007) and Burritt and Schaltegger's (2010) calls for increasing research in sustainability accounting that will engage with organisations in their pursuit of improved sustainability performance.

Future research opportunities

The analysis of prior literature in the preceding section provides an understanding of possible gaps in an understanding of sustainability reporting in the mining industry. In addition to the need for broadening the research context, theorisation and methods for studies into sustainability reporting in the mining industry, a number of other research opportunities exist and these are discussed in this section.

The link between accounting and sustainability has been well established as highlighted earlier in this chapter. There is an abundance of literature on sustainability reporting, including that in the mining industry.

More recently, the critical environmental issue, climate change has emerged to prominence. This has been accompanied by research in this area, and this includes research into climate change/carbon management, reporting and policy. The mining industry is adversely affected by climate change and there is a need for increasing research into carbon reporting by mining corporations. The studies by Hogan and Lodhia (2011) and Pellegrino and Lodhia (2012) have explored carbon reporting in relation to a proposed carbon pricing mechanism in Australia. Further studies are required which address the reporting of climate change in the mining industry, even though carbon pricing requirements do not exist in some jurisdictions such as Australia. These studies could address issues such as mining corporations' accountability in relation to climate change and stakeholder's opinions on this, the approaches used by companies to combat climate change, their perspectives on existing and future carbon pricing requirements and the targets for carbon reduction and abatement.

Another major environmental issue that is of concern to mining corporations is water. Management of water that is used in mining activity is of critical importance given the scarcity of this resource. Similarly, it is of interest to explore the water-related disclosures by mining companies as undertaken by Leong *et al.* (2014), for example. Research is needed to highlight how companies report on their accountability over the use of water and stakeholder views on this, the approaches to water management that are disclosed by these companies and the policies of mining companies in relation to the future availability of water to the mining process.

In addition to emphasis on specific environmental issues, disclosure of specific social issues is another area that has not been investigated in prior literature on sustainability reporting in the mining industry. It would be of interest to explore the reporting of specific social issues by mining companies such as health and safety (including, for example, an assessment of the disclosure of HIV/AIDS issues by South African mining companies), local community impacts and development, poverty alleviation and equitable resource sharing.

A recent development in reporting has the potential to change the corporate reporting landscape. The notion of integrated reporting has emerged, highlighting that financial reporting information has to be integrated with non-financial reporting measures (such as sustainability disclosures) in order to provide stakeholders with a broader measure of organisational success (Lodhia, 2015). Sustainability reporting has in the past operated in isolation from financial reporting. It is envisaged that by integrating the various measures of corporate performance, sustainability can be embedded into business practices (Lodhia, 2013). The International Integrated Reporting Council (IIRC) has taken the lead in the development of integrated reporting and predicts that integrated reporting will replace all other forms of reporting (IIRC, 2013). It has developed a framework for integrated reporting (IIRC, 2013) which provides guidelines for undertaking such a form of reporting.

While the literature on integrated reporting is emerging (De Villiers *et al.*, 2014b), there is a conspicuous lack of literature on the adoption of integrated reporting by mining companies.

There is an urgent need to address the impact of integrating reporting on mining corporations' accountability. Research is required to address how mining practitioners respond to integrated reporting, the approaches they are undertaking to integrate financial information with sustainability matters, the change in existing reporting practices as a result of integrated reporting and stakeholder perceptions of integrated reporting by the mining industry. Moreover, there is a need to explore whether the IIRC's framework for integrated reporting meets the requirements of reporting by mining companies. Given the limitations of the GRI in addressing the sustainability progress by mining companies as expressed by Fonseca *et al.* (2014), it would be of interest to explore whether the IIRC framework addresses some of these limitations.

As highlighted by Fonseca (2010), the assurance of sustainability reporting in the mining industry is an issue that needs to be addressed, given the importance placed on this by the ICMM. Research is required to address issues such as which parties are involved in providing assurance to mining companies over their sustainability reporting, the content of third-party assurance statements and whether a unifying assurance statement can be developed. Stakeholder perceptions of the credibility of sustainability reporting in light of current assurance processes and their insights into reducing the management control over assurance are also worthwhile areas for research investigation.

The studies by Lodhia (2005, 2006a, 2006b, 2012, 2014) have made an important contribution to an understanding the impact of information and communication technologies on communication of sustainability information. The focus has primarily been on the use of the web. Social media has emerged as a key communication tool (Lodhia and Stone, 2017), even for businesses (Lodhia *et al.*, 2016). It would therefore be of interest to explore the potential of social media for communication of sustainability issues and to establish the extent to which this potential is utilised by mining companies as part of their sustainability reporting practice. Stakeholder perceptions on the use of social media as an alternative to traditional means of communicating sustainability information could also be addressed.

Conclusion

This chapter has addressed the contribution of accounting literature through the auspices of sustainability reporting in improving our understanding of sustainability in the mining industry. There is extensive literature on sustainability reporting in the mining industry, highlighting how corporations provide their accountability over social and environmental issues to various stakeholders. This literature has become more sophisticated and critical over time, addressing a number of specific issues in relation to the sustainability agenda of mining companies. However, there are further opportunities for research into sustainability reporting in the mining industry as highlighted in this chapter.

Notes

1 Examples include kilograms, tonnes, etc.
2 The paper by Lodhia (2014) discussed earlier also appeared in this special issue, together with the Lodhia and Hess (2014) article.

References

Adams, C.A. and Larrinaga-Gonzalez, C. (2007) 'Engaging with Organizations in Pursuit of Improved Sustainability Accounting and Performance'. *Accounting, Auditing and Accountability Journal, 20, 3*, 333–355.

Battilana, J., Leca, B. and Boxenbaum, E. (2009) 'How Actors Change Institutions: Towards a Theory of Institutional Entrepreneurship'. *Academy of Management Annals, 3,1*, 65–107.

Bebbington, J., Larrinaga-Gonzalez, C. and Moneva-Abadia, J.M. (2008) 'Corporate Social Reporting and Reputation Risk Management'. *Accounting, Auditing and Accountability Journal, 21, 3*, 337–361.

Bebbington, J., Unerman, J. and O'Dwyer, B., ed (2014) *Sustainability Accounting and Accountability*, 2nd edition. Routledge.

Burritt, R.L. and Schaltegger, S. (2010) 'Sustainability Accounting and Reporting: Fad or trend?'. *Accounting, Auditing and Accountability Journal, 23, 7*, 829–846.

Christopher, T., Cullen, L. and Soutar, G. (1998) 'Australian Mining Companies Environmental Disclosure'. *Accountability and Performance*, 4, 2, 17–41.

De Villiers, C., Low, M. and Samkin, G. (2014a) 'The Institutionalisation of Mining Company Sustainability Disclosures'. *Journal of Cleaner Production*, *84, 1*, 51–58.

De Villiers, C., Rinaldi, L. and Unerman, J. (2014b) 'Integrated Reporting: Insights, Gaps and an Agenda for Future Research'. *Accounting, Auditing and Accountability Journal*, *27, 7*, 1042–1067.

Deegan, C. and Bloomquist, C. (2006) 'Stakeholder Influence on Corporate Reporting: An Exploration of the Interaction between WWF-Australia and the Australian Minerals Industry'. *Accounting, Organizations and Society, 31, 4*, 343–372.

Deegan, C., Rankin, M. and Tobin, J. (2002) 'An Examination of the Corporate Social and Environmental Disclosures of BHP from 1983–1997: A Test of Legitimacy Theory'. *Accounting, Auditing and Accountability Journal, 15, 3*, 312–343.

Deegan, C., Rankin, M. and Voght, P. (2000) 'Firms' Disclosure Reactions to Major Social Incidents: Australian Evidence'. *Accounting Forum, 24, 1*, 101–130.

Deloitte (2013) *The top 10 issues mining companies will face in the coming year.* Deloitte.

Dhaliwal, D., Li, O.Z., Tsang, A. and Yang, G.Y. (2014) 'Corporate Social Responsibility Disclosure and the Cost of Equity Capital: The Roles of Stakeholder Orientation and Financial Transparency'. *Journal of Accounting and Public Policy, 33*, 328–355.

Di Maggio, P.J. and Powell, W.W. (1983) 'The Iron Cage Revisited: Institutional Isomorphism and Collective Rationality in Organizational Fields'. *American Sociological Review*, *48*, 147–160.

Dong, S.-D., Burritt, R. and Qian, W. (2014) 'Salient Stakeholders in Corporate Social Responsibility Reporting by Chinese Mining and Minerals Companies'. *Journal of Cleaner Production, 84, 1, 59–69*

Dowling, J. and Pfeffer, J. (1975) 'Organizational Legitimacy: Social Values and Organizational Behaviour'. *Pacific Sociological Review, 18, 1*, 122–136.

Fonseca, A. (2010) 'How Credible are Mining Corporations' Sustainability Reports? A Critical Analysis of External Assurance under the Requirements of the International Council on Mining and Metals'. *Corporate Social Responsibility and Environmental Management, 17*, 355–370.

Fonseca, A., McAllister, M.L. and Fitzpatrick, P. (2014) 'Sustainability Reporting among Mining Corporations: A Constructive Critique of the GRI Approach'. *Journal of Cleaner Production, 84, 1*, 70–83.

Freeman, R.E. (1984) *Strategic Management: A Stakeholder Approach*. Pitman Publishing, Boston, MA.

Gray, R., Adams, C.A. and Owen, D. (2014) *Accountability, Social Responsibility and Sustainability: Accounting for Society and the Environment*. Pearson.

Guthrie, J. and Parker, L.D. (1989) 'Corporate Social Reporting: A Rebuttal of Legitimacy Theory'. *Accounting and Business Research, 19, 76*, 343–352.

Hogan, J. and Lodhia, S. (2011) 'Sustainability Reporting and Reputation Risk Management: An Australian Case Study'. *International Journal of Accounting and Information Management,19, 3*, 267–287.

IIRC (International Integrated Reporting Committee). (2013) *The International <IR> Framework*. Available: www.theiirc.org/consultationdraft2013.

Jantadej, P. and Kent, P. (1999) 'Corporate Environmental Disclosure in Response to Public Awareness of the OK Tedi Copper Mine Disaster: A Legitimacy Theory Perspective'. *Accounting Research Journal, 12, 1*, 72–88.

Jenkins, H.M. and Yakovleva, N. (2006) 'Corporate Social Responsibility in the Mining Industry: Exploring Trends in Social and Environmental Disclosure'. *Journal of Cleaner Production, 14, 3–4*, 271–284.

Kaur, A. and Lodhia, S. (2014) 'The State of Disclosures on Stakeholder Engagement in Sustainability Reporting in Australian Local Councils'. *Pacific Accounting Review: Special issue on Sustainability Accounting and Reporting, 26, 1/2*, 54–74.

Kaur, A. and Lodhia, S. (2016) 'Institutional Influences on Stakeholder Engagement in Sustainability Accounting and Reporting'. In Crowther, D. and Shalfi, S. (eds), *Corporate Responsibility and Stakeholding (Developments in Corporate Governance and Responsibility, Volume 10)*. Emerald Group Publishing, pp. 105–129.

Kaur, A. and Lodhia, S. (forthcoming) 'Stakeholder Engagement in Sustainability Accounting and Reporting: A Study of Australian Local Councils'. *Accounting, Auditing and Accountability Journal.*

Leong, S., Hazelton, J., Taplin, R., Timms, W. and Laurence, D. (2014) 'Mine Site-Level Water Reporting in the Macquarie and Lachlan Catchments: A Study of Voluntary and Mandatory Disclosures and Their Value for Community Decision-Making'. *Journal of Cleaner Production, 84, 1*, 94–106.

Lindblom, C.K. (1993) 'The Implications of Organizational Legitimacy for Corporate Social Performance and Disclosure'. *Paper presented at the Critical Perspectives on Accounting Conference*, New York.

Lodhia, S. (2004) 'Corporate Environmental Reporting Media: A Case for the World Wide Web'. *Electronic Green Journal, 20, 1*. Available: http://escholarship.org/uc/item/20d3x61r.

Lodhia, S. (2005) 'Legitimacy Motives for World Wide Web Environmental Reporting: An Exploratory Study into Present Practices in the Australian Minerals Industry'. *Journal of Accounting and Finance, 4*, 1–15.

Lodhia, S. (2006a) 'The World Wide Web and Its Potential for Corporate Environmental Communication: A Study into Present Practices in the Australian Minerals Industry'. *International Journal of Digital Accounting Research, 6, 11*, 65–94.

Lodhia, S. (2006b) 'Corporate Perceptions of Web Based Environmental Communication: An Exploratory Study into Companies in the Australian Minerals Industry'. *Journal of Accounting and Organizational Change, 2, 1*, 74–88.

Lodhia, S. (2007) 'Corporations and the Environment: Australian Evidence'. *International Journal of Environmental, Cultural, Economic and Social Sustainability, 3, 3*, 183–193.

Lodhia, S. (2010) 'Research Methods for Analysing Web Based Sustainability Communication'. *Social and Environmental Accountability Journal, 30, 1*, 26–36.

Lodhia, S. (2012) 'Web Based Social and Environmental Communication in the Australian Minerals Industry: An Application of Media Richness Framework'. *Journal of Cleaner Production, 25*, 73–85.

Lodhia, S. (2013) 'Sustainability Accounting and Reporting: An Overview, Contemporary Developments and Research Possibilities'. In Wells, G. (ed.), *Sustainable Business: Theory and Practice of Business under Sustainability Principles*, Edward Elgar, pp. 73–85.

Lodhia, S. (2014) 'Factors Influencing the Use of the World Wide Web for Sustainability Communication: An Australian Mining Perspective'. *Journal of Cleaner Production, 84*, 142–154.

Lodhia, S. (2015) 'Exploring the Transition to Integrated Reporting through a Practice Lens: An Australian Customer Owned Perspective'. *Journal of Business Ethics, 129, 3*, 585–598.

Lodhia, S. and Hess, N. (2014) 'Sustainability Accounting and Reporting in the Mining Industry: Current Literature and Directions for Future Research'. *Journal of Cleaner Production, 84*, 43–50

Lodhia, S. and Stone, G. (2017) 'Integrated Reporting in a Social Media and Internet Communication Environment: Conceptual Insights'. *Australian Accounting Review, 27, 1*, 17–33.

Lodhia, S., Moran, C. and Kunz, N. (2013) 'The Sustainability Agenda of the Minerals and Energy Supply and Demand Network: An Integrative Analysis of Ecological, Ethical, Economic, and Technological Dimensions'. *Journal of Cleaner Production Special issue.*

Lodhia, S., Stone, G. and Parker, L.D. (2016) *Strategizing for Social Media: A Public Accounting Perspective*, CPA Australia. Available: www.cpaaustralia.com.au/~/media/corporate/allfiles/document/professional-resources/education/strategising-for-social-media.pdf?la=en.

Melo, T. and Garrido-Morgado, A. (2012) 'Corporate Reputation: A Combination of Social Responsibility and Industry'. *Corporate Social Responsibility and Environmental Management, 19*, 11–31.

Milne, M.J. and Gray, R.H. (2013) 'W(h)ither Ecology? The Triple Bottom Line, the Global Reporting Initiative, and Corporate Sustainability Reporting'. *Journal of Business Ethics, 118, 1*, 13–29.

Mitchell, R.K., Agle, B.R. and Wood, D.J. (1997) 'Toward a Theory of Stakeholder Identification and Salience: Defining the Principle of Who and What Really Counts'. *The Academy of Management Review, 22, 4*, 853–886.

Moran, C., Lodhia, S., Kunz, N. and Huisingh, D. (2014) 'Sustainability in Mining, Minerals and Energy: New Processes, Pathways and Human Interactions for a Cautiously Optimistic Future'. *Journal of Cleaner Production, 84, 1*, 1–15.

Murguía, D. and Böhling, K. (2013) 'Sustainability Reporting on Large-Scale Mining Conflicts: The Case of Bajo de la Alumbrera, Argentina'. *Journal of Cleaner Production*, *41*, 202–209.

Peck, P. and Sinding, K. (2003) 'Environmental and Social Disclosure and Data Richness in the Mining Industry'. *Business Strategy and the Environment, 12*, 131–146.

Pellegrino, C. and Lodhia, S. (2012) 'Climate Change Accounting and the Australian Mining Industry: Exploring the Links between Corporate Disclosure and the Generation of Legitimacy'. *Journal of Cleaner Production, 36*, 68–82.

Perez, P. and Sanchez, L.E. (2009) 'Assessing the Evolution of Sustainability Reporting in the Mining Sector'. *Environmental Management, 43, 6*, 949–961.

Schaltegger, S., Bennett, M. and Burritt, R. (eds) (2006) *Sustainability Accounting and Reporting*. Springer, Dordrecht, The Netherlands.

Suchman, M. (1995) 'Managing Legitimacy: Strategic and Institutional Approaches'. *Academy of Management Review, 20, 3*, 571–610.

Thornton, P.H. and Ocasio, W. (2008) 'Institutional Logics'. In Greenwood, R., Oliver, C., Sahlin, K. and Suddaby, R. (eds), *The Sage Handbook of Organizational Institutionalism*, Vol. 840, Sage.

Ullmann, A.A. (1985) 'Data in Search of a Theory: A Critical Examination of the Relationships among Social Performance, Social Disclosure and Economic Performance of US Firms'. *Academy of Management Review, 10, 3*, 540–557.

Yongvanich, K. and Guthrie, J. (2005) 'Extended Performance Reporting: An Examination of the Australian Mining Industry'. *Accounting Forum, 29*, 103–119.

11 Mining taxation in mineral-rich developing countries

Past mistakes and future challenges

Pietro Guj

Introduction

The contribution of mining to the economy of many mineral-rich developing countries has grown in recent years ahead of that of other sectors, increasing their dependency on this industry as a mechanism for development and growth. It is thus critical that these jurisdictions develop and enforce mining regulatory and fiscal regimes that, while not discouraging foreign direct investment (FDI), ensure that mining is carried out in a safe, environmentally and socially responsible manner and that a fair amount of mining tax is effectively collected, and appropriately allocated to development priorities.

Many jurisdictions, however, have been disappointed by the level of mining taxes collected relative to the profits accrued by companies falling well under their legitimate expectations for a variety of reasons including:

- mining tax policy, legal and administrative frameworks and combinations of taxation instruments not suited to the country's economic circumstances;
- fiscal incentives designed to attract FDI, sometimes under unfavourable economic circumstances, often having been formulated with inadequate understanding of their potential long-term consequences, and being locked into rigid and one-sided 'stability' agreements;
- global structuring of multinational mining enterprises (MNEs) fragmenting the mining value chain with high levels of cross-border trade, often between related members of the same MNE, frequently resident in low-tax jurisdictions, and its mining subsidiary, creating opportunities to shift profits overseas and reduce their tax bill in the source country and at the consolidated MNE's level;
- inadequate administrative capacity, systems and skill inventories to effectively enforce the mining tax regime;
- inadequate co-ordination, co-operation and information and skills sharing between relevant ministries and departments involved in mining tax administration and revenue collection.

These factors combined create administrative complexity and uncertainty that may be exploited by some MNEs to minimise the tax paid at the consolidated MNE's level.

This chapter provides a broad outline of current mining taxation issues, exploring how mineral-rich developing country governments might best balance conflicting fiscal and development objectives as they design or adjust their mining fiscal regimes. It explores the various mining taxation instruments available to governments, and the extent to which these instruments can increase revenue collection which may be important in order to satisfy public expectations. It does not address how revenues from mining taxation should then be redistributed through the budgetary process to optimise socio-economic objectives including sustainability, nor revenue leakages attributable to corrupt practices, for which the reader is referred to the Extractive Industry Transparency Initiative (EITI). The material presented is based in part on studies carried out and published by the World Bank Group on how to improve mining tax administration and collection frameworks and on transfer pricing in the context of mining in Africa, to which the author had the privilege to direct in a consultant role.

Fiscal objectives

Fiscal systems are designed to achieve a number of objectives falling primarily in the following categories:

- economic efficiency and equity;
- revenue maximisation and stability;
- transparency, and administrative efficiency.

As discussed later, some of these objectives are mutually incompatible and governments, in setting their fiscal policy, need to balance them through trade-offs that suit the prevailing economic and political circumstances.

Economic efficiency and equity

A mining tax system is economically efficient if a change in the tax rate does not alter investment decisions. By contrast, an inefficient tax system would be one where an increase in the tax rate would cause a mine to react by 'high-grading', i.e. by increasing the cut-off grade thus reducing minable reserves tonnages while increasing their average grade, hence their unit value to maintain profit margins. The result would be a reduction in mine life or in its annual rate of production with inefficient utilisation of the resources and realisation of lower economic value.

Most economists would agree that, in theory, in an ideal world of perfect markets and information, an appropriate level of 'normal' profit, including the risk-free rate of interest to compensate for the timing and a premium to compensate for the risk of individual projects, should be adequate to justify an investor to commit and retain capital in individual mining projects. Theoretically, government could levy any profit above the normal profit, the so-called economic rent (Harman and Guj, 2012), if realised in tax systems where government:

1 either refunds to the taxpayer individual losses if and as incurred by a mining project (Brownian tax), thus reducing the risk borne by investors and as a consequence the rate of normal profit at the limit to the risk-free rate; or
2 allows companies to accumulate project losses and to carry them forward for deduction from future revenues generated by the project after being uplifted by the rate of normal profit.

A modification of the second formulation by Garnaut and Clunies Ross (1983), excluding any refund from government to industry of possible cumulative losses at the closure of a mining operation, has been used to structure most of the *resource rent tax* systems currently in force, primarily in the petroleum industry.

An economically efficient tax system would also be equitable in that the level of tax paid reflects the 'ability-to-pay' of individual projects, as producers of valuable commodities and more profitable projects, because of higher grades or proximity to markets, would pay proportionately more tax.

Revenue maximisation and stability

Increases in commodity prices over the last decade have generally leveraged company profits more than government revenues. This has led to a perception that mining does not pay a 'fair' share of taxes, creating political pressure for changes in the tax laws to capture more or even all of the economic rent. In practice, this did not occur to any appreciable degree because different jurisdictions compete globally in attracting limited FDI in mineral exploration and mine development through their mining fiscal regime by sharing the economic rent generated by mining projects to a greater or lesser degree with industry. The major concern is how to maximise revenue collection without deterring FDI, which means collecting what 'market will bear' rather than a 'fair' level of mining taxation.

In addition, government revenue in mineral-dependent economies is inevitably unstable because of the high volatility of mineral commodity prices. This can play havoc with government planning and budgeting. As discussed in greater detail later, the degree of revenue instability tends to be directly correlated with the degree of economic efficiency of the fiscal instruments included in a country's fiscal package. Unless the economy of a country is highly diversified, revenue stability should be given priority when designing a mining tax regime, particularly in relation to decisions about the proportion of revenue to be collected by various tax instruments and possible tax incentives.

Transparency and administrative efficiency

Mining tax policy and related administrative frameworks should be simple, clear and easy to explain and justify to both taxpayers and the citizens. Simple tax rules are easier to administer and harder to manipulate, reducing the likelihood of abuse and taxpayer disputes, as well as the cost of compliance for both government and industry. In many jurisdictions, the competing needs of attracting FDI, and meeting the socio-economic expectations of citizens has led to complexity and inconsistencies in developmental and fiscal policy formulation. The case-by-case approach to negotiating individual mining development agreements, a common practice in many developing countries, can also create an additional layer of administrative complexity because of the co-existence of at times very diverse regimes. The lack of administrative simplicity and the confidentiality of some of the mining agreements may also make it difficult for civil society organisations (CSOs), the media and parliament to monitor mining revenue collection by government. Yet, constructive involvement of these groups in future development and amendment of the mining tax regimes could prove effective in improving their transparency and facilitate their enforcement.

Balancing mutually incompatible fiscal objectives

Table 11.1 highlights how many of the fiscal objectives to be pursued by government are in effect mutually incompatible and cannot therefore be simultaneously optimised. Mining taxation systems can only be based on a compromise that, while not optimal in any single respect, makes acceptable trade-offs among the various economic, political and developmental needs and objectives of the country.

Fiscal instruments and packages

Common components of a mining taxation package

Some tax instruments levied on the mining industry are sector-specific; these include mineral royalties, free government equity and licensing fees (Otto *et al.*, 2007), while others, for instance corporate income tax (CIT) cut across most other sectors of the economy. However, it must be noted that the CIT legislation of most mineral-producing jurisdictions generally includes mining-specific provisions and incentives, as discussed in more detail below.

Table 11.1 Example of inevitable trade-offs confronted by government in setting up its mining fiscal regime

Objective	*Tradeoff/disadvantage*
Economic efficiency and equity	More complex administration and lower revenue stability
Maximising revenue	Discourages investors
Encouraging investment	Fiscal incentives reduce tax revenue and make it unpredictable
Optimal tax base	Few mines heavily taxed versus more mines lightly taxed?
Revenue predictability and stability	Economic inefficiency
Fiscal regime stability/transparency and investor certainty	Multiple tax systems, inequity among projects, lower revenue
Administrative simplicity	Economic inefficiency

A recent study by Goldman and Sachs (in MCA, 2015) indicates that the proportion of total revenue levied from the mining industry derived from mineral royalty is very variable among various jurisdictions, ranging from zero in Mexico to two-thirds in Canada, with the majority of jurisdictions in the one-third to one-half range. This relatively high proportion of mineral royalties in mining tax collections may be an indication that:

- either the mining industry is not as profitable as it is perceived during high points in the commodities price cycle, particularly in the early stages of production when significant capital deductions of exploration and development expenditures take place; or
- corporate income tax presents more opportunities for tax minimisation and avoidance, including from ill-conceived fiscal incentives, often 'stabilised' in mining contracts, and
- globalisation of the industry with consequent fragmentation of its value chain and multiplicity of cross-border transactions often between related parties, frequently resident in low-tax jurisdictions, creates opportunities for significant tax avoidance and, in some cases, even for tax evasion.

To the extent that most of the mineral royalties are computed by basing them either on production volume/weight, or on revenue, they are generally more difficult to avoid than the CIT, given its more complex profit base. It is for this reason, and the delay in receiving revenue from profit- or rent-based royalties and taxes, that some African tax administrations have reconfigured their tax mix to increase government take from royalties. At an extreme, in 2015 Zambia significantly increased royalty rates (from 6 to 20 per cent), abolishing CIT on mining altogether. Following a strong political backlash from mining companies, the Zambian government has since returned to a more balanced mining fiscal regime.

Table 11.2 Possible components of a mining tax regime

Fiscal component	
Mineral royalties	Based on: • Units of volume or weight (e.g. specific $ amount/t), or • Value (e.g. % of gross revenue), or • Profit (e.g. % of a specifically defined measure of profit), or • Hybrids of the above (mostly profit based subject to specific or value-based minimum), or • Resource rent, or • Product sharing
Corporate income tax (CIT)	Generally including mining-specific provisions and incentives such as: • Immediate write-off of capital expenditure • Accelerated depreciation etc.
Capital gain tax (CGT)	At the CIT or at a reduced rate
Free government equity	Normally minority equity of around 10%
Various mining title-related fees	Exploration and mining licenses application, rental and other miscellaneous fees
Other imposts	Administered by the central government: • VAT • Customs duties and excises • dividends and other withholding taxes (WHT) Administered at other levels of government: • stamp duty • payroll tax • property municipal taxes and rates • a plethora of minor 'nuisance' taxes and fees.
Quasi-taxes	Contribution to the establishment of local infrastructure and other community service obligations

Comparing royalty rates across countries is not particularly informative given the multiplicity of potentially very different bases that may be used to compute royalties. By contrast, a comparison of CIT rates may be more meaningful as homogeneous international accounting systems are now adopted by most jurisdictions to determine taxable income. The wide range in CIT rates, between 0 and 10 per cent for a number of 'tax havens' (e.g. United Arab Emirates, Cayman Islands, Bahamas, Mauritius), and more than 35 per cent for some high-tax jurisdictions (e.g. USA, Japan), with the bulk falling in the 20 to 35 per cent range, creates significant opportunities and motivation for tax arbitrage, i.e. exploiting differences in tax rates between jurisdictions. However, the headline rate may be deceiving as some countries, for example the Netherlands, Luxembourg and Singapore, in an attempt to attract FDI, allow the establishment of preferentially taxed Special Purpose Entities (SPEs).

Whether a tax regime is internationally competitive can only be determined by considering simultaneously all the components of its tax mix. According to a comparative study by Goldman and Sachs (in MCA, 2015), the total tax take for the world's main mineral producers (calculated as the ratio between the sum of their mining royalties plus CIT and their taxable income) ranges widely between 22 per cent for Uzbekistan and 61 per cent for India, with a mean of around 38 per cent. Depending on the percentage of revenue derived from royalties relative to CIT, the total tax take ratio will increase in periods of falling commodity prices and vice versa.

Taxable entities and ring-fencing

The obligation to pay mineral royalties is one of the conditions for the granting of a mining tenement. In most mineral-producing countries mineral royalties are embodied in the *Mining Act* and supporting regulations, less frequently in their tax legislation. Consequently mineral royalties are specific to individual mining tenements or projects, which may be just one of many assets held by a mining company.

By contrast corporate income tax (CIT) is generally levied at the entity level, which in the mining sector can be either:

- a national or multinational corporation often operating through branches in dispersed locations both domestically or across multiple fiscal regimes; or
- a project/licence-specific company, registered and taxable in the country, which in turn may be a mining subsidiary of an MNE. This approach, known as 'ring-fencing', is the most commonly observed in developing countries.

From the government's point of view ring-fencing has the advantage of speeding up revenue collection by disallowing write-offs of losses incurred by an associated entity beyond the boundary of the producing area.

However, as Readhead (2016) discusses in a case study based on Ghana, ring-fencing may affect future or long-term revenues by reducing the incentive for companies to invest in exploration activities beyond the project area, which can slow the development of the minerals sector in the country. As discussed later, it can also foster aggressive tax planning.

To enforce ring-fencing provisions there must be clear definitions of what constitutes the taxable entity to be ring-fenced. Figure 11.1 diagrammatically displays how the definition of a taxable entity for the purposes of ring-fencing may range from a single mine and concentrator (encircled by dashed line), down the vertical integration chain to include multiple related mines, smelter and refinery, all the way to marketing and distribution. Ring-fencing at the level of a single mine and concentrator, with the

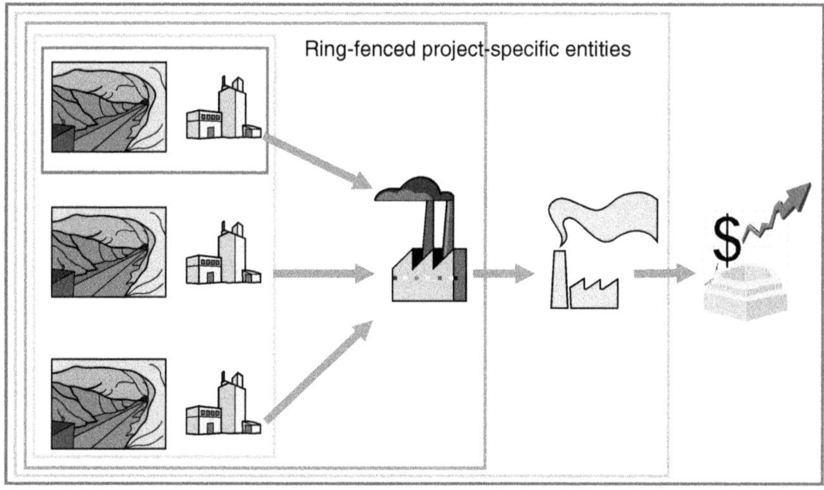

Figure 11.1 Possible extent of ring fencing of a vertically integrated mining operation.

concentrate being exported to a related or unrelated smelter, is the most common approach in many developing countries.

The nature of mineral royalties

There are two distinct philosophies as to what mineral royalties constitute.

- The first contends that a mineral royalty is a payment by a mining company to the state for the right to mine and sell its non-renewable resources. As such it should reflect the value of the resource as taken from the ground, i.e. the value of broken ore or petroleum at the point of extraction either at the mine head or well head. In this light, royalty is strictly speaking not a tax and no royalty should be levied on value added downstream from the mine head.
- The second considers a mineral royalty as just another mineral taxation mechanism to appropriate a share of the profit or economic rent generated by a project, in effect an alternative or a complement to corporate income tax (CIT).

Proponents of the first philosophy will propose *production-based royalties* using a measure of either the physical volume /weight or the value of the mineral extracted or sold as their bases, while those of the second philosophy will lean towards *royalties based on profit* or on economic rent.

Specific or unit-based royalties levy a fixed amount per unit of volume or weight produced or sold (e.g. \$X/m^3 or \$Y/tonne). They are economically inefficient as they are insensitive to changes in the price of the commodity, but easy to understand and simple to administer. They provide predictable and stable revenue as long as a mine continues to operate and may be suitable for low-value, bulk materials, such as sand, gravel aggregate etc.

Transparency and administrative efficiency dictate that in *ad valorem* royalties the value base be derived with reference to the price actually realised for the first mineral product sold at arm's-length to an unrelated buyer. As very few sales of broken ore take place at the mine head, and most minerals are sold after some value has been added by downstream processing, a percentage rate (generally 2 to 10 per cent, mostly 2.5 to 5 per cent) is applied to:

- either the realised or estimated arm's-length sale value; or
- the value of the mineral at selective taxing points upstream from the actual point of sale (shown as V0 to V4 in Figure 11.2), estimated by netting from the arm's-length sales price all processing, transportation and other costs incurred below the selected taxing point.

To ensure royalty payments at any taxation point along the value chain are consistent with the royalty that would have been paid if based on the mine head value, not only all costs incurred upstream of the point of sale must be netted back to the taxation point to get an appropriate royalty value base, but also progressively higher royalty rates must be applied the more upstream the taxation point is. This approach ensures that value added by downstream processing is not taxed, as failing to do this would be inequitable and create a disincentive for mining companies to invest in downstream processing. This problem arises in many instances where the legislation prescribes a single royalty rate for a metal irrespective of the form in which it is sold.

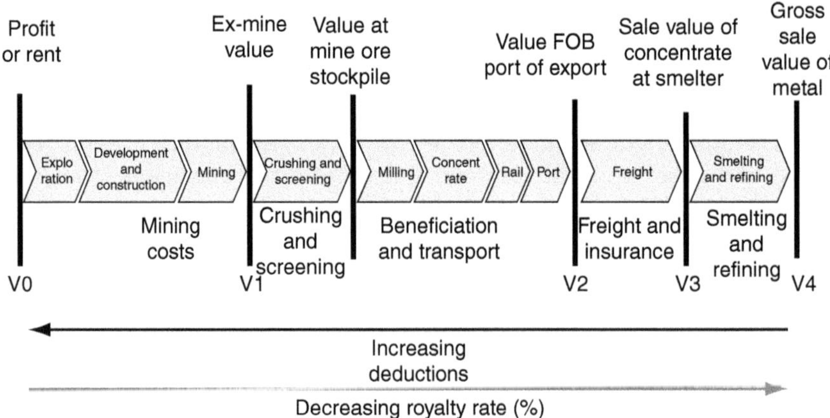

Figure 11.2 Choice of possible taxing points along the mining value chain.

Ad valorem royalties are most commonly applied to high-value mineral commodities. They are more economically efficient than specific royalties as the amount paid is positively correlated with changes in commodity prices. They are relatively easy to explain and justify to industry and the community as they closely relate to the mining processes. They can be simple to relatively complex to administer and will continue to be collected even if commodity prices decline as long as a mine continues to operate.

The measure of profit to be used as a base in profit- or rent-based royalties is different from the profit as calculated in the financial accounts of the mining company holding the project. This is primarily because it is calculated at the level of individual projects and generally makes use of different capital recovery and interest expenses and, in the case of rents, is calculated on a cash rather than an accrual basis. While profit-based royalties are the most economically efficient, they are complex and as a consequence difficult to explain and administer. Because of the generally significant depreciation/amortisation deductions no royalty payments may be made in the early years of production. In addition, as profits are highly leveraged by volatile commodity prices, the stream of royalty payments is very unstable and when prices, and therefore profits, are low there may be no payments at all. As for CIT, auditing profit-based royalties involves consideration of the legitimacy of a significant number of deductible expense items determined through, at times complex, accounting standards and tax rules, requiring a level of tax expertise which is often lacking in the tax authorities of developing countries.

Hybrid royalties, generally composed either of:

- a profit-based royalty subject to a specific or value-based minimum; or
- a value-based royalty with rates increasing in steps as a function of possible increases in the price of the mineral commodity as set out from time to time by government in regulations,

are a compromise designed to achieve revenue stability, while sharing the upside of mineral rents with industry at the cost of transparency and administrative efficiency.

Most mining royalties in the world are value-based or unit-based, and subordinately profit-based, with hybrid royalties imposed by a few jurisdictions. At the time of writing resource rent-based royalties and production sharing were not applied to mining, following their essentially limited and generally administratively unsuccessful use in the past. They are, nonetheless, widely and reasonably successfully applied to petroleum production. Figure 11.3 displays diagrammatically the relationship between various possible tax bases and the degree to which the main fiscal objectives are achieved. In all cases, higher royalty and/or CIT rates would inhibit FDI. Nonetheless there is a clear indication that the mining industry would not be excessively deterred from investing in mineral exploration by

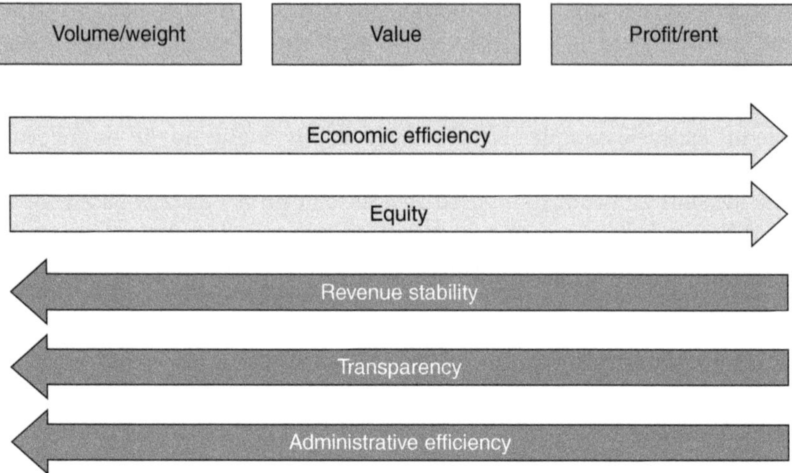

Figure 11.3 Diagram displaying how different types of tax bases (shown in boxes) influence achievement of main fiscal objectives.

high rates of royalty and taxation in cases where a country is perceived as having a high degree of mineral prospectivity. This is particularly true if, based on past experience, the fiscal regime of a country is perceived as stable.

Mining tax incentives

Most fiscal regimes, whether 'coercive' (i.e. based on conditions embodied in current legislation) or 'contractual' (i.e. based on terms negotiated between government and individual mining companies for specific projects) recognise by way of industry-specific provisions and incentives, the unique characteristics of the mining industry, that is to say the fact that:

- mineral resources are not renewable;
- mineral resources are owned by the state but mostly extracted by the private sector;
- mineral exploration and mining are high-risk ventures with low probability of making a discovery and great uncertainty in terms of mine profitability;
- mine development and construction are extremely capital-intensive and involve long pre-production lead times during which the project does not produce any revenue;
- mineral prices and exchange rates are highly volatile thus generating unstable revenues and profit streams; and
- mining operations can have very long lives.

Provisions particularly favourable to industry are often embedded in the CIT system or into mining contracts to attract international exploration and mining investment to a country, often at times of low commodity prices, when the bargaining power of government is also low. For this reason, or because some governments did not appear to have fully appreciated, at the time of negotiation, the potential long-term revenue and administrative consequences of providing various types of incentives, the contribution made by mining to the socio-economic development of some countries has not lived up to expectation, or at least it is so perceived by the political system and the community at large. Fiscal incentives commonly include:

- tax holidays;
- special capital allowances such as:
  - immediate write-off of capital expenses,
  - accelerated depreciation for mining-specific capital expenses;
- depletion allowance; and
- exemption from custom duty, WHT and VAT etc.

Tax incentives may be necessary to stimulate investment in the mining sector and related supporting, often multi-user, infrastructure. However, the decision to grant incentives should be done with full knowledge of the trade-offs involved, such as their impact on much needed revenue collection and opportunities for tax avoidance, and clearly communicated to all stakeholders, particularly citizens.

Stability agreements

In addition, the mining industry often demands, as a prerequisite to investing, that the negotiated fiscal incentives be locked into long-lasting mining contracts by 'stabilisation clauses'. In some cases 'stability agreements' are ratified by parliament, which in effect turns them into laws. This further restricts government from introducing any future changes to the fiscal conditions, other than by reaching mutual agreement with the mining company.

In the past, some agreements were drafted to cover the life of the mine. More recently, the tendency has been to limit the first term to 10–15 years, with a possible extension subject to renegotiation. This is a good practice because of the inherent incapacity of both government and industry to think realistically into the future, which, in mining, invariably proves highly uncertain. A further improvement would be to include triggers to initiate renegotiation in the event of certain key parameters, for example commodity prices exceeding pre-set ranges. The presence of stability agreements also means that, as the fiscal conditions evolve over time, the tax administration must deal with the added complexity of a multiplicity of different co-existing tax systems.

Tax holidays

Tax holidays, which specify a period during which a company will not pay any CIT, thus fully capturing all profits in the early years of the project, can be constructed in two general forms:

- on a time basis (e.g. covering the first five years of production); or
- on a quantity extracted basis (e.g. covering a specific tonnage of ore or metal as identified in the feasibility study).

If the tax holiday is time-based and unconstrained, the amount of tax relief can be increased by the company through an increase in the rate of extraction or by high-grading, effectively reducing the residual mine life and its profitability. This strategy leaves behind lower tonnages of less valuable material to be extracted, reducing potential revenue during the period when taxation applies.

If the tax holiday is tonnage-based, then the taxing authority should satisfy itself that there is no high-grading, but that the grades mined match, within reason, those submitted in the feasibility study at the time the project received mining approval.

Another area to be clear about is to determine how depreciation and amortisation are to be handled during the tax holiday period. Assets should be depreciated as if the operations were being taxed with a tax rate of 0 per cent then applied to the taxable income. The alternative of accumulating depreciation and then deducting it from revenue following the tax holiday period is clearly not recommended as it would further erode the total tax collected.

Clearly defining to what project the tax holiday applies is another area of contention if satellite orebodies are discovered and developed. The question is whether they are an extension of the current operations or a new operation triggering a new tax holiday.

In essence a tax holiday is not a good form of fiscal incentive from the point of view of government, but if it cannot be avoided, then the tax administration should ensure it is not open to abuse, by specifying in the relevant contract and/or legislation:

- what constitutes the mining project;
- the extent to which the quantities mined can be changed; and
- how depreciation expenses and losses are to be treated during the holiday period.

Given a choice it is prudent for tax authorities to consider other incentives, as tax holidays may cause administrative complexity, ambiguity and potential for tax avoidance.

Capital allowances specifically for the mining industry

Mining is capital-intensive, involving very significant upfront investments during the initial period of pre-production when development and construction of the mine take place. Sometimes pre-production may last over a significant number of years during which the mine does not produce any revenue. Significant 'sustaining' capital expenditure is also required during the productive life of the mine to replace assets, fund design changes etc.

For the purpose of this discussion, assets can be generally categorised into tangible and intangible, and further subdivided into:

- normal depreciable assets, which are also commonly used in other sectors of the economy; and
- mining-specific assets that are unique to the mining industry.

The capital allowances or capital recovery rules that apply to the mining industry differ from country to country and may contain special provisions for the second category or for both. These provisions may include:

- immediate write-off of all capital expenses, or only of mining-specific capital expenses; or
- accelerated depreciation of only mining-specific capital expenses, with other assets depreciated normally.

Immediate and/or accelerated write-off of capital expenditure are desirable from the point of view of the mining company because they accelerate cash flows at the critical initial stages when a project is most vulnerable. However, *they have the effect of significantly delaying government revenue*. This may be a significant issue if the mining project is not ring-fenced and losses incurred by associated companies may be deducted from its income.

Fiscal issues relating to globalisation and mining multinationals

Fiscal consequences of corporate structures used by mining multinationals

Multinational enterprises (MNEs) have, in recent years, tended to structure their businesses by consolidating high-value functions and related intangible assets, in entities or hubs which provide goods and services to their global operations, and locating them in low-tax jurisdictions. The result (Guj *et al.* 2016) is that:

- the tax base of the country hosting the mining project is eroded as profit is shifted abroad;

- the functions of an MNE's mining subsidiary are often reduced to mostly routine physical activities utilising primarily tangible assets and less skilled personnel;
- few mining companies in developing countries are fully vertically integrated and tend to export crushed and screened ore (as for instance iron ore and coal), or base metals and other concentrates after limited processing to related smelters or marketing hubs;
- a significant number of cross-border transactions for the provision of high-value, specialised services and assets, and/or financing, are often conducted between related entities part of the same MNE group.

In some cases, the provision of services through these hubs adds value because of synergies created by pooling of specialised resources, proximity to customers, trading and shipping centres and/or research facilities. Mining companies often contend that the finance and key services needed for a project to be developed do not exist and would be unlikely to become available in the country unless provided through related hubs.

On the other hand, the extreme artificiality of some of these structures and evidence that many conduit companies are just 'mail boxes' with no employees, clear business purpose, or value-adding capacity would indicate that they are primarily designed to minimise the MNE's tax at the consolidated level. Some MNEs also make use of a practice known as 'treaty shopping' involving the establishment of complex networks of related conduit companies resident in jurisdictions carefully selected to derive tax minimisation advantages, that would otherwise be inhibited by the limited network of double taxation agreements (DTAs) of some developing countries.

While some of these arrangements may be strictly speaking legal, it may be argued that, in the context of poor developing countries, they are ethically questionable.

Transfer pricing and application of the arm's-length principle

The OECD *Transfer Pricing Guidelines for Multinational Enterprises and Tax Administrations, 2012*, currently being amended in line with the recommendations of the *BEPS (2015) Final Reports*, require that the price adopted in controlled transactions between related parties, the so-called transfer price, should be at arm's-length. In other words the transfer price should be the same as would have been agreed between unrelated parties in an uncontrolled transaction for similar goods or services under similar circumstances. After all, why would the mining company have accepted, acting independently and without compulsion, clearly disadvantageous conditions if better conditions existed in the market at the time?

The OECD *Guidelines* provide five methods that industry can use to apply the arm's-length principle. In most countries the arm's-length principle is either embodied in the general tax law or in specific transfer pricing legislation, and rules which require taxpayers, among others, to compile and to make available on demand contemporaneous documentation as to how transfer prices were derived. Consistent and rigorous application of the arm's-length principle would insure that profits are taxed in the jurisdictions where they are generated and reduce the risk of double taxation.

There is, however, evidence, that transfer pricing is often not conducted at arm's-length but rather used as an opportunity to shift profits to lower tax jurisdictions. Tax administrations must be equipped to examine how transfer prices were determined and whether the profits of mining subsidiaries and of overseas related customers and/or service providers reflect the value actually added by each of them along the mining value chain. If the substance and form of a related-party transaction do not match a tax adjustment and, in extreme cases, recharacterisation of the transaction may be warranted.

Transfer mispricing represents a major taxation risk in the context of MNEs' mining subsidiaries in developing countries, because this sector often represents a major source of revenue and individual transactions may involve very significant cash flows and complexity. The profit of the mining subsidiary and therefore the tax collected in the host country may be significantly reduced by the mining subsidiary:

- undercharging for minerals transferred to related parties; and
- overpaying for specialised (e.g. marketing, treasury/financing, insurance, logistics and technical/R&D) and routine (e.g. most corporate services) goods and services.

Transfer mispricing is possible because of the inherent complexity of some of the mining-related transactions, which creates opacity and opportunities for manipulation. This is particularly the case where intermediate mineral products, for which there are no stringent standard specifications and readily available comparable market prices, are transferred to related marketing hubs. Tax authorities must also satisfy themselves that both quantity and quality of the mineral products exported are correct and that there has been no under-invoicing. Serious, but highly contested, allegations of understating the grade, hence the value, of exported concentrates have recently been levelled at a multinational gold miner by the Tanzanian government.

Transactions, involving hard-to-value specialised marketing, finance, technical/R&D, management and legal knowhow and related intangible assets and intellectual property, are also particularly difficult to audit, as tax administrations are often denied access to adequate financial information relating to the relevant foreign service providers. Irrespective of the presence of 'thin capitalisation' rules, difficulties also arise in determining whether the interest charged on intra-group loans and guarantee fees are at arm's length and whether they constitute justifiable deductions or should be reclassified as non-deductible equity dividends.

In addition to tax authorities' efforts to identify, prioritise and manage revenue risks, NGOs and CSOs are very active in bringing to public attention potential abuses of transfer pricing rules by MNEs, often precipitating government investigations and intervention.

Broad estimates indicate that transfer mispricing and other illicit outflows may represents a $50 billion annual leakage of tax revenues from developing countries in Africa (UNECA, 2014). Developed countries are also not immune from the problem, as indicated by recent significant adjustments to the income tax and royalty payable (i.e. $522 million and $288 million respectively) by an Australian mining company selling its mineral products through a related marketing hub resident in Singapore, and similarly large tax adjustments relating to disallowance of interest deductions by a petroleum MNE.

Given the significant risk to revenue, it is vital that tax administrations in developing countries have the legal powers and the administrative capacity to ascertain whether transfer prices are actually at arm's length, through systematic transfer pricing compliance and risk management processes including audits. It would appear, however, this is not currently the case in many jurisdictions and that relatively few, mining-specific transfer pricing audits are being carried out, mainly because of inadequate resourcing of tax administrations in general and transfer pricing expertise in particular, and inadequate depth of knowledge of the mining industry, its activities and processes.

The problem is also aggravated by the general reluctance of MNEs to disclose to tax administrations key financial information about some of the foreign subsidiaries involved in related-party transactions and of the general scarcity and high cost of relevant transactional comparable information. Although many developing countries have justifiably shied away from entering into DTAs with the countries of residence of some of the main related suppliers to their mining companies, because doing so would have lessened their taxing powers, they should be keenly pursuing negotiation of exchange of information (EoI) agreements with them.

To overcome some of these complexities, while strengthening their administrative capacity, governments in developing countries have tended to capture a greater proportion of profits by applying comparatively high levels of withholding taxes on overseas remittances for dividends, interest, royalties, service fees etc. Many jurisdictions, particularly in Latin America, have also resorted to approaches not complying with the arm's-length principle, such as the application of fixed margins to related-parties transactions and of the so-called 'sixth method'. This method, which makes use of quoted market prices on the day of shipment of minerals, has recently been endorsed by the OECD as a possible anti-avoidance measure. Simplification measures such as the application of 'safe harbours' and of advance pricing agreements (APAs) are being considered, but as yet not widely adopted by developing countries.

Tax administrative capacity and inter-agency co-operation

Asides from the adequacy of the fiscal policy, legislative and regulatory frameworks, issues influencing effectiveness in collecting mining taxation can be grouped (Calder, 2010) into two categories: institutional/structural and administrative capacity issues.

Institutional/structural issues

Different types of taxes may be collected at different levels of government, i.e. central/federal, provincial/state, local etc. An exhaustive discussion about different approaches that government can choose regarding collecting and reallocating mining taxes at the sub-national level can be found in the 2009 International Council of Mining and Metals' review of minerals taxation regimes (ICMM, 2009) to which the reader is referred.

CIT is invariably administered and collected by the central government and falls within the responsibilities of its Ministry of Finance. The picture is somewhat different for mineral royalties which are generally administered and collected centrally, other than in the case of federations, but often by the relevant Ministry of Mines as effective administration of mineral royalties relies on its specialised technical skills and knowledge of the mining industry.

In a federation the constitution determines the respective roles and responsibility of the central and state governments. CIT generally falls into the ambit of the central government, while land-related issues, including mining regulation and administration, are, in most cases, legislated about and administered by state or provincial governments. The jurisdiction in which mineral rights are vested, usually under the terms of a *Mining Act* and supporting regulations, is the predominant factor in determining which level of government collects mineral royalties.

Irrespective of how revenue collection is structured, there must be a clear allocation of the functions to be performed by the various ministries and their departments involved to reduce potentially wasteful instances of inefficient overlaps and duplication of effort (Guj *et al.*, 2013). This may involve the establishment of:

- practical inter-agency protocols, promoting greater co-operation, thus simplifying and expediting processes;
- fewer and more attentive taxpayer's interfaces, ideally establishment of a 'one-stop-shop';
- the harmonisation and sharing of relevant databases, through data warehousing with clear responsibility for the collection and integrity of various datasets; and

- sharing of specialised skills, which would see greater integration of technical mining engineering skills normally resident in the Department of Mines, and physical quantity and value verification skills resident with Custom and Excises within the compliance and risk management processes, including audits, normally carried out by the tax office.

In spite of general agreement in principle, implementation of these types of improvements may be slow and painful, as it affects the boundaries of ministries and departments and therefore their political influence, careers and share of limited budget resources.

Administrative capacity issues

It is generally recognised that investing in tax administration can secure attractive marginal returns for government. However, in reality few tax administrations appear to be adequately funded. Combined with the fact that specialised tax expertise is in high demand and that the employment conditions of the public service in most developing countries are not competitive with those of the private sector, it should come as no surprise that many tax administrations lack an adequate skill inventory. This is despite significant advances in the development of computerised tax administration systems and databases, allowing online submission of both royalties and CIT returns and aiding the verification and audit processes, which should be reducing labour intensity. The 'catch 22' is that potentially lower establishment numbers are to be achieved through scarce availability of higher levels of specialisation.

Tax administrations of developing countries, with the assistance of international institutions and donor countries, must make committed efforts to both improving and simplifying their mining tax frameworks and training their workforce to keep up with the continuous tax challenges presented by globalisation. Training can be in-house making use of private sector specialists and/or officers seconded from other more advanced tax administrations, or by sponsoring promising upcoming officers for, generally bonded, university degrees and mentoring them through clear career paths. More emphasis should also be placed on improving tax officers' communication and negotiation skills, thus achieving a higher rate of voluntary compliance and case resolutions, avoiding unnecessary taxpayer disputes and court proceedings which lock up specialised resources and frequently result in unfavourable outcomes.

Conclusions

The general perception among politicians of many developing countries and their population at large that the contribution made by mining to their socio-economic development has fallen short of what they considered legitimate expectations has brought reform and improvement of their mining fiscal regimes to the forefront of their political agenda.

Based on their past experiences, tax authorities are learning the importance of avoiding conceding counterproductive fiscal incentives such as tax holidays and/or of stabilising their mining tax revenues by relying more on production rather than profit-based taxation instruments, even though they are aware that these are more regressive and less economically efficient measures. They also have started to question the wisdom of conceding immediate write-offs of all project capital expenditures and of taking the companies' financial modelling and evaluations at face value. The time has now come for them to establish basic economic and financial modelling capacity to support better informed mining approval decisions. On balance, economic analysis generally justifies some form of accelerated depreciation for new investment in mining-specific assets, bringing forward the cash flows of projects at their early and most vulnerable time.

Tax administrations should also attempt to renegotiate unfavourable fiscal conditions embodied in past stability agreements, often negotiated with a poor appreciation of their long-term consequences, whenever an opportunity arises. In practice, they should not miss any opportunity to successfully renegotiate fiscal conditions when industry requires amendments in other areas of an agreement. It goes without saying that all new mining agreements should be structured on the basis of successive terms of limited duration (say 10 to 15 years) rather than on the life of the mine, extendable by negotiation and including renegotiation triggers, if and when key parameters, such as commodity prices and exchange rates, exceed pre-set limits.

While the need for early and stable revenue streams and ease of administration will continue to inhibit greater reliance on more economically efficient profit- of rent-based mineral royalties, tax authorities should minimise the use of highly regressive volume/weight-based royalties for valuable minerals in favour of value-based ones particularly applying, where appropriate, progressive, price-related royalty rates.

The degree to which tax authorities will be successful in improving their mining taxation systems and mining contract structures depends on them being proactive and having a sound blueprint for what they consider should be an ideal or at least an acceptable regime in the future, that is to say on introducing policy changes prior to potential individual investors dragging them to the negotiating table. The authority's 'bargaining power' will be higher when negotiations occur in the context of an established fiscal framework which is perceived as reasonably stable and, of course, if commodity prices are high.

Tax authorities should continue, with the assistance of international institutions and donor countries, to improve their transfer pricing legal and regulatory frameworks and strengthening their capacity in the specialised area of transfer pricing compliance and risk management skills, including auditing. This should include a better technical and financial understanding of the various components of the mining value chain which would help direct scarce auditing resources to areas of higher cash flows and risk. They should ensure that domestic legislation is aligned, as far as feasible under their circumstances, with the OECD *Transfer Pricing Guidelines* and refrain from adopting measures that are not compliant with the arm's-length principle. Better communication and negotiation skills are also needed to promote more voluntary compliance and reduce adversarial attitudes and counterproductive litigation through the courts.

While defining clear demarcation lines between the roles and responsibilities of the various ministries and departments involved in mining fiscal policy formulation and administration, to reduce waste and duplication, government should also promote better inter-departmental co-ordination and co-operation, including harmonisation and warehousing of all the relevant databases, improving the integrity of and access to information and sharing of key specialised technical and financial skills residing in different agencies as the need arises.

All these initiatives are, of course, complementary to the significant effort still needed in ensuring that general mining tax administration processes, procedures and skills are continuously improved to keep pace with the demands created by the global dynamics of the mining industry.

References

Calder, J. (2010) 'Resource tax administration: Functions, procedures and institutions'. In Phil Daniel, Michael Keen and Charles McPherson (eds.), *The taxation of petroleum and minerals: Principles, problems and practice.* New York: Routledge.

Garnaut, R. and Clunies Ross, A. (1983) *Taxation of mineral rents.* Oxford: Clarendon Press.

Guj, P., Bocoum, B., Limerick, J., Meaton, M. and Maybee, B. (2013) *How to improve mining tax administration and collection frameworks: A sourcebook.* Jointly published by World Bank Group and Centre for Exploration Targeting of the University of Western Australia.

Guj, P., Martin, S. and Readhead, A. (2016) *Transfer pricing in African mining: A briefing note.* Jointly published by World Bank Group and Centre for Exploration Targeting of the University of Western Australia.

Harman, F. and Guj, P. (2012) 'Mineral taxation and royalties'. In Phillip Maxwell and Pietro Guj (eds.), *Mineral Economics*, Second edition, Monograph 29 of the Australasian Institute of Mining and Metallurgy. Burwood, Victoria, Australia: DPA Digital.

ICMM (International Council of Mining and Metals) (2009) *Minerals taxation regimes: A review of issues and challenges in their design and application.* Commonwealth Secretariat.

MCA (Mineral Council of Australia) (2015) *Submission to Senate Economics Reference Committee inquiry into corporate tax avoidance.*

Otto, J., Andrews, C., Cawood, F., Doggett, M., Guj, P., Stermole, F., Stermole, J. and Tilton, J. (2007) *Mining royalties: A global study of their impact on investors, government and civil society*. Washington, D.C.: International Bank for Reconstruction/World Bank (Directions in Development, Energy and Mining.

Readhead, A. (2016) *Getting a good deal: Ring-fencing in Ghana*. Natural Resource Charter Case Study. Natural Resource Governance Institute.

UNECA (United Nations' High Level Panel of the Economic Commission for Africa) (2014) *Progress report on illicit financial flows: "Track it! Stop it! Get it!"*.

Part V

Sustainability solutions

12 Emissions and the role of renewables

Drivers, potential, projects and projections

Benjamin C. McLellan, Yosoon Choi, Syed Ali Ghoreishi-Madiseh and Ferri P. Hassani

Introduction

Reducing emissions of greenhouse gases to mitigate climate change is a global focus of governments and other organisations (UN, 2015). Likewise, emissions of other pollutants that have a detrimental environmental or human health impact are the traditional focus of regulatory efforts that can support a practical minimum threshold for sustainable societies. The usage of energy, and its conversion from primary energy sources (such as coal or oil) into second energy products (e.g. electricity and petroleum), is one of the leading causes of both localised and globally important emissions. Energy intensive industries, such as the mining and minerals sectors, are facing regulatory and social drivers to improve their emissions per unit output of product. In general this can be achieved by two methods: reducing the usage of energy (i.e. improving efficiency) or reducing the emissions from the energy that is used (i.e. reducing emissions intensity). One of the key mechanisms to achieve the latter of these is the use of renewable energy rather than fossil fuels.

Worldwide interest in renewable energy is increasing due to a number of converging factors, including climate change mitigation, energy security, increasing cost of energy and environmental impact reduction and safety of conventional energy sources. Alternative (typically renewable) energy sources are being developed to provide solutions to these problems. Currently, sustainable, cost-effective and environmentally benign renewable energy technologies such as solar thermal, photovoltaics, wind turbines, hydropower, geothermal energy, ocean energy and biofuels are being developed and are being widely utilised in various industries (Pearce, 2002; Chiras, 2009; Choi *et al.*, 2011).

Companies are responding to government and societal pressures in order to maintain a license to operate in an increasingly environmentally aware society. The mining industry is also introducing renewable energy technologies to resolve power supply problems at mines operating in remote areas (secluded inland areas far away from a coast or city), or in polar regions, and to foster supplementary industries able to benefit from abandoned space in exhausted mines. There are therefore a variety of opportunities for the sector to leverage synergies of renewables and mining.

At the same time, the material requirements of renewable energy technologies (e.g. a variety of base and rare metals) are increasing pressure on minerals supply and minerals markets (McLellan *et al.*, 2016). Increasing demand could potentially drive further mining development, thus benefiting the sector further. However, changes in the geological characteristics of mined deposits over time may present a mixed opportunity for reducing emissions overall, and the pressure on the minerals industry to utilise cleaner energy may grow further.

This chapter presents some of the key drivers, policies and case studies of how renewable energy is being used in the industry, and how this may change in future.

Potential

The mining sector is highly dependent on fossil fuels, with oil product consumption in the sector in particular being significantly larger as a proportion of total energy consumption (29 per cent) than the all-industry average (12 per cent) (IEA, 2014). Another 35 per cent of final energy consumption is provided by electricity, which is globally very fossil-fuel intensive, but considering the majority of renewable energy is focused on electricity generation, this opens up a significant area of opportunity for substitution. Energy use in the mining industry has increased by around 455 per cent in the period 1971–2012, based on data from the International Energy Agency (IEA), while renewable energy used in the sector has only increased by around 430 per cent, meaning that the energy usage has become more "fossilised" (IEA, 2014). At the same time, estimates of production of mined and quarried material show an increase of 320 per cent, showing that the energy increase has outstripped the production – mining and quarrying have overall become less efficient per tonne of material extracted (McLellan, 2017). This trend in the mining sector is likely to be linked with the increasing mechanisation of mining techniques and the greater depth at which mining is now being undertaken, as well as a potential correlation with decreases in cut-off grades. This also contrasts with the downstream minerals sectors, which have become more efficient overall, and increased their share of renewable energy more rapidly than total energy usage (McLellan, 2017).

Figure 12.1 shows the overall rate of renewable energy use across the minerals sub-sectors, including direct energy (fuels mainly) and indirect energy (electricity, assuming global grid mix). It is apparent that the global

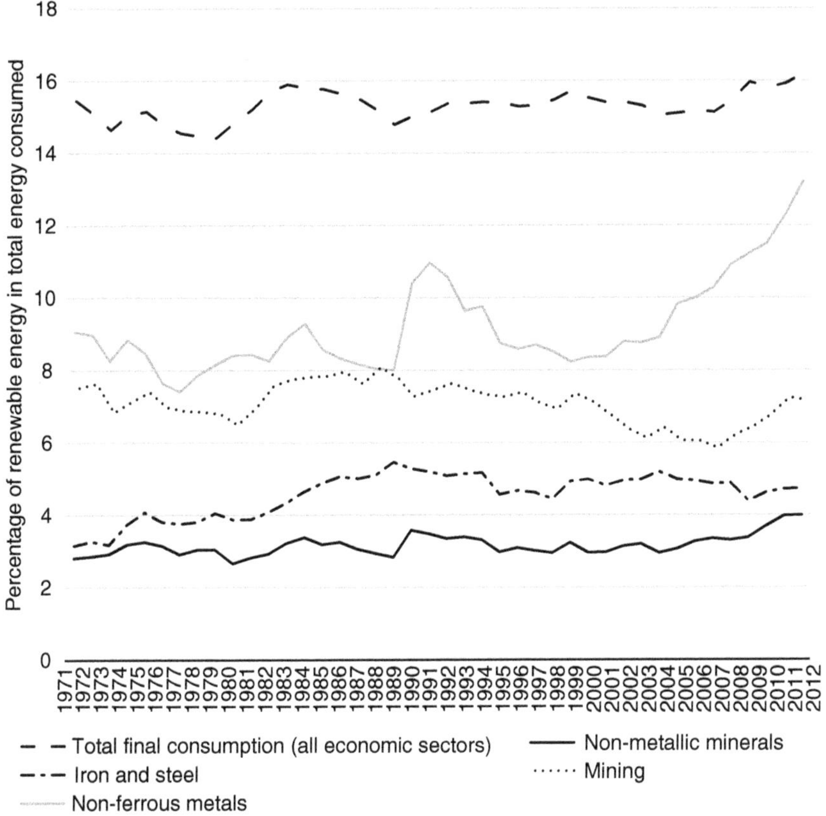

Figure 12.1 Renewable energy in total final energy consumption of minerals industry sectors and across all economic sectors.

Data source: IEA, 2014.

mining sector has historically used around 6–8 per cent renewable energy, with no clear trend of improvement within the time period. In the same period, the other minerals industry sub-sectors have shown moderate improvement, with the non-ferrous metals sector improving the most in recent years. In part, this can be considered to be due to the rate of electrification of each of the sub-sectors, as renewable energy technologies are largely focused on electricity generation. As shown in Figure 12.2, the non-ferrous sector has seen a sharp increase in electrification, while there have been overall moderate improvement in the other downstream sectors, and moderate decline in the mining sector. Figure 12.3 shows the global mix of energy consumption in the mining sector in 2012 (IEA 2014), which indicates that there is very minimal direct renewable energy usage in the sector. Thus, there is apparent opportunity for improving the mining sector's

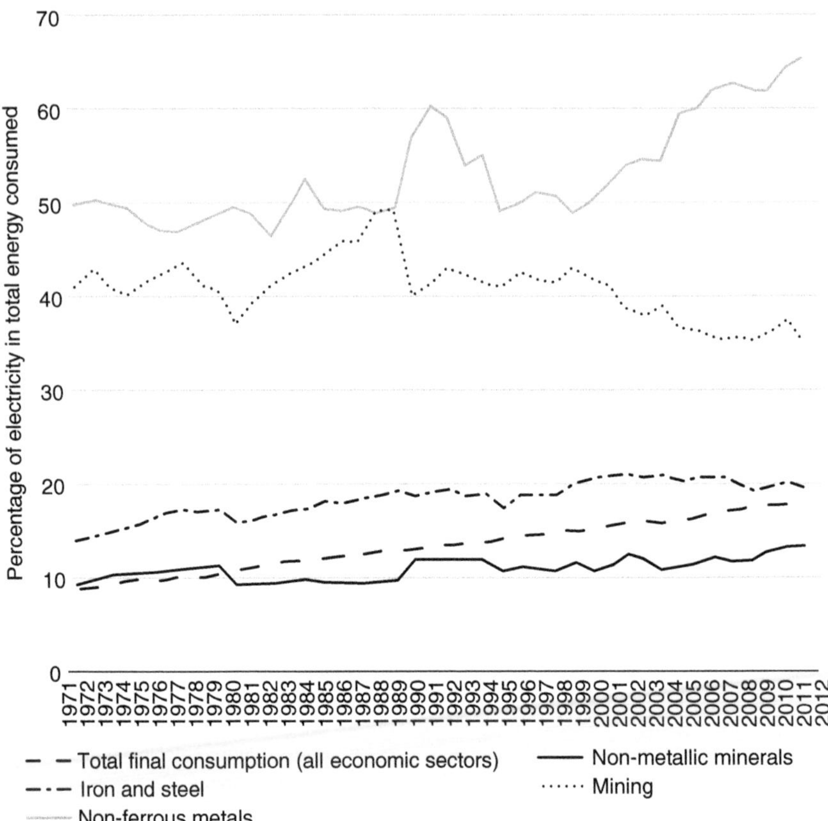

Figure 12.2 Electricity in total final energy consumption of minerals industry sectors and across all economic sectors.

Data source: IEA, 2014.

utilisation of renewable energy – particularly in its electricity mix – and it is likely that greater potential could be obtained if more of the sector's energy usage could be converted to electricity.

For most types of renewable energy, one of the main resources required for its implementation is land – particularly because renewable energy tends to be diffuse (compared with the high energy density of conventional fuels and power plants). In Australia, the land area under mining is approximately 0.2 per cent of the total land mass, or around 1,281 km^2 (ABARES, 2007). Comparing this with production and estimates of mined ore and waste rock (assuming conservative grades for major commodities) the amount of extracted material is approximately 1,000 ktpa/km^2. If we apply this figure across the global mining and quarrying industry, this is likewise approximately 0.2 per cent of the world's land mass (around

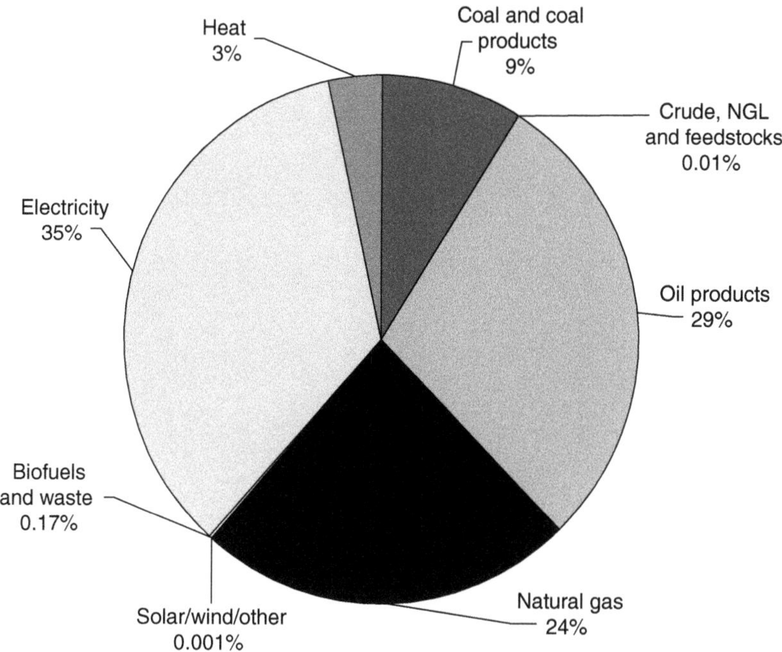

Figure 12.3 Final energy consumption mix in the mining and quarrying sector.
Data source: IEA, 2014.

31,000 km^2 out of 148.94 million km^2). This is a large area of land, and it is useful to make a first-pass estimate of the potential renewable energy capacity that could be installed on this, with regards to the industry total usage. To be accurate, estimating potential for the industry as a whole would require a country-by-country and ultimately mine-by-mine consideration of land use and renewable energy potential. This level of detail was not possible in this case, but instead, an estimate using reported energy use from countries and regions in the world to match the IEA data to the regions in the Global Energy Assessment (IIASA, 2012) was applied. The initial considered potential for each type of renewable energy is extracted from the GEA, shown in Table 12.1. The renewable energy potential was assumed to be directly related to land area, and the land area under mining assumed to be 0.2 per cent as per the Australian case (due to lack of global data).

The amount of estimated renewable energy resource potential was then estimated and compared to the energy use in the mining sector in each of the regions. Figure 12.4 shows this amount of potential as compared to the electricity usage in the mining sector, by region and energy source. Figure 12.5 then shows this amount as a comparison with total energy consumed

Table 12.1 Potential for renewable energy in each country or region

		Potential renewable energy resource by region (EJ/year)												
	Country or Region	USA	Canada	Western Europe	Eastern Europe	Former Soviet Union	Africa	Middle East	China	India	Japan	Other Asia	Oceania	Latin America and Caribbean
	Codes from GEA-2012	USA	CAN	WEU	EEU	FSU	NAF/EAF/WCA/SAF	MEE	CHN	IND	JPN	OEA/OSA/PAS	OCN	LAC
	Terrestrial surface area (1,000 km^2)	11,367	9,331	9,178	1,159	1,614	22,537	5,169	9,351	3,147	394	8,636	7,913	20,295
Hydro	Maximum technical potential	7.3	7.4	11.7	1.3	12.7	14.1	2.5	21.9	9.5	2.6	20.5	1.7	30.2
	Technical potential (20–200 $/MWh)	4.8	3.0	4.1	0.6	8.1	6.6	1.0	8.9	2.4	0.5	5.7	0.6	11.1
	Economic potential (20–80 $/MWh)	1.4	1.9	2.9	0.4	4.7	2.5	0.4	6.3	1.6	–	1.1	0.1	6.6
Biomass	Theoretical total bioenergy potential	64.0	73.0	32.0	11.0	170.0	250.0	5.0	44.0	16.0	4.0	103.0	55.0	299.0
	Theoretical practical bioenergy potential	48.0	52.0	25.0	7.0	117.0	168.0	5.0	37.0	12.0	3.0	69.0	40.0	210.0
Wind (input)	Technical potential (land and offshore)	209.4	373.4	105.4	5.9	86.1	217.6	6.4	35.0	0.1	3.9	16.1	302.3	268.0
	Practical potential (onshore only)	43.2	48.6	9.0	0.7	32.4	1.5	3.6	4.5	0.0	0.2	2.1	27.0	27.0
Solar (input)	Potential for CSP	11,360	2	664	7	8,587	128,618	22,716	11,271	1,756	10	8,342	55,501	28,831
	Technical potential centralised PV	340	140	88	30	606	4,812	1,224	938	379	4	706	1,658	1,169
	Technical potential decentralised PV	29.6	2.8	33.0	3.8	6.6	7.6	11.1	26.3	10.6	19.3	26.2	5.0	31.6
Geothermal (input)	Technical potential (heat)	17.5	12.0	7.5	1.3	24.8	22.8	5.0	11.8	3.5	0.5	18.9	3.5	24.8
	Technical potential (heat for electricity)	75.0	52.0	32.0	5.1	104.0	95.0	21.0	52.0	15.0	2.9	77.4	17.0	109.0
	Economic potential (heat)	1.2	0.1	4.3	0.9	0.5	0.1	0.2	1.8	0.1	0.2	0.4	0.0	0.4
	Economic potential (heat for electricity)	34.9	0.3	6.2	1.2	3.1	0.9	0.6	1.9	0.6	0.6	1.6	7.4	6.2

Source: IIASA 2012.

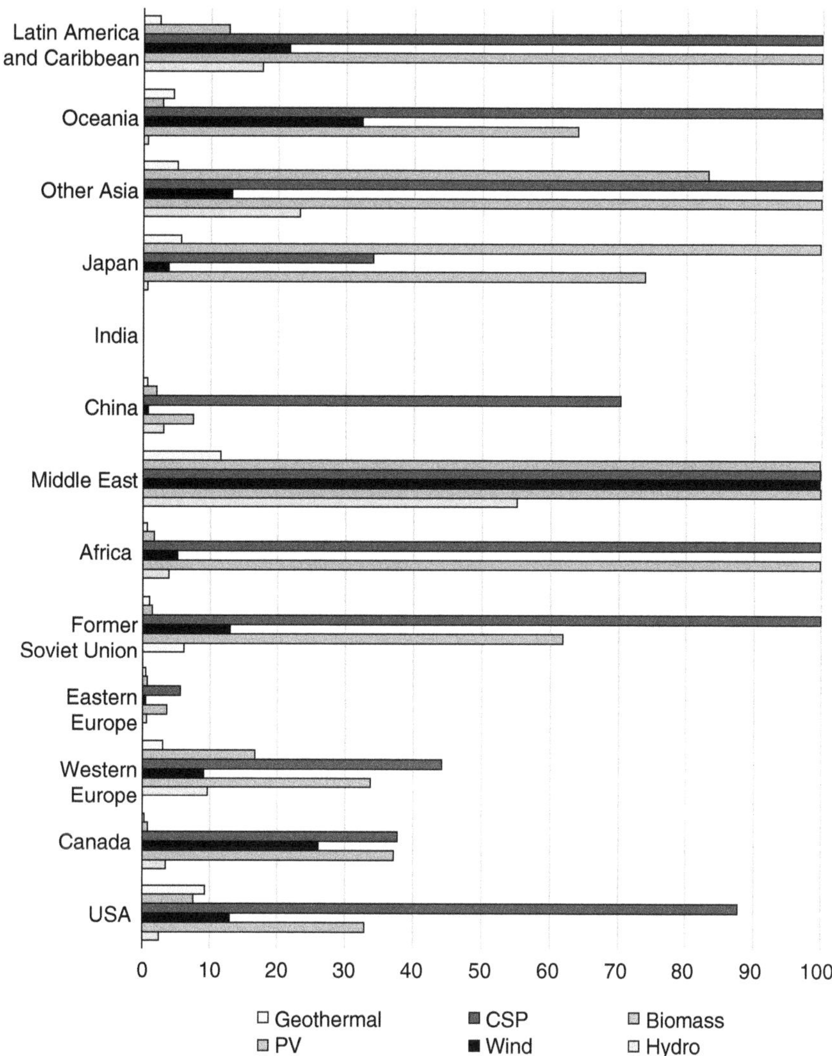

Figure 12.4 Percentage of mining sector electricity suppliable from renewables on mining land.

in the sector. The final column of Table 12.2 then gives the total from all sources, which can range from quite low in the case of Eastern Europe (4 per cent) to many times the current energy usage as in the Middle East (>2,500 per cent). In the case of total energy here, for simplicity and the sake of a conservative estimation, it has been assumed that energy is utilised as electricity. While this is not currently the case for most mining related energy (approximately 65 per cent is not electricity) it can be

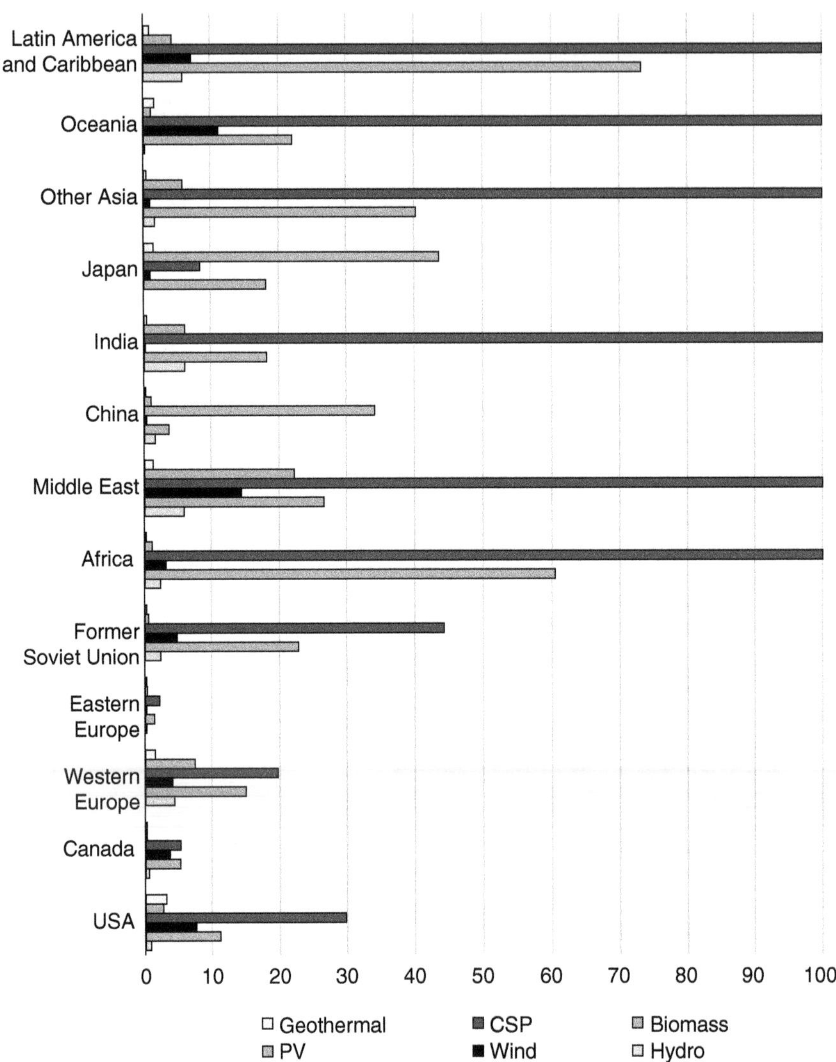

Figure 12.5 Percentage of total mining sector energy suppliable from renewables on mining land.

argued that much of the energy used could be electrified; in cases where this would not be possible, biofuels or hydrogen and synthesised fuels derived from electrolysis could be alternatives (McLellan, 2009). Comparing with previous estimates, across the minerals industry as a whole (not just mining) the substitutability of energy using more biofuels (~65 per cent of thermal energy) and hydropower (~75 per cent of electrical energy) has been estimated when total national renewable energy potential is

Table 12.2 Proportion of total final energy consumption of mining sector possible to be supplied from renewable energy on mining land (%)

Region or country	*Proportion of total final energy consumption of mining sector able to be supplied from indicated renewable energy resource*						
	Hydro	*Biomass*	*Wind*	*CSP*	*PV*	*Geothermal*	*Total*
USA	1	11	8	30	3	3	55
Canada	0.5	5	4	5	0.1	0.01	15
Western Europe	4	15	4	20	7	1	52
Eastern Europe	0.2	1	0.1	2	0.3	0.1	4
Former Soviet Union	2	23	5	44	0.5	0.2	75
Africa	2	60	3	647	1	0.1	714
Middle East	6	27	14	2,440	22	1	2,510
China	2	4	0.3	34	1	0.1	40
India	6	18	0.01	214	6	0.3	245
Japan	0	18	1	8	43	1	72
Other Asia	2	40	1	154	6	0.3	202
Oceania	0.2	22	11	341	1	2	377
Latin America and Caribbean	6	73	7	153	4	1	243

Notes

CSP = concentrating solar power; PV = photovoltaics; assumed to be electricity produced at efficiencies of Hydro:100%, Biomass: 40%, Wind: 30%, CSP: 15%, PV: 15%, Geothermal: 15%.

Mining land assumed to be 0.2% of total land – and renewable resource likewise 0.2% of national or regional total.

considered to be accessible (McLellan *et al.*, 2012). Using the estimates here, it would only be necessary to utilise 5 per cent of total renewable capacity in the worst case (Eastern Europe) in order to supply the full energy quota of the sector. Other estimates across various industrial sectors (not explicitly addressing mining, though addressing the other mineral subsectors) indicated that biomass held the best potential for substitution across all sectors of industry (IRENA, 2015).

If the supply chain of minerals is considered, the mining component is not the largest energy consumer or the largest emitter – typically the smelting or refining stages utilise more energy and subsequently tend to emit more (McLellan *et al.*, 2012). However, with regard to the available land and environmental potential, it is likely that in many cases mining is better placed to install and operate onsite renewable energy generation. Despite this advantage, relocation of mines is effectively impossible, but relocation of downstream processing stages (in order to make use of renewable energy sources available elsewhere) is readily achievable at the early stages of design – although not necessarily desirable from a national government perspective. This approach has been shown to more than mitigate the additional transportation emissions in many cases (McLellan, 2011). In some cases, the business case would also be attractive.

This brief examination of the potential of the minerals industry to substitute the fossil energy it uses for the majority of its energy indicates a significant opportunity – even using the small fraction of land and renewable potential that the mining sector can likely directly access. With this general background in mind, the following sections will highlight the drivers and concrete opportunities that have been demonstrated globally as contextually advantageous to the mining sector.

Drivers

There are multiple reasons for the mining industry to consider utilising renewable energy, driven by a combination of internal corporate and external societal pressures. These factors could largely be classified as associated with: cost, convenience, community relations, regulations, risk reduction or hedging, and responding to global aspirations.

Cost

The cost driver has multiple components that could each be described in detail, but these can be broadly summarised as the comparative cost of conventional energy and renewable energy provision. Dramatic increases in production and improvement in manufacturing processes, as well as a shift of manufacturing from high-cost countries (e.g. Germany, Japan) to lower-cost countries (e.g. China) have been driving a steep decline in the capital cost of many renewable technologies. Efficiencies have also been gained along the supply chain in countries where large-scale installations have taken place (Chapman *et al.*, 2016). In many countries, this has seen technologies previously considered excessively expensive becoming cost-competitive with conventional energy systems (Breyer and Gerlach, 2013). Where this is typically considered in the context of grid-connected, small-scale systems, the cost advantage of renewable energy technologies may be enhanced in the mining context, where remoteness makes supply of electricity via transmission lines, and fuel delivery for onsite use, expensive (Sarder, 2010; Baig *et al.*, 2015). While currently fossil fuel prices are low, electricity costs have been increasing in many markets, and the impact of ongoing increases or high-price shocks could be mitigated through renewable energy. In the case of countries with a price mechanism for greenhouse gas emissions, or strict emissions regulation, the attractiveness relative to alternative options can also be increased.

Convenience

As mentioned above, many mining operations occur in remote locations, often with intermittent transportation options for provisioning of the site. At the same time, the increasing shift to mining occurring in developing countries means that the availability and consistency of electricity supply and infrastructure may be problematic. Within such contexts, onsite power generation is typically favoured. However, for conventional onsite power generation with fossil fuel generators, there is a logistical requirement to transport fuel to site and maintain sufficient storage in case of supply restrictions or failure. In such cases, the provision of energy with onsite renewables avoids the supply chain vulnerability, although it must still maintain sufficient storage to account for periods of non-generation due to unfavourable environmental conditions. Thus, in many cases the convenience of onsite generation via renewables is an important consideration.

Community relations

Social license to operate has long been investigated in the mining industry (Prno and Scott Slocombe, 2012) and is an important consideration both pre-construction and during the operating phase of a mine (Giurco *et al.*, 2014). Renewable energy as an emissions-reducing technology has potential positive implications – in some cases by reducing conflict-invoking adverse onsite emissions directly (e.g. supplanting onsite fossil-fuel based energy generation or by enabling the conversion of fuel-utilising applications to electric power) and in some cases through 'green' image development at the site or corporate level. Certain types of renewable energy may be more controversial – with wind turbines, for example, having been criticised for noise and aesthetic degradation of the landscape (McCubbin and Sovacool, 2013) – although it could be argued that within the context of a mine site, these are likely to be less significant than in more pristine locations. Renewable energy projects that actively engage local communities – through employment, energy contracts or other means – may also help provide mutual gains to all stakeholders (Corder *et al.*, 2012).

Regulations

The direct reduction of onsite emissions through renewable energy could be utilised to bring operations in line with regulated emissions limits in some mines – in the same ways discussed in the previous section. Whilst not common in most jurisdictions, carbon emissions thresholds – particularly for energy or carbon intensive industries – could also drive the implementation of renewable energy. Alternatively, although more indirectly, there have been examples of the utilisation or proposal for utilisation of post-mining landscapes for renewable energy generation, e.g. biofuels (Martinát and Turečková, 2016), wind power (Song and Choi, 2016a), energy storage using pumped-hydropower (Weiss and Schulz, 2012) or compressed air in mining voids (Evans *et al.*, 2009). While post-mining rehabilitation is often mandated in licensing and approval stages of the project development cycle, the integration of renewable energy as a component of the post-mining plan could offer a useful feature in some cases, enabling better re-use prospects for the affected land.

Risk reduction

While the mining industry has long been interested in reducing risk – particularly risk associated with safety and with financial performance – the use of renewable energy can have a role in reducing a number of elements of risk. On the financial basis, there are a variety of costs that can potentially be mitigated through the use of renewable energy, but perhaps more important is the ability to mitigate variability in costs – for example through reduced exposure to fluctuating fossil fuel or electricity prices. One project in a developing country proposed the development of a renewable energy industry locally in order to support both the energy and skilled-labour requirement of a minerals operation – in this case mitigating two major cost components for the project (Corder *et al.*, 2012). Renewable technologies for electricity generation also offer the potential to reduce or eliminate onsite fuel storage, which poses a safety risk (McLellan *et al.*, 2012). On the broadest scale, renewable energy as a contribution to climate change mitigation can also be viewed as mitigating risk associated with changes in weather patterns.

Responding to global aspirations

The threat of climate change, and global aspirations to mitigate it, are fundamental to many of the other drivers mentioned here, but the discussion would be incomplete without considering this component. The aspirations expressed in the Paris Agreement (UN, 2015) and agreed upon by the nations of the world, if put into action, require a significant effort from the minerals sector to fulfil its contribution in reducing emissions. In some cases, the change in operating strategy may be required by legislative changes, whereas in others it may be voluntary. The ability to obtain funding for new projects may also be impacted – particularly through institutions signed-up to the Equator Principles (Equator Principles, 2013) – and there has been ongoing discussion of divestment from coal mining projects in particular in response to the climate change agenda (Clark and Herzog, 2014).

Other drivers at local or national scale are likely to be applicable, but this section has offered an overview of the largest trends at work. The following section will examine the potential for renewable energy in the mining sector, and the potential benefits and costs.

Projects: case studies

As the earlier global data has indicated, there is a theoretical potential to substitute a significant amount of energy for renewables. In this section, a number of concrete, innovative case studies are described. These cases may be seen as representative of some of the broad potential opportunities for renewable energy in the mining industry.

Geothermal energy

Geothermal energy is a safe and reliable source of energy. It causes far less environmental impacts relative to conventional fossil fuels, and has the advantage of providing a continuous and uninterrupted supply of energy unlike several other renewable sources such as wind and solar.

Water management is an important consideration, particularly in underground mines. Harvesting geothermal energy from underground mines has proven to be effective in several regions globally (Watzlaf and Ackman, 2006; Ghoreishi Madiseh *et al.*, 2012; Templeton *et al.*, 2014; Verhoeven *et al.*, 2014). A good example is the Minewater Project in the city of Heerlen (Watzlaf and Ackman, 2006; Verhoeven *et al.*, 2014). The project, which started in 2003, utilises the underground water stored in abandoned mines for the heating and cooling of the buildings and facilities within the city. In its second phase, the award-winning project is estimated to have reduced carbon emissions by 65 per cent (Watzlaf and Ackman, 2006). The project is currently being developed into its third phase which is expected to decrease carbon emissions by 80–100 per cent.

Another example is in Springhill, Nova Scotia, where geothermal energy is harvested from underground water found in abandoned coal mines (Jessop 1995). One of the establishments that utilises geothermal energy in

Springhill is Ropak Packaging, which has replaced a considerable portion of its furnace oil consumption by geothermal energy from an abandoned coal mine. A large proportion of the capital costs for geothermal energy are associated with drilling boreholes and pumping water to the surface. For an active mine with a fully functioning infrastructure, such costs are already covered by the operating expenses. This novel design proposes the installation of geothermal heat pumps or chillers in the dewatering network, before the water discharges to surface collecting ponds.

So far, the majority of the existing mine water geothermal systems have been undertaken in abandoned mines. However, there is significant potential for utilising the mine water found in active mines as a geothermal source to provide heat for onsite operations. This section demonstrates that there are immense benefits to replacing electric or natural gas heating systems with geothermal heating systems within an active mine. It offers a brief overview of deployment of the geothermal capacity of active underground mines, and examines various techno-economic aspects of employing geothermal technologies in mining operations, especially in cold environments like that of Canada. A number of Canadian underground mines were examined and the energy and carbon savings compared, along with the associated economic savings and carbon tax credit benefits versus estimated capital costs of each system. Ultimately, the study aims to highlight the costs and benefits of these technological solutions and draw the engineering guidelines required to evaluate their feasibility for the overviewed mine-specific cases.

Table 12.3 shows the data for the average water flows and temperature values measured at discharge locations at a number of mine sites. Using these measurements, along with the specifications of market-available geothermal heat pumps and chillers, it is possible to estimate the potential geothermal energy that can be harvested from each underground mining operation. Based on the results shown in Table 12.1, depending the discharged flows and temperatures, up to 1,578 kW of sustainable geothermal heat power can be produced (at Mine 5), while most of the mines can produce at least 500 kW of geothermal heat. Table 12.3 also illustrates the economic and environmental benefits from extracting geothermal energy. In addition, the environmental benefits through the reduction of carbon emissions can result in a high public relation value as well as savings from the pending carbon taxes. It is important to note that the conclusion in this preliminary study is based on conservative calculations so as not to be misinterpreted.

Two of the most technically feasible designs for harvesting the geothermal energy content of mine water are discussed below.

1 *Implementation of geothermal chiller*

The first scenario includes the implementation of a large-scale geothermal chiller at a mine site. The chiller will be used to heat mine intake air. In

Table 12.3 Summary of data collected at mine sites

Mine operation	*Water flow(GPM)*	*Water temperature (°C)*	*Heat gain (kW)*	*Annual savings ($/yr)*		*CO_2 reduction (t/yr)*	
				Natural gas	*Electricity*	*Natural gas*	*Electricity*
Mine 1	1,000	16.5	1,160	–	305,360	1,427	252
Mine 2	375	16.7	430	–	115,023	537	95
Mine 3	320	22	430	2,805	113,772	513	91
Mine 4	398	16.7	465	125,930	188,092	554	305
Mine 5	950	20.9	1,578	167,173	415,116	1,897	2,692
Mine 6	290	18.9	360	21,000	205,000	437	620
Mine 7	133	16.6	160	8,000	88,000	190	270
Mine 8	515	16.7	600	31,000	342,000	738	1,048
Mine 9	675	14	730	30,000	414,000	913	1,296
Mine 10	560	15.8	640	30,500	362,000	787	1,116
Mine 11	800	11.5	800	24,500	455,540	1,025	1,455
Mine 12	719	13.8	760	288,000	136,000	1,102	209
Mine 13	116	13.6	125	46,220	21,800	177	34

this case, the geothermal energy of the mine can replace the natural gas or propane consumed for preheating mine intake air in the cold season. The chiller can also be used for mine cooling purposes in summer time. A schematic representation of a chiller application is presented in Figure 12.6. Geothermal heat is received from mine water in the evaporator, and is boosted by the electric power of the motor and then conveyed to the circulating fluid of the condenser before being delivered to mine ventilation air in the heat exchangers. One of the main technical advantages of this design is its capability in handling mine water, which usually contains mud and solid particles. Since a chiller would have a relatively high heating capacity, it is suggested to be applied in the mine ventilation system. Therefore, it can augment the natural gas heating system that is installed in a mine in order to save on the amount of natural gas heating used. Installation costs will depend on the specific electrical and piping work required at each mine site.

2 *Implementation of geothermal heat pump*

Another scenario is to install heat pump(s) at the mine site to provide mine surface facilities with geothermal energy. In the case of heat pumps (Figure 12.7), a tank with a coil heat exchanger is required to harvest the geothermal

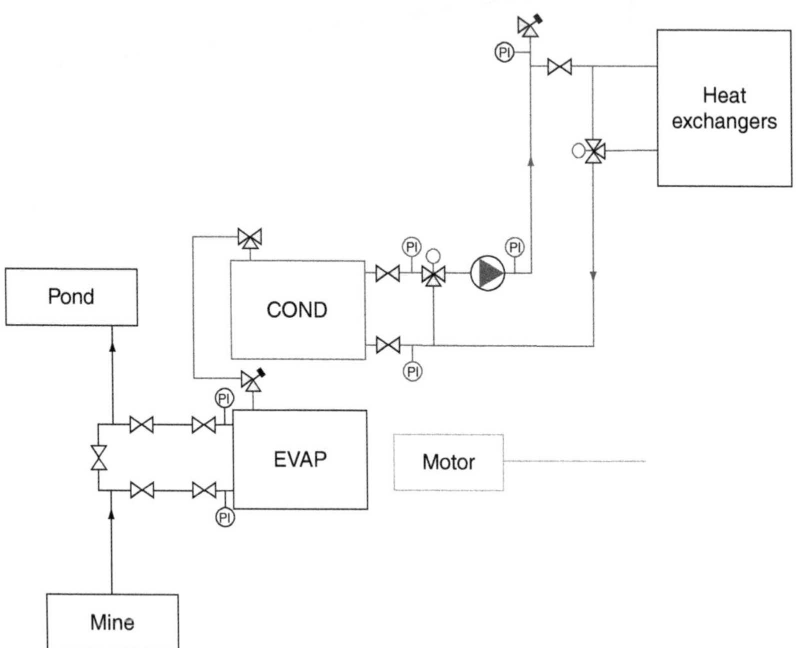

Figure 12.6 Geothermal chiller application.

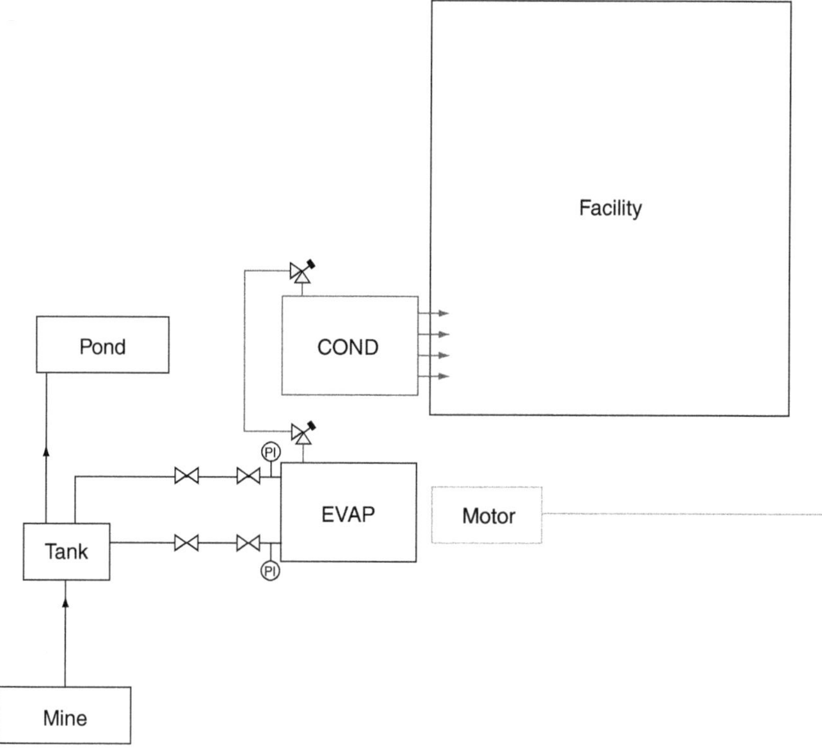

Figure 12.7 Geothermal heat pump application.

heat of milky mine water to prevent pipe blockage on the evaporator side. The extracted heat energy will then be upgraded using compressor power and delivered to end user(s) at the condenser side. These units can be modularised, and the number of units can be varied depending on the heating requirement. The benefit of a heat pump system is that the price per unit is lower when compared to a chiller. In addition, the size of the unit is smaller than the chiller. On the other hand, a chiller can handle more water flow per unit and so one unit can handle all mine discharge water. In addition, due to the larger size, it can produce more heat per unit. However, a heat pump can be placed at any facility within the mine site and can replace either a natural gas heating system or an electric heating system. Since natural gas prices are lower compared to electricity prices, it is expected that the annual savings are more significant when replacing an electrical heating system with a geothermal system.

Geothermal systems can be used in both operating and abandoned mines to supplement natural gas or electric systems. There is also potential to use the gravitational and thermal energy to store energy in mine voids.

Geothermal power systems have been demonstrated in the Lihir mine in Papua New Guinea (Melaku, 2005) and micro-hydroelectric power systems applied in the Summitville mine in USA (USEPA, 2011a). As mines grow deeper, it is likely that the thermal energy potential will increase, although pumping water from greater depth will no doubt offset some of the benefit. Geothermal systems for heat extraction only are more likely to be of use in colder climates, where the heat can be extracted for district heating among other potential uses.

Photovoltaics

Solar-power systems in the form of photovoltaic (PV) systems, solar thermal systems for heat, and concentrated solar power (CSP) are all potentially useful energy systems in remote locations, and many of the countries with extensive mining operations have significant solar potential. In recent years, with the decline in the price of PV systems, many mines have begun investing in large-scale PV to provide or supplement their energy supply. Examples of such applications have been found at many operating mines such as the Chuquicamata mine in Chile (Nielsen, 2011), the Barrick Goldstrike mine in USA (Tsai, 2008), and the Weipa mine in Australia (Australian Renewable Energy Agency, 2014), among others. Because these operating mine sites are located in remote areas, PV systems can supply power to support mining operations where there are few or no alternatives, and in many cases, these remote operations became cost-effective (as compared to standard diesel generators) before urban or grid-connected systems.

A number of applications of PV systems have also been identified at abandoned mines such as the Chevron Questa mine in the USA (USEPA, 2011b) and Meuro mine in Germany (Cichon and Runyon, 2012), where renewable energy technology has been used successfully to cultivate a substitute industry on land abandoned after the mine was closed. Such an application may provide a productive post-closure landscape, but would need to be balanced or considered in the context of other intended rehabilitation targets.

In Korea, a small-scale PV system (85 kW) was installed at the acid mine drainage passive treatment facility at the Hambaek Coal Mine (Jeongseon-gun County, Gangwon-do Province) and another 80-kW PV system at the acid mine drainage physicochemical treatment facility at the Hamtae Coal Mine (Taebaek-si, Gangwon-do). From these applications in South Korea, it has been shown that PV systems have been effectively utilised at mine water treatment facilities to support mine reclamation. PV systems tend to require minimal maintenance, so in particular if facilities require minimum employees, or are fully automated, then such systems have significant advantages.

While the available land for PV systems is often an advantage for mines during operation or as part of remediation, the prospect of utilising floating

PV systems on tailings or supply-water dams has also been investigated (Trapani and Millar, 2015; Song and Choi, 2016b). In some cases where water is scarce, this could also provide a method of preventing or reducing evaporation. Alternatively, the cooling effect of the water may also increase the performance of the PV cells in particularly hot environments.

Wind power

Wind power is typically the cheapest, most economically competitive form of medium-scale renewable energy generation. Applications of wind power generation systems have been implemented at operating mines, including the Veladero mine in Argentina (Barrick, 2007) and Diavik mine in Canada (Canadian Wind Energy Association, 2013). Moreover, a number of large-scale wind farms have been constructed at abandoned mines sites in the USA. Representative US cases are the wind farms of Dave Johnston Mine in Wyoming (capacity: 237 MW, electricity supply: 66,000 households), Somerset Mine in Pennsylvania (34.5 MW, 10,000 households), and Buffalo Mountain Mine in Tennessee (29 MW). The scale of the wind farms at abandoned mines has generally been larger than that at operating mines. This is no doubt in part due to the additional available space and elimination of the potential for operational interference.

While the need for energy storage has become more important as the increase in intermittent renewable energy in electricity supply has grown, the cost of batteries (as the simplest off-the-shelf storage method) has decreased rapidly. At the same time, use of flooded mines as pumped-storage hydropower systems has also been mooted, which would utilise an efficient onsite storage method.

Besides the aforementioned cases, a variety of studies have been carried out to find out the renewable energy source best suited for abandoned mine sites and to assess the feasibility of renewable energy projects prior to the installation and operation of renewable energy generation systems. In the United States, the Environmental Protection Agency and the National Renewable Energy Laboratory jointly ran the RE-Powering America's Land programme which included operating renewable energy generation facilities at mine sites (e.g. wind farms and PV systems) (USEPA, 2016). As a result, a PV power plant is currently under construction at the Chino abandoned mine site in New Mexico (Kiatreungwattana *et al.*, 2013), and a PV power plant project is currently underway to re-use the Vermont Asbestos Group (VAG) mine site (Simon and Mosey, 2013). In Korea, studies have been conducted to analyse the potential of PV systems and wind power systems at seven abandoned mine-promotion districts at regional scale (Song *et al.*, 2015; Song and Choi, 2016a). Moreover, at local scale, the feasibilities of PV systems were assessed at acid-mine-drainage passive treatment facilities in abandoned mine sites (Song and Choi, 2015) and on the pit lakes in open-pit mines (Song and Choi, 2016b).

Projections

It can be expected that the minerals industry will face the same ongoing pressures to utilise a greater component of renewable energy that will face all economic sectors into the future. There are a number of apparent trends that could affect the potential uptake and the required potential energy provision for the sector, some of which are discussed hereafter.

Deeper

As the most readily accessible shallower ores are gradually depleted, mining is progressing further and further underground. This trend is not likely to be reversed or even to stagnate until the limits (economic and technical) to deeper mining are reached – in comparison with alternative resource extraction methods such as recycling, waste reprocessing or seawater extraction. Deeper mining has a number of key implications for energy usage. First, the ore (and most likely the waste rock) will require extraction to the surface, meaning an obvious increase in the energy required to move the rock for the additional distance. Second, the functioning of the mine – ventilation, water removal, potentially cooling, transport of workers and equipment – will require increasing amounts of energy associated with the conditions at depth. Third, any additional waste rock, and any additional renewable energy requirement onsite, may be required to fit within the current mine footprint, or at least within the bounds of an existing lease. This latter point may make self-sufficiency of energy a more challenging task.

At the same time, digging deeper may provide greater opportunity for geothermal energy utilisation. Moreover, the more extensive final voids that could potentially arise could be utilised for the storage of waste (including nuclear waste), CO_2 in carbon capture and storage, or compressed air for energy storage under the appropriate conditions.

Dirtier

Ore grades have been gradually declining globally (Mudd, 2010) and more complex ores are being mined, as a natural progression of economic exploitation of a limited and grade-differentiated resource (i.e. the cheaper and easier deposits are extracted first, then the more difficult). The implication for energy usage from this trend is an increase in energy requirement across all stages of the supply chain. Lower grade requires higher quantities of ore to be extracted and processed, and often the refractory and finer-grained ores require higher levels of grinding to liberate valuable components. While some shifts in processing – for example towards heap leaching – may counter this trend, there is an overall expectation of higher energy requirement (Norgate and Jahanshahi, 2010).

Cleaner

The use of clean energy technologies – both in the production of energy and in its utilisation – are a noted driver in the expanded demand for minor metals, such as indium and tellurium in photovoltaics or neodymium and dysprosium in the magnets for motors in electric vehicles and generators in wind turbines (McLellan *et al.*, 2016). This increasing demand is currently being met by greater rates of mining and better extraction of minor elements from tailings or parent metals. Current recycling rates of such metals are typically low, and so expanding demand is expected to be met by greater primary resource extraction. While not necessarily impacting the energy intensity of individual mines dramatically, as a whole, industry energy use is likely to rise further on the back of this demand.

Automation

The increasing use of mechanisation in mines may be a contributor to higher reported energy usage over time, but automation is considered to have the potential to increase efficiency and utilisation rates of equipment, as well as making mines safer by reducing machine-human interactions. A number of mines across the world have been testing automation to greater or lesser extents in conjunction with equipment manufacturers. While automation may drive efficient use of energy, it may increase use of electricity at control centres offsite – although this is unlikely to negate the efficiency gains.

Off-earth

Deep ocean and space mining are two potential future resource supply chains that are currently in the conceptual stage. In the case of deep ocean resource extraction, the use of onsite renewable energy becomes very difficult, apart from minor services, as the distance from shore and the offshore conditions (waves, winds, depths) do not enable permanent or even floating infrastructure to be readily deployed (McLellan, 2015). While most of the seabed mining tools and the pumping and lifting equipment proposed for deep sea mining are run on electricity, it is difficult to conceive of any method for providing this adequately and appropriately by renewable energy.

On the other hand, space mining (mining asteroids or the moon, for instance) would necessarily rely on renewable energy – most probably in the form of solar power, as with existing space operations.

Alternative mining techniques

A variety of alternative techniques are being developed to extract minerals or mine ores from deposits. Techniques such as block caving, mass mining, in situ leaching and others, may have a significant impact on the land forms and applicability of renewable energy, as well as in the form of energy required.

Conclusions

According to these cases of applied renewable energy in the mining industry, it could be expected that the utilisation of renewable energy technology in the mining industry would have positive effects in both environmental and economic terms. In terms of the environment, environmental restoration projects could be promoted at neglected sites through redevelopment of sites polluted by mine waste. Reduction of fossil fuel use at mine sites could contribute to a reduction in greenhouse gas emissions. In terms of the economy, the economics of mine operations could be improved by substitution of fossil fuels needed for power production – particularly in periods of high oil prices. Particularly with globally decreasing costs of renewable energy systems, and improvement in their efficiency. Moreover, the creation of new business models and jobs related to the design, construction and operation of renewable energy utilisation systems will stimulate growth in local economies (Corder *et al.*, 2012). For these reasons, the use of renewable energy technology in the mining industry is expected to continue to spread, and there is certainly further potential – both in technical terms on the demand side and in resource potential on the supply side.

References

ABARES (2007). *Australian Land Use: National Scale Land Use Statistics 2005–2006*. Canberra, Australia, Government of Australia.

Australian Renewable Energy Agency (2014). 'Weipa 6.7MW solar photovoltaic (PV) solar farm'. http://arena.gov.au/project/weipa-solar-farm.

Baig, M., D. Surovtseva and E. Halawa (2015). 'The potential of concentrated solar power for remote mine sites in the Northern Territory, Australia'. *Journal of Solar Energy*. http://dx.doi.org/10.1155/2015/617356.

Barrick (2007) 'Barrick invests in innovative energy projects in Chile, Tanzania'. www.barrick.com/investors/news/news-details/2007/BarrickInvestsinInnovativeEnergyProjectsinChileTanzania/default.aspx.

Breyer, C. and A. Gerlach (2013). 'Global overview on grid-parity'. *Progress in Photovoltaics: Research and Applications* 21(1): 121–136.

Canadian Wind Energy Association (2013) 'Canadian Diavik Wind Farm: Wind energy helps reduce carbon footprint'. http://canwea.ca/wp-content/uploads/2013/12/canwea-casestudy-DiavikMine-e-web2.pdf.

Chapman, A. J., B. McLellan and T. Tezuka (2016). 'Residential solar PV policy: An analysis of impacts, successes and failures in the Australian case'. *Renewable Energy* 86: 1265–1279.

Chiras, D. (2009). *Power from the sun: Achieving energy independence*. Gabriola Island, BC, Canada, New Society Publishers.

Choi, Y. and J. Song (2016) 'Sustainable development of abandoned mine areas using renewable energy systems: A case study of the photovoltaic potential assessment at the tailings dam of abandoned Sangdong Mine, Korea'. *Sustainability* 8(1320): 1–12.

Choi, Y., J. Rayl, C. Tammineedi and J. R. S. Brownson (2011). 'PV analyst: Coupling ArcGIS with TRNSYS to assess distributed photovoltaic potential in urban areas'. *Solar Energy* 85(11): 2924–2939.

Cichon, M. and J. Runyon (2012) 'Renewable Energy Projects of the Year highlight the industry's best achievements'. www.renewableenergyworld.com/rea/news/article/2012/12/renewable-energy-projects-of-the-year-highlight-the-industrys-best-achievements-part-1.

Clark, V. R. and H. J. Herzog (2014). 'Can stranded fossil fuel reserves drive CCS deployment?' *Energy Procedia* 63: 7261–7271.

Corder, G. D., B. C. McLellan, P. J. Bangerter, D. van Beers and S. R. Green (2012). 'Engineering-in sustainability through the application of SUSOP®'. *Chemical Engineering Research and Design* 90(1): 98–109.

Corder, G. D., B. C. McLellan and S. R. Green (2012). 'Delivering solutions for resource conservation and recycling into project management systems through SUSOP®'. *Minerals Engineering* 29(0): 47–57.

Equator Principles (2013). *The Equator Principles III: A financial industry benchmark for determining, assessing and managing social and environmental risk in project financing*. Washington, D.C., The Equator Principles Association.

Evans, D., M. Stephenson and R. Shaw (2009). 'The present and future use of "land" below ground'. *Land Use Policy* 26, Supplement 1: S302–S316.

Ghoreishi Madiseh, S. A., M. M. Ghomshei, F. P. Hassani and F. Abbasy (2012). 'Sustainable heat extraction from abandoned mine tunnels: A numerical model'. *Journal of Renewable and Sustainable Energy* 4(3). https://doi.org/10.1063/1.4712055.

Giurco, D., B. McLellan, D. M. Franks, K. Nansai and T. Prior (2014). 'Responsible mineral and energy futures: Views at the nexus'. *Journal of Cleaner Production* 84(0): 322–338.

IEA (International Energy Agency) (2014). *Energy balances of non-OECD countries*. Paris.

IIASA (International Institute for Applied Systems Analysis) (2012). *Global energy assessment: Toward a sustainable future*. Vienna.

IRENA (International Renewable Energy Agency) (2015). *Renewable energy options for the industry sector: Global and regional potential until 2030. A background paper to 'Renewable energy in manufacturing'*. Abu Dhabi.

Jessop, A. (1995). *Geothermal energy from old mines at Springhill, Nova Scotia, Canada*. www.geothermal-energy.org/pdf/IGAstandard/WGC/1995/1-jessop.pdf.

Kiatreungwattana, K., J. Geiger, V. Haeley and G. Mosey (2013) *Feasibility study of economics and performance of solar photovoltaics at the Chino Mine in Silver City, New Mexico*. Tech. Rep. NREL/TP-7A30–57959, National Renewable Energy Laboratory, Denver, Colorado. www.nrel.gov/docs/fy13osti/57959.pdf.

Martinát, S. and K. Ture ková (2016). 'Local development in the post-mining countryside? Impacts of an agricultural ad plant on rural community'. *Geographia Technica* 11(1): 54–66.

McCubbin, D. and B. K. Sovacool (2013). 'Quantifying the health and environmental benefits of wind power to natural gas'. *Energy Policy* 53(0): 429–441.

McLellan, B. C. (2009). 'Potential opportunities and impacts of a hydrogen economy for the Australian minerals industry'. *International Journal of Hydrogen Energy* 34(9): 3571–3577.

McLellan, B. C. (2011). 'Optimizing location of bulk metallic minerals processing based on greenhouse gas avoidance'. *Minerals* 1(1): 144–156.

McLellan, B. C. (2015). 'Comparative life cycle impacts of deep ocean minerals and land-based counterparts'. Third International Future Mining Conference. Sydney, Australia.

McLellan, B. C. (2017). 'The minerals–energy nexus: Past, present and future'. In: Mitsutaka Matsumoto, Keijiro Masui, Shinichi Fukushige and Shinsuke Kondoh (eds), *Sustainability through innovation in product life cycle design*. Springer, Singapore: 619–631.

McLellan, B. C., G. D. Corder, D. P. Giurco and K. N. Ishihara (2012). 'Renewable energy in the minerals industry: A review of global potential'. *Journal of Cleaner Production* 32: 32–44.

McLellan, B. C., E. Yamasue, T. Tezuka, G. Corder, A. Golev and D. Giurco (2016). 'Critical minerals and energy: Impacts and limitations of moving to unconventional resources'. *Resources* 5(2): 19.

McLellan, B. C., Q. Zhang, H. Farzaneh, N. A. Utama and K. N. Ishihara (2012). 'Resilience, sustainability and risk management: A focus on energy'. *Challenges* 3(2): 153–182.

Melaku, M. (2005). 'Geothermal development at Lihir: An overview'. *Proceedings of World Geothermal Congress*, Antalya, Turkey, 24–29 April 2005. www.geothermal-energy.org/pdf/IGAstandard/WGC/2005/1343.pdf.

Mudd, G. M. (2010). 'The environmental sustainability of mining in Australia: Key mega-trends and looming constraints'. *Resources Policy* 35(2): 98–115.

Nielsen, S. (2011). 'A solar mother lode for Chile's Mines'. *Bloomberg Businessweek Magazine*, 11 February 2011. www.businessweek.com/magazine/content/11_08/b4216012473761.htm.

Norgate, T. and S. Jahanshahi (2010). 'Low grade ores: Smelt, leach or concentrate?' *Minerals Engineering* 23(2): 65–73.

Pearce, J. M. (2002). 'Photovoltaics: A path to sustainable futures'. *Futures* 34(7): 663–674.

Prno, J. and D. Scott Slocombe (2012). 'Exploring the origins of "social license to operate" in the mining sector: Perspectives from governance and sustainability theories'. *Resources Policy* 37(3): 346–357.

Sarder, M. (2010). 'Remote mines: The case for wind power'. *AusIMM Bulletin: Journal of the Australiasian Institute of Mining and Metallurgy* 1(February): 28–29.

Simon, J. and G. Mosey (2013). *Feasibility study of economics and performance of solar photovoltaics at the VAG mine site in Eden and Lowell, Vermont*, Tech. Rep. NREL/TP-7A30–57766, National Renewable Energy Laboratory, Denver, Colorado, USA. www.nrel.gov/docs/fy13osti/57766.pdf.

Song, J. and Y. Choi (2016a). 'Analysis of wind power potentials at abandoned mine promotion districts in Korea'. *Geosystem Engineering* 19(2): 77–82.

Song, J. and Y. Choi (2016b). 'Analysis of the potential for use of floating photovoltaic systems on mine pit lakes: Case study at the Ssangyong open-pit limestone mine in Korea'. *Energies* 9(2): 1–13.

Song, J., Y. Choi and S. H. Yoon (2015). 'Analysis of photovoltaic potential at abandoned mine promotion districts in Korea'. *Geosystem Engineering* 18(3): 168–172.

Templeton, J. D., S. A. Ghoreishi-Madiseh, F. Hassani and M. J. Al-Khawaja (2014). 'Abandoned petroleum wells as sustainable sources of geothermal energy'. *Energy* 70: 366–373.

Trapani, K. and D. L. Millar (2015). 'Floating photovoltaic arrays to power the mining industry: A case study for the McFaulds Lake (Ring of Fire)'. *Environmental Progress and Sustainable Energy*. doi:10.1002/ep.12275.

Tsai, P. (2008). 'Goldstrike Mine – Nevada's giant golden goose'. *Mining.com*, 1 September 2008. www.infomine.com/publications/docs/Mining.com/Sep2008i.pdf.

UN (United Nations) (2015). *Adoption of the Paris Agreement*. Framework Convention on Climate Change, Paris.

USEPA (US Environmental Protection Agency) (2011a). 'Micro-hydroelectric power at Summitville'. www.epa.gov/sites/production/files/documents/Summitville_MicroHydroBrochure23Aug11.pdf.

USEPA (US Environmental Protection Agency) (2011b). 'Chevron Questa mine reuse success story'. http://epa.gov/superfund/programs/recycle/pdf/molycorp-success.pdf.

USEPA (US Environmental Protection Agency) (2016). 'RE-powering America's land: Siting Renewable Energy on potentially contaminated lands, landfills, and mine sites'. http://epa.gov/renewableenergyland.

Verhoeven, R., E. Willems, V. Harcouët-Menou, E. De Boever, L. Hiddes, P. O. Veld and E. Demollin (2014). 'Minewater 2.0 project in Heerlen the Netherlands: Transformation of a geothermal mine water pilot project into a full scale hybrid sustainable energy infrastructure for heating and cooling'. *Energy Procedia*, 46: 58–67. https://doi.org/10.1016/j.egypro.2014.01.158.

Watzlaf, G. R. and T. E. Ackman (2006). 'Underground mine water for heating and cooling using geothermal heat pump systems'. *Mine Water and the Environment* 25(1): 1–14.

Weiss, T. and D. Schulz (2012). 'Using already existing artificial structures for energy storage in areas with high shares of Renewable Energies'. Third IEEE PES Innovative Smart Grid Technologies Europe (ISGT Europe).

13 Implementing shared-use of mining infrastructure to achieve the Sustainable Development Goals

Perrine Toledano and Nicolas Maennling

Introduction

According to the Africa Infrastructure Country Diagnostic conducted by the World Bank, Sub-Saharan Africa faces an annual infrastructure-funding gap of around US$31 billion (Briceño-Garmendia *et al.*, 2008). Many of the Sustainable Development Goals (SDGs),[1] adopted on September 25, 2015 by the United Nations, will only be achieved if the population has access to basic infrastructure services, such as water, power, transport, and telecommunications services. However, in many developing countries there is a lack of infrastructure to guarantee these services and there are insufficient public funds to satisfy growing needs.

In resource-rich countries,[2] the mining sector can play a key role in increasing access to infrastructure, as operations require transportation, water, energy, and telecommunications. This mining-related infrastructure is often developed to serve the exclusive need of mining companies, but if shared and developed to serve the broader needs and uses of the host economy, it could fill up to 9 percent of the infrastructure funding gap (McKinsey Global Institute, 2013).

This chapter outlines how shared-use of mining-related infrastructure could contribute towards achieving ten out of the 17 SDGs. The first section sets the scene by explaining the concept of shared-use and how it relates to the SDGs; the second section goes through the relevant SDGs in detail; the third section delves into the challenges of implementation; the fourth section concludes.

Shared-use infrastructure

The concept of shared-use

The concept of "shared-use" refers to the various ways to leverage extractive industry-related infrastructure investments in resource-rich countries for the broader benefit of the national and regional community. In opposition to the "enclave approach," the concept of "shared-use" seeks to integrate the mining sector within the rest of the economy through sharing the use of the infrastructure serving the mines.

To be beneficial for a country's long-term development, the extraction of depletable resources should involve investments in infrastructure and human capital that will support sustainable and inclusive growth. For infrastructure investments, countries face two non-mutually exclusive options: (1) optimizing the resource taxation potential of mining projects and reinvesting the tax revenues collected into infrastructure; or (2) requiring shared-use of infrastructure that is financed by the mining sector (CCSI, 2014). The first option is particularly relevant for mining, as in many resource-rich developing countries, mining is the only sector that generates sufficient cash flow to be able to pay for the construction of "trunk" or "backbone" infrastructure.

Shared-use infrastructure can be *multi-user*, whereby several mining companies use the infrastructure, or *multi-purpose*, whereby non-mining users such as the agriculture, forestry, or public sectors gain access to the infrastructure. Both should be promoted according to the country or region's economic conditions. Multi-user infrastructure enables mining companies to reduce the capital expenditure and operating costs of the mines, thereby leading to increased tax revenues to the government. It also has the potential to reduce the environmental footprint of the infrastructure development. Multi-purpose infrastructure has the potential to lower the costs of water, energy, transportation, and ICT services to other users, thereby promoting economic development in the region. Shared-use arrangements can result in economies of scale and economies of scope. Economies of scale occur when an infrastructure investment at a larger scale results in unit cost savings. Economies of scope refers to the situation when one type of infrastructure can be used to save costs for the development of another, such as laying the fiber optic cables needed for telecommunications infrastructure along a railroad.

The challenge in relation to achieving shared-use relates to the fact that mining concessionaires "have traditionally adopted an enclave approach to infrastructure development, providing their own power, water, ICT and transportation services to ensure that the basic infrastructure needed for their operations is reliably available" (CCSI, 2014). Countries therefore have often missed the opportunity to promote shared-use infrastructure and exploit potential synergies between any applicable national infrastructure plans and the mining sector's infrastructure plans.

Shared-use and the SDGs

The last 20 years have witnessed considerable efforts by academia to show the direct contribution of infrastructure access to growth, economic development, and reduction of income inequality (UN Habitat, 2011), with access to ICT, followed by roads and power, having the bigger impact

(Estache, 2005). One study showed that infrastructure investments accelerated the annual growth convergence rate by over 13 percent in Africa over the 30 years preceding the study (Estache, 2005). Another study showed that improving transportation infrastructure could increase agricultural income by as much as 10 percent (Abdulai *et al.*, 2005).

> This reflects economic infrastructure's role in raising the productivity of the poor by improving their access to markets, local and foreign, reducing the risks of private investments which will provide them employment, and (...) better information about market opportunities and ways to improve livelihoods.
>
> (Willoughby, 2004)

Calderón and Servén (2008) showed that the worldwide average inequality, measured by the Gini coefficient, was reduced by 3 basis points from 2001–2005 compared to 1991–1995 because of increased infrastructure development.

In this context, it appears clear that encouraging policies that will lead to an accumulation of infrastructure stock or improved infrastructure quality will contribute to achieving the SDGs. The next section outlines how shared-use infrastructure has the potential to impact ten out of the 17 SDGs. These ten SDGs have been selected considering that shared-use impacts them more directly. This is not to say that shared-use infrastructure does not have the potential to impact the other SDGs indirectly. All goals are interconnected and therefore contributing to one goal can also affect other goals. For example, we have not included SDG 3, good health and wellbeing, and SDG 4, quality education, in this analysis, although increasing the access of health clinics and schools to electricity, transport, water, and ICT infrastructure is likely to have a positive impact on these goals. Furthermore, access to road infrastructure will greatly facilitate access to these facilities for surrounding populations.

The targets for each SDG that are particularly relevant to the nexus of the mining and infrastructure sectors are highlighted in the following section. In order to cover the variety of shared-use arrangements across infrastructure types, each goal features a case study involving one particular type of infrastructure. This is not to say that the other types of infrastructure do not also contribute to the goal discussed.

Shared-use mining-related infrastructure by SDG

SDG 1 – no poverty

SDG 1 focuses on eradicating extreme poverty by 2030 and warranting equal access to services and opportunities for all citizens. Target 1.4 is particularly relevant to shared-use and requires that "all men and women, particularly the poor and the vulnerable, have equal rights to economic resources, as well as access to basic services, ownership, and control over land and other forms of property."

Mining and its related infrastructure often require resettlement of communities living in the area of operation. Problems associated with resettlement can include joblessness, marginalization, food insecurity, loss of common land and resources, increased health risks, social destruction, violation of human rights, and disruption of formal education and access to basic public services (Mishra and Reddy, 2011), all of which are counterproductive to achieving SDG 1. Attempts by even the most careful company to carry out resettlement programs in ways that minimize negative impacts on affected persons' development and human rights often fail to restore them to a position that is at least as favorable as the position they were in before the project began. When livelihood restoration programs fail – for instance, where the resettlement sites are isolated, and far from towns, markets, schools, and medical services – families are left worse off, with often no ability to access other income opportunities (Lillywhite *et al.*, 2015).

According to Stanley (2004), infrastructure development causes a lot more displacement of communities than mining itself. In Guinea, the 670 km-long Simandou railway corridor built by Rio Tinto for its iron-ore mine is estimated to occupy 8,000 hectares of land and to have displaced 10,000 people (Els, 2013). Shared-use helps to avoid duplicating infrastructure when it is not needed: parallel railways, power, and fiber optics lines are avoided, which reduces the amount of land impacted by infrastructure and, consequently, the potential number of people to be resettled.

In addition to the direct displacement caused by many large infrastructure projects mentioned above, there is also an indirect form of displacement that is often not addressed in formal resettlement operations. Indirect displacement stems from situations where the impacts of investments or related infrastructure make it untenable for persons to remain on the land on which they reside – for instance, where contamination of drinking water or the destruction of land used for farming causes households to leave their homes and lands to find healthier conditions elsewhere (FMO, 2011). As explained in SDGs 6 and 12, shared-use in the context of water infrastructure can reduce instances of indirect displacement.

SDG 2 – zero hunger

SDG 2 aims to "end hunger, achieve food security and improved nutrition and promote sustainable agriculture," Target 2.6, relevant for shared-used, requires "to increase investment, including through enhanced international cooperation, in rural infrastructure (...), in order to enhance agricultural productive capacity in developing countries, in particular least developed countries."

The development of a commercial agriculture sector is highly reliant on agriculture-supporting infrastructure that connects to the trunk infrastructure (main roads, railways, power lines, and treatment facilities) such as feeder roads, irrigation systems, and electricity distribution lines (BAGC, 2013). Furthermore, farmers can face constraints in accessing irrigation because such access is often reliant on diesel generators that can be three times as costly as the power grid. In many cases high transportation costs also prevent farmers from reaching markets and selling their goods at competitive prices. Furthermore, investments in water infrastructure such as small dams and storage reservoirs are needed to regulate water supply and avoid water shortages during the dry season. The Beira Agriculture Growth Corridor initiative has estimated that the average off-farm infrastructure cost in the Beira region in Mozambique is around US$5,000/ha. Such a cost is too high for small and medium-sized farmers to operate profitably (BAGC, 2013).

Trunk infrastructure developments, including multi-purpose infrastructure, by mining operations can be leveraged to reduce such costs for farmers. The construction of distribution lines from the trunk infrastructure built by the mining company is going to be less costly than having to also invest in trunk infrastructure or relying on diesel generators (see SDG 7). If water storage and treatment facilities are designed at additional capacity for agricultural uses, the cost is likely to be lower than having to invest in separate water management facilities (see SDG 6). Sharing access to railways and service roads with farmers can also improve access to markets.

Several case studies have evidenced how the agriculture sector can benefit from shared-use mining infrastructure.[3] For instance, towards the end of the nineteenth century in Western Australia, the rich gold deposits of Kalgoorlie led to mass immigration of workers. But Kalgoorlie was close to the desert and 600 km from the coast, and lacked sufficient water reserves to serve the growing demand from both the mines and the migrants. One visionary engineer devised a scheme to pump water from coastal dams and pipe it inland; this provided water not only to Kalgoorlie, but also to the intermediate region, converting marginal grazing land into one of the world's most productive wheat growing areas (Doepel and Bolton, 2013).

SDG 6 – clean water and sanitation

Achieving SDG 6 means "ensur[ing] access to water and sanitation for all." Two of SDG 6's targets can be directly affected by shared-use infrastructure: Target 6.3, "by 2030 improve water quality by reducing pollution, eliminating dumping and minimizing release of hazardous chemicals and materials, halving the proportion of untreated wastewater, and increasing recycling and safe reuse," and Target 6.4 "by 2030 substantially increase water-use efficiency across all sectors and ensure sustainable withdrawals and supply of freshwater to address water scarcity and substantially reduce the number of people suffering from water scarcity."

According to Moody's Investor Service (2013), about 70 percent of the mining operations of the "Big Six" mining companies,[4] are located in countries where water stress is considered to be at moderate to high risk. In such contexts, mining operations can aggravate the water stress of local communities and the environment by competing for water. Through shared-use arrangements, mining companies can avoid competing with the ecosystem. This can be realized by either diminishing the water footprint of mining companies (in quantity and/or quality) or by increasing the water supplies to the community from alternative sources (Toledano and Roorda, 2014a). We expand on the former arrangement under SDG 12 and the latter in this discussion of SDG 6.

To increase the sources of available water to themselves and to the community, mines can either realize the potential related to the fact that some parts of the mining process require water of lower quality than that of human consumption, such as sea water in copper flotation processes, or they can treat sea water or residential waste/sewerage water (Toledano and Roorda, 2014a).

When a mine does the latter, economies of scale can be leveraged to increase the sources of water available to the communities. Freeport McMoRan's Cerro Verde expansion project is a good example. Since 1994, the company has operated a copper mining project southeast of Arequipa, Peru's second largest city. In order to receive the approval for the mine expansion plan, the company agreed to build a US$400 million water treatment plant for the city of Arequipa with a capacity of around 83 percent of Arequipa's domestic sewage and industrial discharges (BTG Practical, 2016). The construction of the wastewater plant was completed in December 2015 and the mine expansion in May 2016. Prior to the plant, the city's wastewater was discharged without treatment into the Chili River, negatively affecting downstream communities whose livelihoods are primarily reliant on agricultural activities. Under the agreement, Cerro Verde can source an annual average of one cubic meter per second of the treated wastewater from the plant. The remaining water is discharged into the Chili River (Freeport-McMoRan, 2015).

SDG 7 – affordable and clean energy

SDG 7 and its Target 7.1 focus on ensuring access to affordable, reliable, sustainable, and modern energy for all. While access to energy is core to the fight against poverty, "[t]he availability of power lies at the core of a mine's development strategy; mining operators need to make sure that the energy demand of mining operations is met" (Toledano, 2013). Shared-use of mining-related power infrastructure will help to satisfy both the needs of the country and the mining industry.

The mining industry adopts different strategies to meet energy needs, depending on several factors. Such factors include: the power situation of the country, the project's energy demand, and the project's distance from the grid. When sourcing from the grid is too expensive or when there is no connection to the grid, the mining company will finance and build its own power generation facilities or source from a third party (an independent power producer). When sourcing from the grid is less inexpensive as compared to self-generation, the mining company will either source from the grid or finance/co-finance the upgrade of the power infrastructure with the public utility. Each of these sourcing arrangements is conducive to shared-use arrangements (Toledano, 2013; CCSI, 2014).

The main reason for this lies with the premise of leveraging economies of scale in the context of constructing either a power plant or the backbone infrastructure. Economies of scale render the marginal MegaWatt (MW) produced less expensive than the averaged unit cost of a new power plant; similarly, economies of scale make the last-mile infrastructure less expensive than the average unit cost of the backbone infrastructure. Thus shared-use enables regions and communities to access a more robust power system with extended coverage. Robustness combined with broader coverage leads to energy access that is both reliable and affordable.

Shared-use can also enable a wider adoption of renewables in the energy mix through the deployment of mini-grids. Many mining companies are now considering this type of off-grid solution to ensure a smaller environmental footprint and reduced energy costs; this is facilitated by the fact that production costs of alternative energy sources are falling rapidly, and will often be less than the cost of importing diesel used for generators (Kirshke, 2016).

A case study illustrating the benefits of one of the shared-use arrangements comes from the Democratic Republic of Congo (DRC). Despite having a huge hydropower potential of 40,000 MW, the DRC has a limited installed capacity of 1,775 MW, with an electricity grid that only reaches 11 percent of the population and is characterized by intermittent electricity supply and regular power outages (Banerjee *et al.*, 2014). The energy-intensive copper mining industry in the Katanga region, on which DRC is highly dependent, is constrained by this lack of regular power supply. The power outages, coupled with the high cost of diesel, mean that less copper is produced, and the cost of production is higher.[5] Given the long-term nature of the mining operations and their consistent power needs, a number of mines, including those operated by Glencore Xstrata plc, have agreed to invest in upgrading the national electricity grid through a series of measures including the repair of two turbines at the Société Nationale d'Electricité's (SNEL) Inga 2 hydropower plant and the improvement of about 2,000 km of transmission lines. By doing so, the mines ensure more reliable access to power. This power will also be cheaper than the self-procured diesel costing up to 48 c/kWh, whereas the hydro-based power is sold by SNEL at around 3.5 c/kWh (Maennling *et al.*, 2016).

The commercial arrangement that Glencore and SNEL devised to conduct this investment is as follows: in 2012, through its subsidiary Katanga Mining Ltd., Glencore Xstrata signed an agreement with SNEL for a US$283.5 million investment in the above-mentioned power infrastructure upgrading. A large part of this amount will be reimbursed by SNEL through utility bill credits payable by Katanga mining and its affiliates that will also benefit from the additional and more reliable electricity produced. According to the agreement signed between SNEL and Katanga mining, 10 percent of the excess power generated (i.e., the power above what is needed by the mines) will be generated and sold back to SNEL. Accordingly, grid-supply is expected to reach 450 MW of power capacity once the investment is completed (Maennling *et al.*, 2016). With an upgraded backbone infrastructure, SNEL will be able to plan for the construction of distribution lines to the communities.

SDG 9 – industry, innovation, and infrastructure

SDG 9 is about "build[ing] resilient infrastructure, promot[ing] sustainable industrialization and foster[ing] innovation." Shared-use will be particularly impactful on Target 9.8, which aims to "significantly increase access to information and communications technology and strive to provide universal and affordable access to the Internet in least developed countries by 2020."

The World Bank has estimated that a 10 percent increase in high-speed Internet connections is associated with a 1.3 percent increase in economic growth in developing countries and is critical to foster innovation (World Bank, 2009). Despite this, an estimated 4.4 billion households, mainly in developing countries, still lack access to the Internet, let alone high-speed Internet (Ferdman, 2014).

ICT is employed in all phases of a mine's life, from exploration to operation and closure. Instantaneous access to video, voice, and data communications enables the mining company to use materials and human resources more effectively, reduce waste and delays, and improve the safety of employees (Toledano and Roorda, 2014b). ICT can also make mining operations more efficient.

Shared-use may expand telecommunications and broadband access to surrounding communities, therefore contributing to the realization of SDG 9. Economies of scope may be leveraged along the longitudinal infrastructure (which includes railways, roads, pipelines, and power lines) built to serve the operations of a mine. Shared-use arrangements can be designed where the mine builds its own ICT infrastructure along its longitudinal infrastructure, where telecommunications companies add ICT capacity along the mine's infrastructure, or where an infrastructure logistics company builds the infrastructure for the mine. If clearing the right of way and excavation is undertaken for another longitudinal infrastructure type, the additional cost of laying out fiber optic cables can be reduced significantly. Roughly 80 percent of the costs associated with laying out fiber optic cables are related to excavation (Toledano and Roorda, 2014b). Examples of where such economies of scope were leveraged include: (1) CEC Liquid Telecom's laying fiber optic cables along the power lines of the mines in the Zambian copper belt and leasing the capacity to telecommunications operators; and (2) Compania Minera Antamina in Peru leasing part of the fiber optic cable laid to control its slurry pipeline to Telefonica de Peru for it to bring telecommunications services to the surrounding areas (Toledano and Roorda, 2014b).

SDG 12 – responsible consumption and production

SDG 12 highlights the importance of reducing our ecological footprint by changing the way that resources and goods are produced and consumed. Target 12.2 – "By 2030 achieve sustainable management and efficient use of natural resources" – is directly linked to both mining projects and associated infrastructure projects. Building and operating shared-use infrastructure, as opposed to building multiple infrastructures at a lower capacity in the same region, will reduce the amount of resources required. For example, it requires less material to build a multi-user railway line at a higher capacity than building two railway lines that serve individual mining projects.

The most relevant natural resource and opportunity to share infrastructure in relation to SDG 12 is water. Responsible consumption may result from shared-use water infrastructure arrangements as described in SDG 6, but may also result from putting in place strong environmental regulations that incentivize water re-use. A good illustration comes from Victoria, Australia where under the *Environment Protection Act 1970* companies should only consider the disposal of the water used (as any industrial waste) as a last resort measure after exhausting measures such as avoidance, reduction, reuse, recycling, and treatment.

It has been estimated that, combined with a sound water management system, water re-use enables the mining industry to almost halve its daily freshwater intake (Szyplinska, 2012). Consequently, water licenses should only be granted once mines have adopted a water efficiency policy that determines the mine's net demand after recycling, retreating, and re-using water. In some regions of Chile, where water consumption is estimated to be six times greater than water renewal, the Chilean government has prohibited mines from benefiting from the granted water licenses and rejected new mining projects planning on using freshwater (Edwards *et al.*, 2013). Some of the bigger mining operations have been embarking on desalination projects to cope with this situation.

Companies in Brazil and China provide additional illustrations that responsible consumption through water efficiency mechanisms is possible. At its Sossego metallurgical plant in Brazil, Vale recycles 99.99 percent of the water used to produce copper concentrate: it saves 900,000 cubic meters of freshwater annually whereas this water had previously been pumped from a nearby river. This makes up enough water to supply a town of 25,000 inhabitants with water for six months. In China, at its Dexing mine, Jiangxi Copper Company partnered with BioTeQ Environmental Technologies to construct a water treatment plant that both treats and recovers copper from the wastewater. Within its first six months of operation, the plant treated 3 billion liters of wastewater and recovered 700,000 pounds of copper, which covered the treatment costs (Toledano and Roorda, 2014a).

SDG 13 – climate action

SDG 13 requires stakeholders to take urgent action to combat climate change and its impacts. Target 13.3 foresees the integration of "climate change measures into national policies, strategies and planning." Private sector stakeholders should align their strategies accordingly. Mining companies can contribute to SDG 13 through three channels, namely by moving away from thermal coal extraction, reducing emissions from operations, and integrating climate resilience in all aspect of operations. Sharing infrastructure investments has the potential to lower emissions; as in the case of SDG 12, the construction of shared infrastructure at a larger capacity, as opposed to constructing two or more pieces of infrastructure for use by a single mining company, is likely to reduce the required inputs and with it the associated emissions during the construction phase.

During operations, shared power infrastructure is particularly relevant for SDG 13. Mine self-supply power plants are often based on heavy fuel oil (HFO) or diesel (Banerjee *et al.*, 2014). These types of power plants are able to provide sufficient and reliable power to mining projects at a relatively low up-front capital cost, but have high operating costs and produce relatively high levels of emissions.

If a mining project can secure reliable power at a reasonable price from the public utility, this would be the preferred option, as highlighted in the above discussion of SDG 7. This could also significantly reduce CO_2 emissions of the project, given that HFO and diesel are among the most polluting power sources. In Liberia, the World Bank estimated that by 2030, mines could represent more than 80 percent of national power demand (World Bank, 2011). To satisfy this demand, the study assesses different power generation scenarios and finds that energy costs could be reduced from US$0.15 per kilowatt hour in a self-supply scenario to US$0.08 per kilowatt hour in a scenario where one large hydropower plant is built to serve the mining projects and the rest of the economy. Estimates suggest that, compared with self-supply systems, an integrated system could save up to 2,000 tons of CO_2 emissions per annum or 22,000 tons of CO_2 over the lifetime of the mine.

SDG 14 – life below water

SDG 14 focuses on the conservation and sustainable use of the oceans, seas and marine resources. Target 14.5 aims to, "by 2020, conserve at least 10 per cent of coastal and marine areas, consistent with national and international law and based on best available scientific information." A large proportion of marine pollution comes from land-based sources; shared water infrastructure solutions are relevant to address water discharge of mining projects on land (see discussions of SDGs 6 and 12, above). Mining water discharge has had disastrous effects all over the world. A most egregious and recent example comes from Brazil where, in 2015, two Samarco[6]-owned dams containing by-products of iron mining collapsed, causing many casualties in the surroundings and water contamination of nearby rivers which led to the suspension of water supply in several cities depending on those rivers (Rezende, 2015).

Shared port infrastructure can also contribute to achieving SDG 14. Ports impact the marine environment through the terminal infrastructure and shipping activities. Adverse impacts include: (1) the clearing and modifying of coastal habitats; (2) dredging leading to loss of species and changes in habitat within the port area, along the port channel and where dredge material is disposed; (3) the risk of chemical and oil spills due to shipping activity; and (4) noise pollution disturbing marine life (Queensland Government, 2012). While shared port infrastructure may not reduce all these potential adverse environmental impacts, a significant share of it can be curbed by "common" infrastructure investments. For example, one multi-purpose port could benefit from the same dredged channel and wave breaker. Different piers would still be required, but the overall marine impact of additional piers and/or terminals are smaller than building two separate ports.

This fact is illustrated by the ports strategy of the state government of Queensland, Australia. Queensland is the largest coal exporting state in Australia and is also home to the largest coral reef in the world, which is declared a World Heritage Site. Seaborne coal demand grew significantly during the commodity super cycle leading to new mining projects, port expansions, and increased shipping activity along the Great Barrier Reef. Due to concerns about the adverse impacts of shipping activity on the fragile reef ecosystem, the Queensland Government highlighted in its ports strategy that port development would be restricted to existing port limits given that "few, larger port areas will mean less disruption to the environment and marine wildlife than would occur if new port areas were established."

SDG 15 – life on land

Shared-use mining infrastructure can both positively contribute to SDG 15, as well as having adverse impacts, including accelerating biodiversity loss and deforestation. Particularly Targets 15.2 – "by 2020, promote the implementation of sustainable management of all types of forests, halt deforestation, restore degraded forests, and substantially increase afforestation and reforestation globally" and 15.5 – "take urgent and significant action to reduce degradation of natural habitat, halt the loss of biodiversity, and by 2020 protect and prevent the extinction of threatened species" are relevant to the impacts of mining on SDG 15.

As discussed under SDG 9, above, combining longitudinal infrastructure rather than building two separate systems can significantly reduce the infrastructure footprint of the mining industry. Forests need to be cleared on either side of a transmission, road, and railway network in order to avoid falling trees causing damage. For Cameroon's Mbalam iron ore project it has been estimated that it would require at least a 100-meter wide transport corridor for the proposed 508-km railway and adjacent maintenance road to transport iron-ore to the point of export. This would result in the clearing of 5,080 hectares of forest (Rainbow Environment Consult, 2011). A double-track system to increase capacity and service multiple mining projects in the region would only marginally increase the footprint of the existing railway as compared to building two separate railway lines.

However, shared-use infrastructure may render projects viable that would not have gone ahead without multiple actors working together. The Tridom region where the Mbalam iron ore project is located provides a useful example. While the mining company is planning to use heavy fuel oil generators for power self-supply purposes, it would welcome the possibility of tapping the potential Chollet Dam hydropower project in the Republic of Congo, which would only be viable if several mining projects in the region were to move ahead. While potentially having a positive impact on SDG 13 due to reduced greenhouse gas emissions, the development of such a dam would flood large parts of habitat-rich pristine rainforest in the region (Bottrill, 2013).

The biggest potential adverse impact of shared-use infrastructure on SDG 15, however, is that improved road infrastructure, in particular, but also railway infrastructure may unlock economic activity and create access to areas that previously were not easily accessible by humans. Forest degradation and habitat loss may result through incursion into forest areas for agriculture, artisanal mining, and other potentially harmful activities (Hund and Megevand, 2013). In order to minimize such adverse impacts, countries should implement land-use planning strategies that set out "no-go" zones and plan transport corridors accordingly.

SDG 17 – partnerships for the goals

To achieve the SDGs, partnerships among all stakeholders are necessary and, as highlighted in the introduction, it is envisaged that the private sector will play a greater role than was set out in the previous MDGs. Particularly Target 17.16 – "enhance the global partnership for sustainable development complemented by multi-stakeholder partnerships that mobilize and share knowledge, expertise, technologies and financial resources to support the achievement of sustainable development goals in all countries, particularly developing countries" – is relevant for the question of partnerships and shared-use.

The necessity to collaborate in order to achieve shared-use mining infrastructure cannot be overstated. There are a number of stakeholders involved in realizing shared-use infrastructure. Apart from the government (various ministries and agencies at the national level, as well as, potentially, regional or local governments), utility companies, and the relevant mining company that will build the infrastructure, other private sector players need to be involved. These include the subsequent mining companies and companies from other sectors that want to access the infrastructure and will require access terms that are economically viable. It may also include companies that could benefit from economies of scope due to the construction of the infrastructure as discussed in the above consideration of SDG 9. Financiers will also need to be part of the discussion given that large-scale infrastructure projects will generally not be financed through equity. Landowners and communities affected by the infrastructure development will need to be meaningfully consulted to build a shared consensus regarding potential infrastructure projects over their lands, and overcome information asymmetries as well as to avoid adverse impacts on their human rights. An added layer of complexity occurs when the infrastructure crosses country borders given that the neighboring country will also need to be part of the negotiations to discuss transit tariffs and/or access provisions.

Given the numerous players involved and the complexity of shared-use infrastructure agreements, these projects may provide an opportunity to create lasting partnerships beyond the construction of the infrastructure project itself and can act as a driver to regional integration (Gözde *et. al*, 2015). The Maputo Development Corridor, which connects South Africa's mining region to Maputo port is a case in point. It set up a multi-stakeholder group in 1997 to facilitate public and private actors of South Africa, Mozambique, and Swaziland to oversee infrastructure projects, build public sector capacity on trade facilitation, research policy measures to enhance investment around the corridor, and facilitate cross-border development initiatives. The multi-stakeholder group also involved local governments, informal entrepreneurs, and affected communities in its undertakings (Byiers and Vanheukelom, 2014). To improve operational efficiency of railway transport along the Maputo corridor, a Joint Operating Center was inaugurated in Maputo in September 2014, which houses operators from Maputo port, the Mozambican railways company, the South African railways company, and the Swazi railways company. To ensure the effectiveness of the Center, the operators have aligned investment plans, maintenance and safety standards, as well as skill development initiatives. It is expected that these measures will enhance adherence to scheduled train movements across rail and port facilities throughout the corridor. Transnet is also looking to roll out similar initiatives on the North-South Corridor (Zimbabwe, Zambia, DRC, and South Africa) and the East-West Corridor (Botswana and South Africa) (Railways Africa, 2016).

Roadblocks to shared-use infrastructure

While the implementation of shared-use infrastructure can contribute to achieving the SDGs as outlined in the previous section, it is fraught with challenges and trade-offs. This section addresses why mining companies may be against sharing infrastructure investments, the potential trade-offs that need to be made in order to achieve shared-use, and pre-conditions that need to be put in place in order to make shared-use infrastructure work.

The competitive nature of the mining sector

The competition that exists between large mining companies is a roadblock to the implementation of multi-user arrangements, particularly if there are no strong regulatory requirements and clear policy guidelines in place. The Australian experience shows that mining companies will use all strategies to avoid implementing shared-use policies, including "aggressive legal challenge, engineering and design features, pre-emptive access arrangements, capacity management and mergers and acquisitions" (Collier and Ireland, 2015). When large multinational mining companies compete to supply different grades of ore to their consumers, their natural behavior is to use their monopoly power on the infrastructure in the region to acquire further regional concessions at a lower price. Moreover, large-scale mining companies are often price makers and so view it as in their interest to restrict regional production to receive higher prices for their products.

Trade-offs involved when negotiating shared-use infrastructure

Governments and companies negotiate over the allocation of economic rent (the estimated excess profits over the minimum required return to induce investment). This negotiation will entail fiscal and non-fiscal obligations, such as local content and shared-use of infrastructure (CCSI, 2014). Depending on the country's objectives, the government can prioritize one type of benefit over another. If strategic, the government can prioritize shared-use infrastructure in the negotiations. If this comes at a significant cost to the company however, the government should be prepared to concede on another negotiation point, such as the fiscal terms.

From the perspective of the company, two important factors will determine its willingness to embark on shared-use arrangements: (1) the extent to which the infrastructure is costly and strategic; and (2) whether multi-purpose access to infrastructure will unlock economic development and help preserve the company's social license to operate. Rail infrastructure is considered to be most strategic and costly given that it makes up a significant proportion of total capital expenditure and third-party access may adversely impact operations. From the perspective of the government,

> shared-use in the context of expensive infrastructure such as rail and ports is worth the price of foregone revenues if (1) there are significant economies of scale or scope so that the provision of extra capacity is inexpensive, and (2) a real market for that marginal low-cost capacity exists.
>
> (CCSI, 2014)

Given the potential cost imposed on the company in implementing shared-use and the price paid by the government in terms of both foregone tax revenues and establishing a regulatory authority to enforce shared-use of the mining-related infrastructure, governments should prepare for the negotiation by conducting a detailed cost-benefit analysis of the negotiation package. As mentioned above, negotiating shared-use should proceed from a planning effort for infrastructure expansion and public–private coordination, and in response to a predicted demand.

Preconditions for shared-use infrastructure may not be in place

Several preconditions are needed to successfully determine whether shared-use requirements make sense and to implement shared-use if deemed appropriate.

Planning and coordination

An infrastructure master-plan across sectors that outlines infrastructure requirements is necessary to identify synergies and opportunities for shared-use between the mining sector and other users. These plans should be based on future demand forecasts of potential users of the infrastructure to determine the economic importance of implementing shared-use. Furthermore, as outlined during the above discussion of SDG 17, implementing shared-use infrastructure involves many players and interests, which need to be consulted and included in coordination efforts.

Legal framework

To realize infrastructure-mine synergies, countries need to provide a sufficiently predictable regulatory environment to attract investments by mining companies and infrastructure companies. In some instances, it might mean the liberalization of certain segments of infrastructure that traditionally fall under the scope of prerogatives of the state-owned utility (train operations, power generation, water treatment facilities, and telecommunications services). In other instances it means the clarification of the rules (including guiding principles to set access tariffs; identification of the role and responsibility of the infrastructure owner, infrastructure operator, national government, and local government; procedures in case of disputes; and cost sharing mechanisms). When the legal framework is not sufficiently developed, adapted, and implemented, critical elements may be left to negotiation. This can complicate planning efforts for governments and create an uncertain environment for the investor. It is also generally advisable for the government to keep the right of way or servitude along the longitudinal infrastructure (such as roads, pipelines, power lines, and railways) in order to be able to monetize the right of way to other infrastructure types and optimize infrastructure development (Gözde *et al.*, 2015).

Regulation

Implementing shared-use requires regulatory oversight. The regulator must: (1) monitor the tariffs charged by the operator (this could be the mining company, a special purpose vehicle company (SPV), or the state-owned rail company) to third parties on a non-discriminatory basis; (2) define the access charges between the infrastructure owner and operator if the two are separated; (3) determine technical standards, necessary improvements or expansion; (4) assess complaints and manage arbitration; and (5) guarantee the implementation of open access infrastructure. Independence and transparency in regulatory processes are required to gain trust from the private sector; in advanced jurisdictions the regulatory bodies are therefore often independent institutions. For countries where resources and institutional capacity is limited, intermediary solutions, such as outsourcing regulatory functions to a third party or expert panel can work well (Eberhard *et al.*, 2011).

State-owned utility

In many shared-use arrangements, the power and water utilities, as well as state-owned railway, port, and telecommunications companies will be the main partners of the mining company and associated infrastructure companies. Therefore their reliability, financial health, and creditworthiness are essential and will determine the range of possible arrangements in which the mines and the private sector will be willing to engage (CCSI, 2014).

Conclusion

Significant progress has been made to promote the mining sector moving away from its enclave model towards sharing its infrastructure investments. This chapter highlights the importance of continuing this trend by outlining how shared-use infrastructure can play an important role in contributing to the development framework that countries worldwide have agreed to for the next 14 years. Transport, power, water, and ICT investments by mining companies can provide a springboard to economic development, particularly in resource-rich countries with large infrastructure financing gaps. If shared, these investments can improve access to services and unlock economic potential in areas that were previously unconnected. To minimize the potential adverse impacts of shared-use infrastructure on the SDGs, countries should plan these investments taking into account environmental and human rights considerations.

It is noteworthy that shared-use water arrangements play a dominant role in achieving a number of SDGs. With increasing pressure on water resources due to increasing demand from the mining and non-mining sectors, as well as exacerbated flooding and drought events caused by climate change, shared-use water solutions deserve particular attention by all stakeholders in mining jurisdictions in the years to come.

The commodity price downturn has put many mining projects and associated infrastructure projects on hold. The squeeze on mining projects' margins has also exacerbated competitive pressures among mining companies. Given that the relative position of mining projects on the global cost curve will determine how the owners of those assets will withstand the downturn and which new projects will become viable (Collier and Ireland, 2015), access to low-cost infrastructure solutions has become an important factor in deciding whether a project is profitable or not. There is therefore an added incentive for controlling companies to try and limit their competitors' access to infrastructure in order to gain market share.

In such an environment of heightened competition it is even more important for governments of resource-rich countries to enforce shared-use infrastructure solutions given that the public cost to the mineral-producing country of such competitive behavior outweighs the benefits. Furthermore, coordinated large-scale shared-use infrastructure investments have the potential to create economies of scale and reduce the overall costs of the services to the mining sector of a country. As this chapter highlights, above and beyond the monetary aspects, such shared-use solutions will also go a long way to help to achieve each SDG and the 2030 Agenda.

Notes

1 The 17 SDGs and their 169 associated targets shape the international community's development agenda for the next 15 years and form a common framework for achieving sustainable development. Building on the Millennium Development Goals (MDGs) that guided development over the last 15 years, the SDGs are not only relevant for developing countries, but also developed countries given that they cover a wider range of issues, including an increased focus on the environment. The private sector is also given a more prominent role in helping to achieve the SDGs.
2 For the purpose of this chapter, we use a broad definition of "resource-rich," which also includes countries that have recently discovered mineral or fuel deposits.
3 More examples can be found in Toledano and Roorda, 2014a.
4 BHP Billiton, Rio Tinto, Anglo American, Vale S.A., Xstrata plc and Glencore International.
5 In 2012, power shortages resulted in a loss of 250,000 tons of copper; this led to lost exports worth US$1.8 billion, translating into a loss in GDP of US$700 million (4.4 percent of GDP) and a loss in tax revenues of US$250 million (1.6 percent of GDP) (Banerjee *et al.*, 2014).
6 A joint venture between BHP and Vale.

References

Abdulai, A., Diao, X., and Johnson, M. (2005) *Achieving Regional Growth Dynamics in African Agriculture.* Discussion Paper No. 17, International Food Policy Research Institute.

BAGC (Beira Agricultural Growth Corridor Initiative) (2013) *Beira Agricultural Growth Corridor: Delivering the Potential.* Available at: www.agdevco.com/uploads/reports/BAGC_Investment_Blueprint_rpt19.pdf.

Banerjee, G. S., Romo, Z., McMahon, G., Toledano, P., Robinson, P., and Arroyo, P. I. (2014) *The Power of the Mine: A Transformative Opportunity for Sub-Saharan Africa.* World Bank Publications.

Bottrill, L. (2013) *Heart of Iron: Mining in the Congo Basin Rainforest.* USA/Congo, WWF and World Bank. Available at: https://vimeo.com/66945898.

Briceño-Garmendia, C., Smits, K., and Foster, V. (2008) *Financing Public Infrastructure in Sub-Saharan Africa: Patterns, Issues, and Options.* Africa Infrastructure Sector Diagnostic Background Paper No. 15, World Bank Publications.

BTG Practical (2016) *Cerro Verde – Massive Expansion on Stream – but Priced.* Available at: www.btgpactual.com/Research/OpenPdf.aspx?file=32380.pdf.

Byiers, B. and Vanheukelom, J. (2014) *What Drives Regional Economic Integration? Lessons from the Maputo Development Corridor and the North-South Corridor.* Discussion Paper No. 157, European Centre for Development Policy Management.

Calderón, C. and Servén, L. (2008) *Infrastructure and Economic Development in Sub-Saharan Africa.* World Bank Policy Research Working Paper No. 4712.

CCSI (Columbia Center on Sustainable Investment) (2014) *A Framework to Approach Shared Use of Mining-Related Infrastructure.* Columbia University.

Collier, P. and Ireland, G. (2015) *Shared-Use Mining Infrastructure: Why it Matters, and how to Achieve it.* BSG Working Paper Series, BSG-WP-2015/009, Oxford University. Available at: www.bsg.ox.ac.uk/sites/www.bsg.ox.ac.uk/files/documents/BSG-WP-2015-009.pdf.

Doepel, D. and Bolton, G. (2013) "Extracting the Value from the Extractive Industries: Insights from the Australian Experience." *GREAT Insights*, 2, 2.

Eberhard, A., Rosnes, O., Shkaratan, M., and Vennemo, H. (2011) *Africa's Power Infrastructure: Investment, Integration, Efficiency*. Directions in Development: Infrastructure, World Bank Publications.

Edwards, E. C., Cristi, O., and Libecap, G. D. (2013) "Groundwater Conservation via Desalination: Regulator Behavior and Welfare Implications." Working Draft.

Els, F. (2013) "Simandou Railway will Uproot 10,000 People." Available at: www.mining.com/simandou-railway-will-uproot-10000-people-52462.

Estache, A. (2005) "Africa's Infrastructure: Challenges and Opportunities." Paper presented at high-level seminar "Realizing the Potential for Profitable Investment in Africa," organized by IMF Institute and Joint Africa Institute, Tunis, February 28–March 1, 2006.

Ferdman, R. A. (2014) "4.4 Billion People around the World Still don't Have Internet: Here's Where They Live." Available at: www.washingtonpost.com/news/wonk/wp/2014/10/02/4-4-billion-people-around-the-world-still-dont-have-internet-heres-where-they-live.

FMO (Forced Migration Online) (2011) "Types of Development Projects Causing Displacement." Available at: www.forcedmigration.org/research-resources/expert-guides/development-induced-displacement-and-resettlement/types-of-development-projects-causing-displacement#section-2.

Freeport-McMoRan (2015) "2015 Working Toward Sustainable Development." Available at: www.fcx.com/sd/pdf/wtsd_2015.pdf.

Gözde, I., Opalo, K., and Toledano, P. (2015) *Breaking out of Enclaves: Leveraging Opportunities from Regional Integration in Africa to Promote Resource-Driven Diversification*. World Bank Report No. ACS14156.

Hund, K. and Megevand, C. (2013) *Deforestation Trends in the Congo Basin: Reconciling Economic Growth and Forest Protection*. World Bank Working Paper 4: Mining.

Kirschke, J. (2016) "The Global Mining Industry Begins to Embrace Renewables." Available at: www.triplepundit.com/2016/08/global-mining-industry-shines-light-climate-change-energy-insecurity.

Lillywhite, S., Kemp, D. and Sturman, K. (2015) *Mining, Resettlement and Lost Livelihoods: Listening to the Voices of Resettled Communities in Mualadzi, Mozambique*. Oxfam, Melbourne.

Macauhub (2014) "Port of Maputo, in Mozambique, has Greater Processing Capacity," September 24, 2014. Available at: https://macauhub.com.mo/2014/09/24/port-of-maputo-in-mozambique-has-greater-processing-capacity.

Maennling, N., Toledano, P., and Thomashausen, S. (2016) *Mine Power: Partnering to Upgrade Energy Infrastructure in the DRC*. Natural Resource Governance Institute, Natural Resource Charter Case Study.

McKinsey Global Institute (2013) *Reverse the Curse: Maximizing the Potential of Resource Driven Economies*.

Mishra, P. P. and Reddy, G. M. (2011) "Mining-Induced Displacement: The Case of Aluminium Refinery in Andhra Pradesh." In Somayaji, S. and Talwar, S. (eds.), *Development-Induced Displacement, Rehabilitation, Resettlement in India: Current Issues, Challenges*. Routledge, New York, 91–108.

Moody's Investor Service (2013) *Water Scarcity to Raise Capex and Operating Costs, Heighten Operation Risks*. Report number 149714, Special Comment.

Queensland Government (2012) *Great Barrier Reef Ports Strategy 2012–2022: For Public Consultation*. Department of State Development, Infrastructure and Planning.

Railways Africa (2016) "The Maputo Development Corridor Sets the Bar for Economic Development Corridors in Africa." *Railways Africa*, Issue 2, p. 28. Available at: https://issuu.com/railwaysafrica/docs/ra_2-2016_final_issuu.

Rainbow Environment Consult (2011) *Mbalam Iron Ore Project Environmental and Social Assessment: Volume 1. Executive Summary*. CamIron, Yaoundé, Cameroon.

Rezende, F. (2015) "Rompimento de barragens causa 'maior dano ambiental da história de Minas,' diz promotor." Available at: http://noticias.r7.com/minas-gerais/rompimento-de-barragens-causa-maior-dano-ambiental-da-historia-de-minas-diz-promotor-06112015.

Stanley, J. (2004) *Development-Induced Displacement and Resettlement*. Forced Migration Online Research Guide, Refugee Studies Centre, University of Oxford.

Szyplinska, P. (2012) *CEO 360 Degree Perspective of the Global Mining Water and Wastewater Treatment Market*. Frost & Sullivan.

Toledano, P. (2013) *Leveraging the Mining Industry's Energy Demand to Improve Host Countries' Power Infrastructure*. Columbia Center on Sustainable Investment, Columbia University.

Toledano, P. and Roorda, C. (2014a) *Leveraging Mining Investments in Water Infrastructure for Broad Economic Development: Models, Opportunities and Challenges*. Columbia Center on Sustainable Investment, Columbia University.

Toledano, P. and Roorda, C. (2014b) *Leveraging Mining Demand for Internet and Telecommunications Infrastructure for Broad Economic Development: Models, Opportunities and Challenges*. Columbia Center on Sustainable Investment, Columbia University.

UN Habitat (2011) *Infrastructure for Economic Development and Poverty Reduction in Africa*. Global Urban Economic Dialogue Series.

Willoughby, C. (2004) *Infrastructure and the Millennium Development Goals*. Session on Complementarity of Infrastructure for Achieving the Millennium Development Goals, United Nations.

World Bank (2009) *Transformation-Ready: Using ICT to Fast-Track Africa's Development Path*. Available at: http://siteresources.worldbank.org/INFORMATIONANDCOMMUNICATIONANDTECHNOLOGIES/Resources/WorldBank_ICT_brochure.pdf.

World Bank (2011) *Republic of Liberia: Infrastructure Policy Notes – Leveraging Investments by Natural Resource Concessionaires*.

Index

Page numbers in *italics* denote tables, those in **bold** denote figures.

For Product Safety Concerns and Information please contact our EU representative GPSR@taylorandfrancis.com
Taylor & Francis Verlag GmbH, Kaufingerstraße 24, 80331 München, Germany

www.ingramcontent.com/pod-product-compliance
Ingram Content Group UK Ltd.
Pitfield, Milton Keynes, MK11 3LW, UK
UKHW021009180425
457613UK00019B/869
* 9 7 8 0 3 6 7 5 9 3 3 7 7 *